AMERICAN SIDESHOW

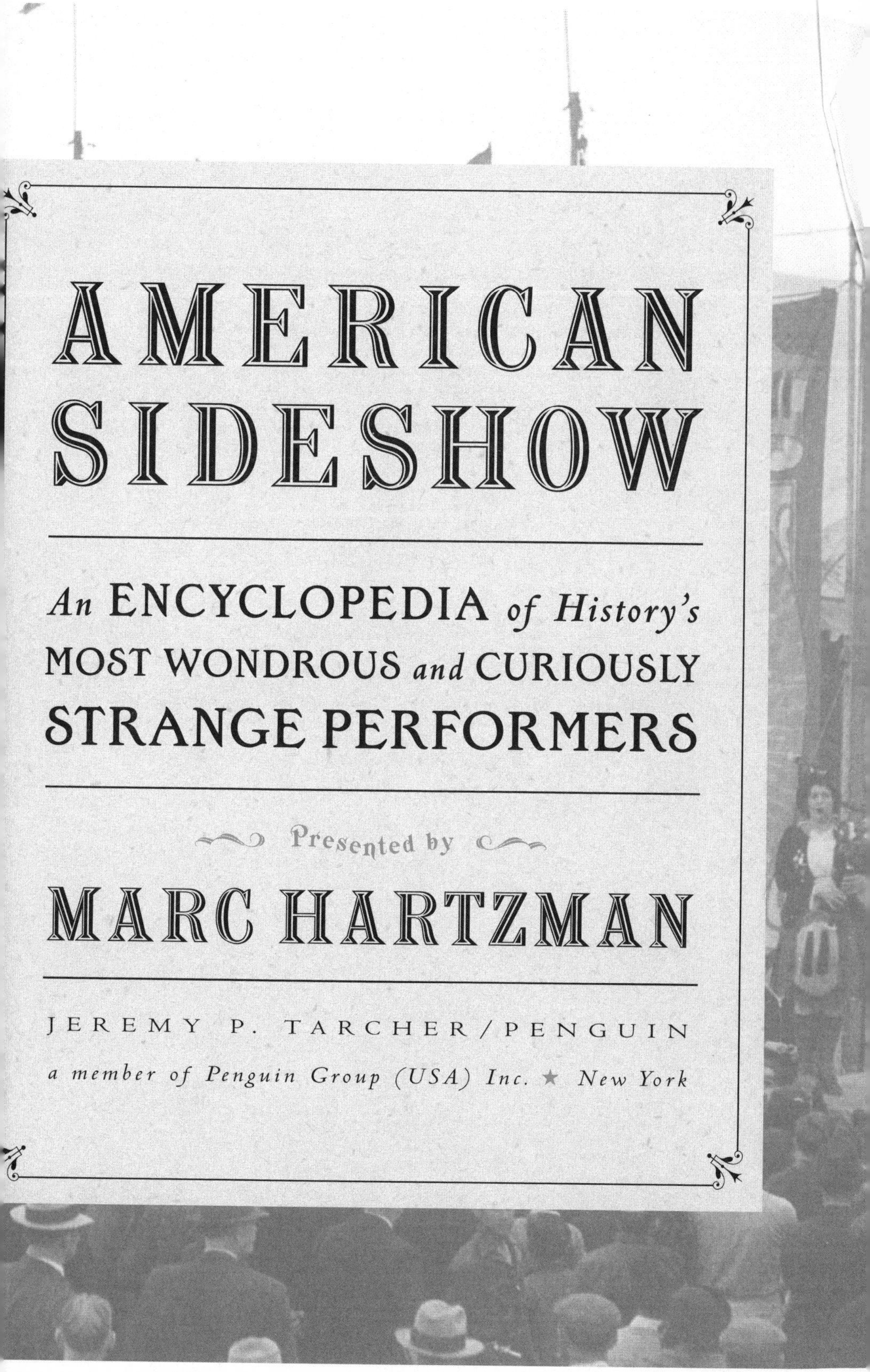

AMERICAN SIDESHOW

An ENCYCLOPEDIA of History's
MOST WONDROUS and CURIOUSLY
STRANGE PERFORMERS

~ Presented by ~

MARC HARTZMAN

JEREMY P. TARCHER/PENGUIN
a member of Penguin Group (USA) Inc. ★ New York

JEREMY P. TARCHER/PENGUIN
Published by the Penguin Group
Penguin Group (USA) Inc., 375 Hudson Street, New York, New York 10014, USA · Penguin Group
(Canada), 90 Eglinton Avenue East, Suite 700, Toronto, Ontario M4P 2Y3, Canada (a division of
Pearson Penguin Canada Inc.) · Penguin Books Ltd, 80 Strand, London WC2R 0RL, England ·
Penguin Ireland, 25 St Stephen's Green, Dublin 2, Ireland (a division of Penguin Books Ltd) · Penguin
Group (Australia), 250 Camberwell Road, Camberwell, Victoria 3124, Australia (a division of Pearson
Australia Group Pty Ltd) · Penguin Books India Pvt Ltd, 11 Community Centre, Panchsheel Park,
New Delhi–110 017, India · Penguin Group (NZ), Cnr Airborne and Rosedale Roads, Albany,
Auckland 1310, New Zealand (a division of Pearson New Zealand Ltd) · Penguin Books
(South Africa) (Pty) Ltd, 24 Sturdee Avenue, Rosebank, Johannesburg 2196, South Africa ·
Penguin Books Ltd, Registered Offices: 80 Strand, London WC2R 0RL, England

ISBN-13: 978-0-7394-6196-9

Printed in the United States of America

BOOK DESIGN BY MEIGHAN CAVANAUGH

While the author has made every effort to provide accurate telephone numbers and Internet addresses
at the time of publication, neither the publisher nor the author assumes any responsibility for errors, or
for changes that occur after publication. Further, the publisher does not have any control over and does
not assume any responsibility for author or third-party websites or their content.

To my loving wife, Liz,

and to Myrtle Corbin—

the four-legged woman who

brought us together

ACKNOWLEDGMENTS

This project could not have been completed without the help of the many people I e-mailed and spoke with. First, I thank my wife, Liz, who not only encouraged me to pursue this book from the beginning, but supported me along the way by taking countless photos, traveling, pushing me to bid higher for photos on eBay, and putting up with me while I disappeared into my office to interview, research, and write.

Within the sideshow community, I thank those who took the time to share their many stories, historical knowledge, and industry contacts: Ward Hall and Chris Christ, who also graciously welcomed my wife and me into their home, allowed us to rummage through piles of photos, and attempted to continue telling stories over loud Spanish karaoke at a Mexican restaurant; Bobby Reynolds, who also hosted us and let us go through numerous books and photos; Johnny Fox, for sharing pieces from his collection, supporting my interest in sideshows long before this book began, and inspiring me over the years; Harley Newman, who offered information and advice, and gave a private performance in my driveway; Derek Rose, who put me in touch with performers from day one of this project; Bob Blackmar, who answered every question I threw at him and generously assisted with archived articles, the Kobel collection photographs, and images from his own collection; Tom Hernandez, who happily dispensed his wealth of sideshow knowledge whenever I had a question and who contributed images from his collection; Ken Harck, who shared pieces from his personal archives and helped with contacts; Johnny Meah, who reminisced about his friendships with various performers; James Mundie, who kindly provided photos from his collection; Dick Zigun, for arranging interviews and photography with the Sideshows by the Seashore cast; Judy Rock, for always being helpful with her stories and time; Slim Price, for recounting his days at Coney Island; Marie Roberts, who gave me access to photos from her personal collection and told me family stories; James Taylor, for sharing knowledge and offering suggestions; George McArthur, who took a road trip to meet with me and who put me in touch with other performers; Jennifer Miller, who met my wife and me at the subway station in freezing weather to bring us to her home; and Jeffrey Gordon of johnnyeckmuseum.com, who generously allowed his photograph of Johnny Eck to be published for the first time. Many other people took time to furnish information, give interviews, and meet for photo shoots: David Adamovich, Carol Armstrong, Eduardo Arrocha, Adena Baker, Scott Baker, Cathy Berry, Dick Brewer, Ses Carny, David Clark, Tim Cridland, Matt Crowley, David Denholtz, Jimmy Dixon, Don Driver, The Enigma, Mark Frierson, Lorett Fulkerson, Tyler Fyre, The Great Nippulini, Jan Gregor, Insectivora, Fred Kahl, Katzen, Bob Leonard, Sahar Mitchell, Stephanie Monseu, Alexzander Morrow, Keith Nelson, Todd Robbins, John Robinson, Jim Rose, Särka, Daniel Browning Smith, Erik Sprague, David Straitjacket, John Strong, Red Stuart, Tina Tomaini, Stephanie Torres, Ula, Vivian Wheeler, and Jerry Willman.

Many amazing people beyond the sideshow world also helped make this project possible, and I thank them: Katie Boyle, my agent, who had read Katherine Dunn's *Geek Love* just before I brought this idea to her, then loved the idea, made it happen, and offered support and advice throughout; my editor, Terri Hennessy, for all her wonderful work and for giving me the freedom to do what I needed to; my copy editor extraordinaire, Anna Jardine, for her incredible thoroughness; Meighan Cavanaugh, who designed this book beautifully; Chris Steighner, who saw the potential in my idea and pushed me to continue pursuing it; contributing photographers Laure Leber, Allen Falkner, and Carl Saytor; Buck Wolf, who provided contact information, advice, and support and who shares an interest in the bizarre; Kathy Maher of the Barnum Museum, Bridgeport, Connecticut; Lois Szudy of the Courtright Memorial Library, Otterbein College, Westerville, Ohio; Wilma June Kapfer of the Downing House Museum, Memphis, Missouri; Metta McDowell and Don Storwold of the Eddy County Museum and Historical Society, New Rockford, North Dakota; Alan F. Rumrill of the Historical Society of Cheshire County, New Hampshire; Devon Dawson of the Holyoke, Massachusetts, History Room and Archives; Dawn Triplett of the Kalkaska, Michigan, Genealogical Society; Aaron DeGroft, Debra Walk, and Marcy Murray of the Ringling Museum, Sarasota, Florida; Marvin Allen of the Starke County Historical Society, Knox, Indiana; Diane Cooter, Carolyn Davis, and Peter Verheyen of Syracuse University's Bird Library; the White Plains, New York, Public Library; Cristina Boothe, for sharing photos from her family's collection; Gabrielle Bowen; Andy Foot; Steve Harvey; Timothy Kahn; Bernie Lander; Nancy McCreery; Shawn Ness; Dr. Zoe Palmos and Georgia Melissaris; Robert Perry, at Tattooed Mom in Philadelphia, for letting me use his space for a photo shoot; Sam Steger and Fred and Ann Dinstell, for contact help; Aileen Tarver; Reva Wolf, Eugene Heath, and Audrey and Scott Dinstell for much-needed books; Mom and Dad, for sending books and photos found on eBay, for seeing *Freaks* with me—twice—and for letting me see *The Elephant Man* when I was seven, and weekly *Ripley's Believe It or Not!* during dinner; and finally, my friends and co-workers who've listened to me talk about sideshows perhaps a little more than they wanted to hear.

CONTENTS

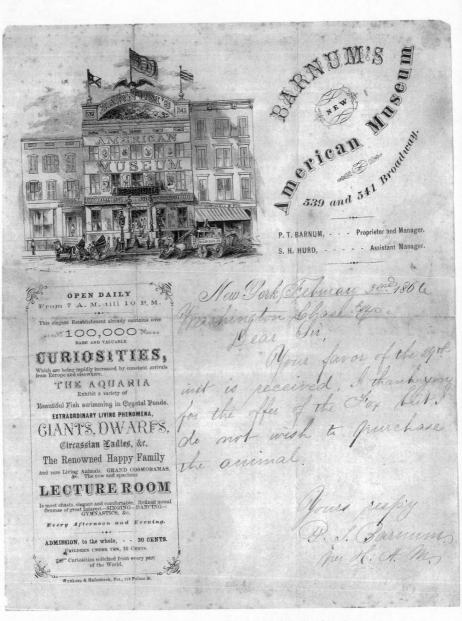

The New American Museum as it appeared on Barnum's stationery.

Ken Harck archives/Bros. Grim Side Shows

OPENING BALLY

Thank you for stepping right up to the cash register or online checkout and purchasing this book. Consider it your ticket to the greatest collection of physical wonders, magnificent marvels, peerless prodigies, and peculiar performers ever assembled between two covers. Not to mention exaggerations and adjectives galore. Welcome to the American Sideshow.

Many historians claim the sideshow began with P. T. Barnum, yet the concept has existed for as long as there has been human curiosity. When something different or unusual is presented before you—whether it's living or inanimate—you're intrigued, amazed, or maybe even disgusted. But you want to see it.

If I'm walking down a street and I see a little person, I look. I don't blatantly stare or gawk—no, I follow the societal rules of proper conduct and sneak only a few furtive glances to satisfy my curiosity. Just like everyone else around. What's it like to live in a world not built for your size? To be unable to reach high countertops? To be an adult and have to shop in the children's section? For that matter, how do the armless or legless compensate for their missing limbs? How does a conjoined twin maintain sanity without a second of privacy? Regardless of their physical abnormalities, the people presented in this book triumphed over their disadvantages, defied expectations, succeeded financially, and often found love.

Throughout history, those who have been born somehow different from the rest of us have had the opportunity to profit from human curiosity, the sense of wonder at their difference. Human oddities have been featured in fairs for hundreds of years, dating at least as far back as 1102, when the first St. Bartholomew Fair was held in London. Freaks of nature were always a strong draw, and members of royalty were among the biggest fans of the deformed and talented. A German entertainer, Matthias Buchinger, called the Little Man of Nuremberg, was born on June 3, 1674, without arms or legs, just two flipperlike stubs. By the early 1700s he was performing for crowned heads across Europe. Buchinger could play more than half a dozen instruments, shoot a pistol expertly, write with exquisite calligraphy, and perform astonishing sleight-of-hand. He also married four times and had eleven children.

When nature didn't provide enough anomalies, broods of miscreants took upon themselves the job of creating their own monsters. Victor Hugo described such a group, the seventeenth-century Comprachicos, in his novel *The Man Who Laughs*. These nomadic types would purchase children (hence their name, meaning "child-buyers" in Spanish) and purposely stunt their growth or distort their features, then sell them as attractions. "It is convenient; one can order one's dwarf beforehand, of any desired shape," Hugo wrote.

By the late eighteenth and early nineteenth centuries, Americans began profiting from exhibitions of the unusual. One important example was Charles Willson Peale, a Philadelphia portrait painter and collector of natural history artifacts. In 1786 he converted a wing of his house into a museum to display his artwork and his curious collection of stuffed and mounted animals, mineral specimens, and old coins. When the museum outgrew the home, Peale moved it into its own space. Donors sent odd pieces from their personal collections, then went to see them displayed in public. Suddenly, a four-legged chicken, a two-headed pig, a root resembling a human face, and an eighty-pound turnip were all the rage. Peale rolled with the trend and became a showman. His son Rubens later operated Peale's New York Museum and Peale's Baltimore Museum (which he took over from his brother, Rembrandt), both of which thrived on the eccentric and bizarre. Today Charles Willson Peale is credited with establishing the first major museum in America.

In the 1840s, an Albany, New York, chemist named Gilbert Spaulding bought a small circus from an owner who had fallen into debt. Working under the name Doc Spaulding, he found success with the show and later added to it with the purchase of an Albany museum collection. In addition to the circus, he exhibited relics from Egypt, Greece, and Rome; statues of the 728-pound English Fat Man Daniel Lambert, Siamese twins, and famous historical figures; and zoological specimens representing wild and rare animals from Europe, Asia, Africa, and South America. By 1852 he had built a "floating palace," complete with 3,000 spectator seats, to tour with his show and museum along the Ohio and Missouri rivers. Five years later he was back on land, using the railroad to transport his circus from city to city, skipping the places that weren't profitable.

Other showmen capitalized on weird wonders, animate and inanimate, by renting out meeting halls or other venues for exhibitions. But it was P. T. Barnum who mastered the ability to tap into human intrigue and market an oddity. He made his fortunes by securing the greatest attractions for his beloved American Museum. The museum, first known as Scudder's American Museum, was located at Broadway and Ann Street in lower Manhattan. Barnum purchased it in 1841 and opened it on New Year's Day in 1842. Success came quickly. The showman added to the original Scudder collection with a menagerie of live animals (including the nation's first hippopotamus), taxidermy exhibits, ancient fossils, exotic insects, wax figures, human and nonhuman freaks (including the legendary Fejee Mermaid, which was nothing more than a monkey's torso with a fish tail attached), and much more. America loved the American Museum as much as Barnum did, and it became the most visited place in the entire country. Dime museums sprouted across the land, featuring oddities of all kinds, with the living ones as the star attractions.

In the 1870s, Barnum brought his wondrous marvels on the road with his circus and created a sensation. The show was on the side of the main circus tent and entertained guests before the circus began. The big top was soon the main venue for such "side" shows. At the time, there were already more than thirty circuses in America.

The concept of the midway was perfected at the 1893 World's Columbian Exposition in Chicago, held in honor of the 400th anniversary of Columbus's discovery of America (it ran a year late). The 600-foot-wide Midway Plaisance served the same function for the Exposition as the sideshow for the circus. Fairgoers were entertained by acts and exhibits from around the world, including Turkish, Japanese, and Egyptian villages; mosques; snake charmers; the first Ferris wheel; a young magician who had recently changed his name to Harry Houdini; and of course, freaks. The success of the

Columbian Midway, with its many attractions, amusements, and innovative electrical fanfare, became a model for future circuses.

The sideshow maintained its place on the midway through 1956, when Ringling Bros. and Barnum & Bailey featured its last outdoor tent show (until 1985, when showmen Ward Hall and Chris Christ produced an exhibition under canvas for western tour dates). After the 1956 finale, the sideshow was limited mostly to the circus's engagements at Madison Square Garden in New York. In 1999, however, Ringling incorporated various sideshow attractions into its main show, among them Michu, the Smallest Man in the World, and Khan, the Tallest, both of whom were featured circus acts.

The decline of sideshows can be attributed to various factors. Increased medical knowledge has led to fewer births of freaks, or to corrections of their abnormalities, and to the diagnosis of certain birth defects; diseases began to evoke pity rather than wonder. Attractions from the old days retired or passed away. Carnival rides, movies, and television offered new forms of entertainment. Movies and television were especially threatening, as they brought the world to local theaters and living rooms, thereby weakening the sideshow's credibility in presenting such exotic acts as the Wild Men of Borneo. Now people could see that the people of Borneo weren't so wild.

To complicate matters further, the new attitude of political correctness made it wrong to stare at and profit from human oddities. This was relevant, for example, in the 1960s and early 1970s in cases in North Carolina and Florida, where two girls were offended after attending sideshows. One of these was fifteen-year-old Carol Grant, who had deformed arms and legs. "Handicapped people are seeking more in life than being stared at in a sideshow," she wrote in a 1968 letter to the North Carolina agriculture commissioner, and a copy of her letter was sent to the governor's wife, sparking controversy in the press. Grant's concern may have been justified for certain people, some said, but why take away the option of appearing in a sideshow if someone wanted to? Those who did want to fought back. They had a right to earn a living, and the sideshow was a place to do it.

Harvey Boswell, a North Carolina sideshow operator and paraplegic, responded to Grant's statement: "I'm stared at but it doesn't bother me. Nor does it bother the freaks when they are stared at on their way to the bank to deposit the $100, $150, $250, and even $500 per week that some of the more sensational human oddities receive for their showing in the sideshows."

Dick Best—who spent decades providing human oddities for Royal American Shows and the Ringling Bros. shows—also stood up for the exhibition of freaks. His reasoning: "An alligator girl can't be a waitress, or a receptionist, or a nurse, or a babysitter. How many job opportunities are open to Siamese twins? How many personnel managers are looking for monkey-faced boys? Would you climb into a taxi driven by a dwarf with a pointed head, or a guy nine feet tall?"

Showman Bobby Reynolds would have agreed. "Today, if you're a mutation of sorts, the biggest thrill you get out of life is opening up the mailbox and getting a check from the government," Reynolds says. "Or they put you in an institution. When we had them out, people would say, 'Oh, you took advantage of those people!' We didn't take advantage of those people. They were stars! They were somebody. They enjoyed themselves." The freaks were indeed the kings and queens of the sideshows.

Despite all the debate, sideshows never really went away. There were just fewer of them. In the 1980s, Dick Zigun opened Sideshows by the Seashore at Coney Island. The Jim Rose Circus sideshow took off by attracting a younger, rock-'n'-roll crowd with its appearance at Lollapalooza in 1992. The show subsequently launched a new wave of performers. A decade later, the first Sideshow Gathering was held in Wilkes-Barre, Pennsylvania, as a convention for fans and performers.

It's all part of the rejuvenation the sideshow has experienced in recent years. Curiosity still sells. State fairs and new sideshows occasionally feature human oddities. But it is television—once an enemy of the sideshow—that has become the new home for freaks. Every time conjoined twins are operated on, CNN and *Dateline* are there. Jerry Springer and Maury Povich have frequently kept their ratings up by featuring conjoined twins, little people, and others who formerly would have found a home in the sideshows. *The Howard Stern Show* made celebrities out of the late Hank the Angry Drunken Dwarf and the dentally challenged dwarf Beetlejuice. Working acts found a national stage on such programs as *Guinness World Records: Primetime* and *30 Seconds to Fame.* Fox's *Man Vs. Beast* pitted forty little people against an elephant in a contest of strength, and in a sequel organized four little people in a relay race against a seven-foot-tall camel. Ridiculous? Yes. Entertaining? Absolutely. Fox even pursued the reality dating show craze with *The Littlest Groom,* in which a diminutive bachelor was wooed by a group of both little and normal-size women. Even freakish animals have had their fifteen minutes. Just weeks before I wrote this paragraph, a four-eared cat and an alleged three-headed frog made national news.

And now there's this book. In it, I've attempted to cover as many performers in the United States as possible, from the early 1800s to today. It's intended to serve as a tribute to those brave and amazing people who overcame whatever quirk of nature was bestowed on them—be it a parasitic twin or missing limbs, proportions wee or gigantic—as well as self-made freaks and those who trained their bodies to achieve the seemingly impossible. Covering all such people would take a lifetime, or longer. Countless big, little, fat, skinny, and tattooed people have worked the sideshows. And acts such as sword swallowers, fire eaters, and human blockheads have been in no shortage, either.

Were the freaks exploited? Sometimes. But in some cases, that may have been for the best. Schlitzie, an imbecilic pinhead, was certainly exploited. But he thrived off the adoration of the crowd and was miserable when briefly institutionalized. While plenty of books are available to analyze such cases from a sociological point of view, I simply wish to highlight who these performers were and the extraordinary things they did. Not only did they entertain, but they did more in their physically disadvantaged state than many ever do who are born normal.

It should also be noted that the facts presented here come from a variety of sources, including old newspaper articles, promotional booklets, advertisements, magazines, books, and interviews with showmen, historians, surviving family members, and retired and current performers. As such, the truth may occasionally be exaggerated. After all, journalists likely were getting information from embellishing publicists, and ads were designed to romanticize the shows. Giants were frequently given several extra inches in height, and fat people always tacked on a few extra pounds. Sorting out what's true and what's not isn't always easy. But it doesn't necessarily matter. It's all part of the wonder of the sideshow.

PART ONE

We are all ladies and gentlemen, and we act so. None of us are frights.

Charles Tripp, *the Armless Wonder, at the Protective Order of Prodigies meeting, 1903*

The

GOLDEN AGE

From P. T. BARNUM'S LIVING PRODIGIES
to the DEATH *of* JAMES BAILEY

(circa 1830s *to* early 1900s)

Banners promoting Lionel the Lion-Faced Man
at Coney Island. *Collection of Marie A. Roberts*

★ ★ ★ ★ ★ ★ ★ ★ ★ ★ ★ ★ ★ ★ ★ ★ ★

Imagine living in America in the mid–nineteenth century. There are no movies, forget about television and radio. But thrill seekers had a form of entertainment that was perhaps more memorable than any we have today. Freaks! A trip to a dime museum or an exhibition hall promised sights that would etch themselves into the brain. Midgets, giants, armless wonders, legless wonders, bearded ladies, tattooed marvels, fat folks, thin men, and other amazing figures astounded audiences across the nation not only with their unique obvious appearance, but with their remarkable talent and upbeat attitude as well. Hundreds, if not thousands, of them worked for the likes of P. T. Barnum and other entrepreneurial showmen. Though not officially known as such, it was the golden age of the sideshow.

★ ★ ★ ★ ★ ★ ★ ★ ★ ★ ★ ★ ★ ★ ★ ★ ★

Carrie Akers looking unhappy.
Becker Collection, Special Collections
Research Center, Syracuse University Library

CARRIE AKERS

Circa 1860s–?

In the late 1800s, Carrie Akers was a sideshow double feature. Hailing from Virginia, she weighed 309 pounds and stood just thirty-four inches tall—making her both a Fat Lady and a dwarf. Her unusual dimensions were comparable to the average warthog's.

Nicknamed "Quarrelsome Carrie," Akers was known to have a bad temper. Of course, given her unfortunate shape, who could blame her for being a little cranky? According to Leslie Fiedler, author of *Freaks: Myths and Images of the Secret Self*, Akers "was well on the way to becoming a Bearded Lady, too, when she decided to retire from show business." She could have been a triple threat, albeit an angry one. All Akers needed was a conjoined twin and she could have been an entire show.

THE AZTEC CHILDREN, MÁXIMO *and* BARTOLA

Máximo: circa 1840–1913
Bartola: circa 1840–?

New discoveries of ancient Central American civilizations intrigued nineteenth-century Americans and created new fodder for capitalistic showmen. This was exemplified by Máximo and Bartola, the Aztec Children, who were brought to the United States in 1849 and remained a sensation for more than fifty years.

Máximo and Bartola were born in San Salvador, El Salvador, in the late 1830s or early 1840s. A Spanish trader bought the micro-cephalic sibling simpletons and subsequently sold them to an American entrepreneur when they were about ten years old. Their small, sloped heads recalled pre-Columbian sculpture. Their lips jutted out, they barely had chins, and bushy afro-style hair helped ac-centuate their deformity. Aztec-design tunics adorned their tiny bodies. Máximo was about thirty-three inches tall and weighed twenty-nine pounds, while his sister stood twenty-nine and a half inches high and weighed just seventeen pounds. The 1896 book *Anomalies and Curiosities of Medicine* characterized them as "little better than idiots in point of intelligence."

The Aztec Children, Máximo and Bartola, with an unidentified woman. *The Doghouse Collection / showhistory.com*

The Aztec novelty was brought to the United States, where it baffled scientists and captured the curious. When showcased at the Exhibition Room of the New York Society Library, the siblings were de-scribed as "the most extraordinary and inexplicable phenomena that the history of the human race has yet produced. They were recently taken from a newly dis-covered and idolatrous people in Central America, by whom they were kept with super-stitious veneration, distinct and secluded as a caste of their priesthood, and employed as Muses and Bacchanals in their Pagan ceremonies and worship."

The Aztec Children appeared in Barnum's American Museum in the early 1850s and later toured with the Barnum & Bailey Circus. They danced and spoke Aztec gibberish. On January 1, 1867, in a grand publicity stunt, the two were married in London as Má-ximo Valdez Núñez and Bartola Velásquez. Perhaps showmen hoped the two would cre-ate more Aztec Children for future exhibits, but evidently Máximo was sexually immature and the marriage was never consummated. The Aztecs continued touring until 1901. At one point in their career they were earning $200 a week. Máximo is believed to have died in 1913. The date of Bartola's death remains a mystery.

Through the years many imitators tried to ride the wave of the Aztecs' popularity. Two microcephalic youngsters named Aurora and Natali were once exhibited as Aztec

Children. A report from 1884 mentions two "Caucasian idiots" who performed as Aztec Children who were returned to the Ohio insane asylum from which a showman had taken them. If imitation is the sincerest form of flattery, it's unfortunate that Máximo and Bartola could not comprehend the compliments.

JONATHAN R. BASS, THE OSSIFIED MAN
1830–1892

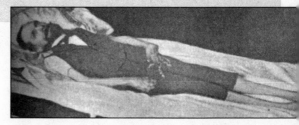

Jonathan R. Bass, the Ossified Man.
Note what appear to be overgrown fingernails on his left hand
From Gould and Pyle, Anomalies and Curiosities of Medicine

When Jonathan Bass was born, on November 25, 1830, in the town of Cambria in western New York, he didn't appear in any way to be sideshow material. Bass, the eldest of three brothers, was a healthy, normal child.

But at age seven, he suffered from a minor case of rheumatism, and things began to change. Another attack assaulted his hip when he was nine, leaving him stiff for three days. By 1848, when he was seventeen, the internal enemy returned, this time ravaging his feet. He couldn't stand and was stuck at home for three months. Treatment proved no help. Bass could move only with the aid of crutches and a cane. Still, he defied the disease and kept his job managing a stable of horses and mules. When his condition worsened, he took on less physical work as a bookkeeper at a hardware store.

Eventually Bass became completely ossified. The rheumatism led to ankylosis of all his joints. The *International Journal of Surgery* claimed: "All the muscles, tendons and joints have been converted into solid bone; he is incapable of any motion whatever, being a prisoner in his own frame." Luckily, Bass didn't suffer any pain. He had a good appetite, and ate by sucking food into his mouth and swallowing it whole. His days and nights were spent confined to a specially made bed.

As bad as his condition was, his life got worse. Cataracts took his eyesight in 1869. His mother died in 1872, one brother several years later. The universe was on a mean streak with poor Bass. By 1887 he had decided it was time to exhibit his stonelike, emaciated body in order to earn a living. At seventy-five pounds he could have had a double billing as the Ossified Man and the Living Skeleton.

Along with a manager, Bass started his tour in Niagara Falls and worked his way across the country. At World's Museum in Fort Wayne, Indiana, he was the "Sensation of the Season"; your life was "not complete without forming the acquaintance of this marvelous man." Bass was intelligent and remained cheerful through his plight.

In 1892, Bass's cheeriness grew to frustration. He was unhappy with his $25 cut of the weekly earnings, so he parted ways with his manager. His remaining brother became his new partner. While on exhibit at Huber's 14th Street Museum in New York City, the Ossified Man became ill with pneumonia and a fever. The Bass brothers returned home to Lewiston, New York, where Jonathan died on September 13.

When physicians wanted to perform an autopsy, their request was refused. The Ossified Man was buried in an ironclad vault to prevent grave robbers from stealing the body.

Like a good special-edition DVD, the story of Jonathan R. Bass comes with an alternative ending. According to a 1908 *Scientific American* article, Bass died after being "injured by a careless museum attendant, who let him fall as he was being removed from a carriage."

BARNUM'S BEGINNINGS

The world's most famous showman was born on July 5, 1810, in Bethel, Connecticut. Before breaking into show business, young Phineas Taylor Barnum worked in an uncle's grocery store in Brooklyn, New York, sold lottery tickets, and published his own liberal newspaper in Danbury, *The Herald of Freedom*. The paper taught him the power of the writ-

(continued)

ten word and, after he was a defendant in a libel case, the power of publicity. By age twenty-five, Barnum reckoned he was born to be a showman. He couldn't have been more right. As a reporter wrote in his obituary in 1891, "He had a fondness for popular applause—he had it down to the last day of his life—and thought he possessed the instinct of divining what the public wanted and arousing a furor of interest in what he had to show." During his lifetime, Barnum also ventured into politics and real estate, and through his marketing and promotion genius has been hailed by many as the father of advertising.

His first claim to fame came in 1835, after he heard of an old African-American slave named Joice Heth, who was being exhibited as the 161-year-old former nurse of George Washington. She was blind, had no teeth, weighed less than fifty pounds, and moved very little. Yet she was very sociable around visitors and enjoyed recounting anecdotes of the young president-to-be and his family. In his autobiography, *Struggles and Triumphs*, Barnum wrote of Heth: "I was favorably struck with the appearance of the old woman. So far as outward indications were concerned, she might almost as well have been called a thousand years old as any other age." The burgeoning showman purchased the slave for $1,000 and put her on tour.

Heth was a hit. Many in the public, and even the press, accepted the claim of her age. Although the truth didn't necessarily matter—the prospect itself was fascinating and entertaining. According to Kathleen Maher, curator of the Barnum Museum, in Bridgeport, Barnum "was putting the new kind of democratic dream out there—you can believe whatever you want, come and see, make up your own mind. That is what made it so exciting to people." Barnum's exhibition featured a statement describing how Heth had been found, a reading of her bill of sale, and a question-and-answer session about Washington. Members of the audience were also permitted to quiz Heth, but none was able to stump her.

Unlike Heth herself, the exhibition was short-lived. On February 19, 1836, age finally caught up with the old slave. An autopsy was published and revealed that the doctor's report determined that Heth was no older than eighty. Interestingly, not everyone wished to acknowledge the examination results. In March, after her actual age was announced, a newspaper proclaimed: "Joice Heth is no more! This ancient of days, on whose knees the infant Washington once rested and played, has at last laid down the burden of more than 160 years. She was the oldest woman in the world, when she met her death, which took place of Monday last [*sic*]. Actual age, 162. May she have fitting exequies, and repose in peace."

In contrast to Heth, Barnum's next attractions were legitimate. The showman made stars of an Italian acrobatic performer, Signor Vivalla, and the opera singer Jenny Lind, the Swedish Nightingale. At the time, opera was a manner of entertainment largely unknown in the United States; Barnum's marketing savvy made the European star a household name before she ever sang a note on American soil. "What he did, cleverly, was not really sell her on her artistic merits," Maher explains, but promote her "on her pious character." Lind was a religious and benevolent woman who donated generously to orphanages and musical societies, and who planned to give proceeds from her opening-night concert in New York to local fire departments. To help with these good deeds, Barnum matched a portion of what she gave. "Those were all little tiny pieces that endeared her to American society in 1850," says Maher. Lind's performances earned $1,000 a night for 150 nights.

Such were the beginnings to Barnum's remarkable career. The timeline below is a rough guide to his struggles and triumphs.

1835   Barnum exhibits Joice Heth.

1841   Barnum purchases Scudder's American Museum.

1842   Barnum opens his American Museum, on New Year's Day. Later promotes the Fejee Mermaid and discovers Charles Sherwood Stratton, aka Tom Thumb.

1849   With Tom Thumb's father, Barnum launches the Great Asiatic Caravan, Museum and Menagerie.

1855   Barnum goes bankrupt after a bad business venture.

1857   Fire destroys Iranistan, Barnum's Bridgeport, Connecticut, mansion.

1865   Fire destroys Barnum's American Museum.

1868   Fire strikes again, at Barnum's New American Museum.

1871   Barnum initiates his Grand Traveling Museum, Menagerie, Caravan and Circus.

1881   Barnum joins with two London circus promoters, James Bailey (an American) and James Hutchinson, to create the Barnum & London Circus.

(continued)

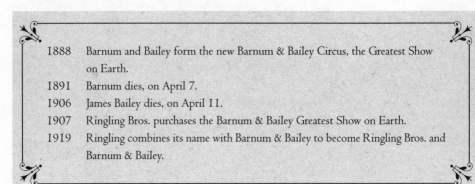

1888   Barnum and Bailey form the new Barnum & Bailey Circus, the Greatest Show on Earth.

1891   Barnum dies, on April 7.

1906   James Bailey dies, on April 11.

1907   Ringling Bros. purchases the Barnum & Bailey Greatest Show on Earth.

1919   Ringling combines its name with Barnum & Bailey to become Ringling Bros. and Barnum & Bailey.

MARTIN VAN BUREN BATES *and* ANNA SWAN

Bates: 1845–1919
Swan: 1846–1888

If ever a man and a woman were destined to be with each other, it was the seven-foot-eleven-inch Bates and the slightly taller Swan.

Martin Van Buren Bates was born in Letcher County, Kentucky, on November 9, 1845. His size at birth was normal, but he grew rapidly. By age fifteen he was six feet tall, and soon he was known as the Kentucky Giant. Bates was a gentle giant, but his good nature was temporarily shelved when he joined the Fifth Kentucky Infantry in the Confederate army to fight in the Civil War. His unnatural size helped him enroll at an underage sixteen, and his enormous physique and fearlessness made him a ferocious fighter. Bates's accomplishments and bravery were rewarded with a promotion to the rank of captain. After the war, having had enough of fighting, he sold his property in Kentucky and moved to Cincinnati to join a circus. Captain Bates was one sideshow performer who actually earned his military title, unlike the little people who were aggrandized with titles of general, admiral, and commodore.

Anna Haining Swan was born on August 6, 1846, in Tatamagouche, Nova Scotia. She was the third of twelve children—and at an astonishing eighteen pounds, she was certainly the most challenging birth for her mother. By age four she was already four feet, six inches tall. Her steady growth continued, and she naturally dwarfed her classmates. Her school desk was propped up and she was given a tall stool to sit on.

It didn't take long for Anna to capture the attention of P. T. Barnum. At sixteen, she began working in his American Museum, exhibiting her full height, a glorious seven feet, eleven and a half inches. Swan would often be paired in contrast with the twenty-nine-inch Commodore Nutt or the equally small Tom Thumb. Working for Barnum was profitable, but tragedy would strike. Twice. The museum caught fire while Swan was there, and

Promotional card for Anna Swan and Captain Bates with W. W. Cole's
Great New York & New Orleans Circus, 1879. Hype on the reverse. *Author's collection*

it burned to the ground. Firemen heroically broke through a wall and used a crane to lower her to safety. The giantess lost all her possessions. Barnum opened a second museum, which was also destroyed in a fire while Swan was there. After this, she left Barnum and returned home to Nova Scotia. A year later, in 1869, Swan rejoined the showman for a tour of the United States.

Fate finally brought the giants together during her travels. Swan and Bates met at a party in New Jersey and were later reacquainted in 1871, when a promoter, Judge H. P. Ingalls, booked them both for a three-year European tour. The two saw that clearly they were made for each, and they fell in love. They were married in London shortly afterward, on June 17, 1871. Queen Victoria also fell in love with Bates. And Swan. She showered the couple with wedding gifts, including a gown and a diamond ring.

The following year, Mrs. Bates gave birth to a daughter. The baby was just like Mom—eighteen pounds, twenty-seven inches—but sadly, she died shortly after birth.

The colossal couple settled in Seville, Ohio, where they built a home designed just for them. Doorways were eight and a half feet high, ceilings reached to fourteen feet, and oversize furniture was constructed to provide a rare treat for giants, comfort. But soon the pair would need money. They took advantage of the gift nature had given them and joined W. W. Cole's circus, touring as the Tallest People on Earth. They were advertised as "the greatest people since Goliath's day" and "the two greatest curiosities in existence."

In 1879, another baby Bates was born. This time a boy, weighing in at twenty-two pounds and measuring twenty-eight inches. He would not get the chance to follow in his parents' giant footsteps either. This second child also died in infancy.

Nine years later, Anna Swan Bates herself died, the day before her forty-second birthday. Captain Bates built her a monument in the Seville cemetery. Chances were slim that he would find another woman he could gaze at eye-to-eye. In 1900 he married a much smaller woman, Lavonne Weatherby, a relatively fragile five feet tall and 135 pounds.

Bates died on January 14, 1919. Before his death, he had chosen six friends to carry his coffin. Eight were needed. He was buried in Seville, with his first wife and their children. Their giant-size home was torn down in 1948, as no one else could live comfortably inside.

Today, Anna Swan's hometown honors the giantess with a museum devoted to her memory.

HANNAH BATTERSBY
1842–1889

Hannah Battersby.
Author's collection

In the late 1800s, Hannah Battersby was considered the largest woman in the world. Her path to fame began in Vermont, where she was born as Hannah Perkins. She was a normal young girl until age twelve, when puberty unleashed its mighty fury. Rambunctious hormones transformed her into a whole lot of woman.

By the time she turned seventeen, the scales were thrust up to 500 pounds. Not only was she heavy, but she stood over six feet tall. As Hannah continued to beef up, she found someone to share her curvaceous cushion with—a Living Skeleton named John Battersby. Her husband was an extreme opposite, weighing just fifty-two pounds. He claimed that his emaciation began after he was thrown off a wagon near Frankford, Pennsylvania. The bizarre Battersbys traveled together, exhibiting their contrasting bodies around the nation; one appearance was at P. T. Barnum's American Museum in 1865.

Hannah's girth was rivaled by that of another Fat Lady on the circuit, Kate Heathley. While most Fat Ladies earned $75 to $100 dollars a week, Heathley and Battersby were paid a dollar for every pound they weighed. The pounds-for-profit scale helped make Battersby a nice fortune. She and her skinny husband were said to be worth $10,000 by the mid-1880s. This was the peculiar couple's peak. John began to put on weight, and eventually ballooned up to 130 pounds. He left show business and returned home to Frankford to run a blacksmith shop.

In 1889, Hannah took ill. While her husband had been gaining weight, she had been losing it. On April 15, she passed away in her home. Once billed by promoters as weighing 800 pounds, Hannah Battersby had shrunk to 343 at the time of her death.

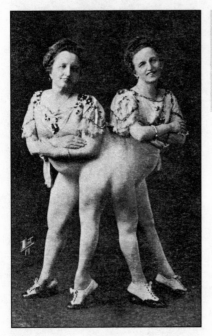
Rosa and Josefa Blazek. *Author's collection*

ROSA *and* JOSEFA BLAZEK, THE BOHEMIAN TWINS

1878–1922

Rosa and Josefa were born on January 20, 1878, in Czechoslovakia. Attached at the lower part of the spinal column, they shared an anus and a urethra, but each had a rectum and a vagina of her own. They grew up healthy and active, and moved about with ease. Rosa emerged as the stronger sister, able to choose a direction and leave Josefa with no choice but to follow. So controlling was Rosa that she needed only think about walking and Josefa would take the first step. Rosa was also the more gregarious. The two had very different tastes in food and were hungry at separate times.

In 1891 the twins began exhibiting themselves in Paris and London as the Bohemian Twins. At fifteen, they traveled to America to appear in the 1893 World's Columbian Exposition in Chicago. Shortly after returning to Europe, though still quite young, the sisters wanted to marry. The lucky groom would get a two-for-one deal. It wasn't until 1910 that a marriage opportunity presented itself. That was the year Rosa gave birth to a son, Franz, in Prague. The father wanted to marry Rosa, but her parents were not supportive. The court to which Rosa and the man turned wasn't, either. It denied the marriage, since the groom would be marrying two women, not one. Marrying Rosa would mean marrying Josefa, and that would be bigamy. The situation made Josefa uncomfortable. She said she didn't like being an involuntary member in the ménage à trois—though Rosa claimed her sister received pleasure as well. Like many conjoined twins, Josefa was able to separate herself mentally from her sister, and could choose to pay no attention to her sister's actions.

By 1922, as the twins aged, they toured the United States with the C. A. Wortham

Shows. But their touring didn't last long. Rosa contracted a case of jaundice, and in character with her controlling will, Josefa fell ill soon after. The twins were treated in a Chicago hospital. One doctor suggested their heavily meat-based diet since entering the United States was responsible. Josefa spent a week in a stupor, and it grew evident that she would die. Doctors considered a separation, but Rosa had made it clear that she did not wish to be divided from her sister. On March 30, 1922, Josefa died. Rosa followed, fifteen minutes later.

X-rays performed after the twins' deaths showed their spines formed a con-

> ★ P. T. Barnum once exhibited infant conjoined twins known as the St. Benoit Twins. They lived just under a year, dying after suffering from a cold in August 1879.

tinuous U shape. A doctor examining the radiographs did not believe either twin could have given birth, unless by cesarean section. But there was no evidence of a scar on Rosa, so Franz's legitimacy as her son was brought into doubt. Had Franz just lost his mother, or had he lost one long before? The answer is not known.

ELI BOWEN, THE LEGLESS ACROBAT

1844–1924

★ Born on October 14, 1844, in Richland, Ohio, Eli was one of ten children. But unlike his siblings, he had no legs. He did, however, have two feet, of different sizes, protruding from his pelvis. The deformity was due to a rare birth defect known as phocomelia. Bowen made the most of what he had, and became one of the world's best-known Legless

Eli Bowen with his family and pet goat. *Author's collection*

Oil painting of Eli Bowen.
Gabrielle Bowen

Wonders. His legless body weighed 140 pounds and his height peaked at twenty-four inches.

At an early age, Bowen learned to use his arms and shoulders to compensate for his lack of legs. He gained great strength and was able to perform stunts and acrobatic tumbling. At age thirteen he began exhibiting his talent with Major Brown's Coliseum, and the act earned him his moniker. The Legless Acrobat's career continued for more than fifty years with dime museums and various circuses, including Barnum & Bailey, Ringling Bros., and late in life, the Coney Island Dreamland Circus Side Show. He occasionally was teamed with the Armless Wonder Charles Tripp. The two were featured in a famous photo with Bowen steering a bicycle being pedaled by his armless partner (see page 282).

At age twenty-six, Bowen married Mattie Haines, who was just sixteen. The two produced four fully limbed sons. According to his great-great-granddaughter Gabrielle Bowen, he did not like little boys and wanted daughters. Nevertheless, he often posed for photos with his wife, the boys, and a pet goat—who may have been treated like a daughter.

The acrobatic anomaly took his final tumble in the living quarters at Coney Island's Dreamland on May 4, 1924, at age seventy-nine. He died of pleurisy, possibly caused by pneumonia, just days before he was scheduled to open an engagement.

BARNUM'S "FREAK"-LESS PHRASEOLOGY

Barnum made a fortune off the exhibition of freaks, but he never referred to his bread and butter as such. Rather, he used more distinguished terms, such as "living wonders" and "human curiosities," along with extended grandiose phrases to enhance his performers' status and show them respect. After his death, his business partner James Bailey began using "freaks" on programs, billboards, and other advertisements. In 1903, the so-called

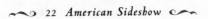

freaks organized into the Protective Order of Prodigies. Chairman Signor Tomasso (a Human Pincushion) and Secretary Charles Tripp (an Armless Wonder) drafted a letter to Bailey protesting the use of the f-word, demanding to be called "prodigies." Bailey had been guilty of the same offense four years earlier in London, but he acquiesced after similar dissent there. He seems to have forgotten the incident upon returning to the United States.

These are a few of Barnum's flamboyant phrases:

★ Parliament of Peculiar and Puzzling Physical Phenomena and Prodigies
★ Colossal Continental Congress of Curious Creatures
★ Weird and Winsome Wonders of the Wide, Wide World
★ Peerless Prodigies of Physical Phenomena and Great Presentation of Marvelous Living Human Curiosities

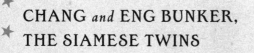

CHANG *and* ENG BUNKER, THE SIAMESE TWINS

1811–1874

★ Without question, Chang and Eng are the most famous of all conjoined twins. It's because of them that conjoined twins are still called Siamese today, regardless of their nationality. The brothers were born on May 11, 1811, in a fishing village in Siam, what is now Thailand. They were two of seventeen children.

Chang and Eng Bunker relaxing in their later years, circa 1860s. *Johnny Fox's Freakatorium*

Among their siblings were three other sets of twins and one set of triplets. Chang and Eng were the only conjoined siblings.

A four-inch ligament, which could stretch to eight inches, connected the twins at the chest. They stood half facing each other, with Chang on the left and Eng on the right (they were named after the Siamese/Thai term for their respective sides). Physically, their bodies functioned separately. If one was sick, the other felt no effects. Eng developed a good-natured personality, while Chang was often more irritable. Eng was the decision maker, a fact that may have contributed to Chang's crankiness.

In 1829, the American explorer Captain Abel Coffin discovered the novel brothers. He purchased them and exhibited them in England and America. After three years under his management, Chang and Eng chose to run their own career. Their binding ligament brought them fantastic fame and fortune. By 1838 they were able to retire with $60,000. Still, the twins had wanted to be separated. They fought often, sometimes quite bitterly. Numerous physicians examined them but determined they could not be separated without risking the life of one or the other.

The brothers took their earnings and moved to Wilkes County, North Carolina. They became American citizens and adopted the last name Bunker (the name of their banker in New York City). The Bunkers wasted no time in finding sisters who would become their wives. Sarah and Adelaide Yates were not even twenty when they agreed to marry the famous twins. Both wanted Sarah, the larger and heavier of the two women. Eng, in keeping with his role as decision maker, won her. Chang's consolation prize was Adelaide. The marriage seemed unbelievable, and many newspapers reported the union was a hoax. It was anything but. Chang and Eng would go on to father twenty-two children between them. None were twins.

The Bunker clan lived on a plantation that Chang and Eng had purchased. The brothers also acquired slaves, despite their once being owned themselves. The separate families lived in two houses, about a mile and a half apart. The men's time with their individual families was split into three-day periods. This rule was very strict; even the death of a child was not grounds to break it.

With such large families to support, the brothers needed more money. In 1850 they agreed to travel with P. T. Barnum for five years. The famed showman hadn't worked with them before, but he had tried to associate himself with them by exhibiting wax likenesses in his museum in the 1840s. In 1860 the Bunkers teamed up with Barnum once again, displaying themselves at his American Museum for six weeks. Eight years later, after the Civil War, the Confederate twins experienced heavy financial damages. Although Chang and Eng didn't particularly like Barnum, they did enjoy recouping their losses, so they joined forces with the showman one last time for a European tour.

In 1870, Chang suffered a paralyzing stroke. Fortunately for Eng, his brother had a partial recovery, though his right leg was useless. Had both been crippled, Eng would have had to drag his brother along for the remainder of their years. On January 17, 1874, Chang passed away at home. Eng lived four more hours, lying next to his dead brother. An autopsy claimed that the twins could not have been successfully separated while alive.

Chang and Eng Bunker died wealthy, leaving money for their wives and their many children.

CHANG
THE CHINESE GIANT
1845–1893

Chang Woo Gow (also known as Chang Yu Sing) was born in 1845 in Fychow, China. As a teenager he earned the name the Chinese Giant for obvious reasons, and he became a sensation in the court of the emperor. The well-proportioned eight-footer claimed to have a sister who was even taller, but it was he who made a career out of his stature.

In 1864, standing seven feet, nine inches

Chang the Chinese Giant, as advertised for a show featuring some of nature's other giants. *Becker Collection, Special Collections Research Center, Syracuse University Library*

and growing, he left China for England. He appeared before the Prince and Princess of Wales, at their request, and after looking down on royalty, continued his tour of England for nearly two years. He towered above thousands of men and women while on exhibition. He later toured Europe, often appearing with a dwarf, Chung, to further demonstrate his size. Chang's traditional Chinese gown also worked to his advantage by making him appear larger. The taller, the better.

Chang was an intelligent, cultured man. He spoke several languages besides Chinese, including English, French, and German. He was also well-read, familiar with both English and Chinese literature.

It is not known whether Chang was affiliated with a particular showman or circus before 1881. But in that year, Barnum's Greatest Show on Earth brought him to the United States for the new season, purportedly at a salary of $600 a week. Barnum's ad described him as having the "strength of Hercules and the beauty of Apollo." Not a bad combination. The giant worked with Barnum through the mid-1880s.

As with many giants, Chang's height was probably exaggerated. An 1883 New York *Journal* article entitled "How Giants Are Made" featured a fellow giant, Colonel Ruth Goshen, stating that "Chang, the Chinese monstrosity, has a mouth that could not be enlarged without danger to his ears. His actual height is about six feet, six inches, and his shoes are made in such a way as to raise him about five inches higher." Of course, Goshen may have been exaggerating as well; after all, Chang was competition.

Regardless of Chang's true height, he was living as large as his appearance, enjoying wealth, renown, smarts, and even romance. The giant was often pictured with a Chinese bride named King-Foo—likely just for show. An article in the Kansas City, Missouri, *Times* in 1886 reported that Chang was single but considering marriage, though he declined to comment on the young lady. The article also claimed that Chang had intended to become an American citizen and make his home in Kansas City. It seems the giant changed his mind, as there are no further mentions of Chang the Kansas City Giant. Other sources say he did indeed find love, but it was in Australia that he met his wife. The couple had two sons and settled in Bournemouth, England. Chang opened a tearoom in his home, which was decorated with his collection of art from the Far East.

In 1893, Chang's wife took ill and died. He lasted only four months without her, apparently dying of a broken heart.

CHE-MAH,
THE CHINESE DWARF
1838–1926

Che-Mah was born on April 15, 1838, in Ningpo, China. His dwarfism was of the achondroplastic (normal torso, shortened limbs) variety. The little man was first exhibited in London in 1880 and subsequently brought to the United States by the Barnum & Bailey Circus in 1881. He later exhibited his twenty-eight inches and forty pounds with Buffalo Bill's Wild West Show and with the Kohl and Middleton dime museum in Chicago.

At one time, Che-Mah earned a handsome $125 a week. He quickly amassed a fortune, and married his first wife in 1882—a normal-size trapeze artist from Brooklyn, New York, named Louisa Coleman. The mismatched couple had a son, Frankie. When the marriage ended in divorce after five years, Che-Mah lost custody of his much larger boy.

At the age of sixty-two, the small man retired to a small town. He bought a farm near Knox, Indiana, but his vertically challenged stature wasn't conducive to farming: it simply took too long for him to do anything. He gave up his dream of being a farmer and bought a house and several other pieces of property in Knox. An old theatrical friend's daughter, Norah Cleveland, moved in to help him around the house. She was the size of many Che-Mahs, weighing a hefty 200 pounds. Despite the age difference—he was seventy-one, she not quite thirty—romance flourished. When the odd couple married, Che-Mah stood atop a table next to his bride. Their differences caused problems over the years. Che-Mah was jealous of his younger and taller wife, and their unhappiness led to divorce in 1923, when he was eighty-five.

Che-Mah, in traditional Chinese dress, with an unknown woman. *Starke County Historical Society, Inc., Knox, Indiana*

The Chinese Dwarf died on March 21, 1926. Ten years later, the book *This Way to the Big Show: The Life of Dexter Fellows,* claimed that Che-Mah was actually Jewish and from London. This would explain why he was first exhibited there. At the time, a Chinese heritage was indeed much more exotic and interesting. If this story is true, his origin was certainly a well-kept secret.

WHAT'S THE DIFFERENCE BETWEEN A MIDGET AND A DWARF?

Everyone knows it's not polite to point and stare at a little person. But one thing many average-size people aren't sure of is whether that little person is a dwarf or a midget.

According to Little People of America (LPA), dwarfism is a medical or genetic condition that usually results in an adult who stands no taller than four feet, ten inches. The most frequent kind of dwarfism is achondroplastic, which causes disproportionately short limbs and a large head. Achondroplasia occurs in one per 26,000 to 40,000 births, though there are more than a hundred diagnosed types of dwarfism.

A midget is basically a proportionate dwarf—a little person whose arms, legs, and head are relatively proportional for his or her size. Midgets look like anyone else, only in miniature. LPA dates the common use of the term "midget" to 1865, when freak shows were enjoying great popularity and people of diminutive stature were exhibited to the public. Thus, "midgets" were a source of other people's amusement. Because of this, many consider the term offensive.

Now that you can differentiate the two, keep the knowledge to yourself. Most midgets and dwarfs prefer to be called little people.

MADAME JOSEPHINE FORTUNE CLOFULLIA, THE BEARDED LADY OF GENEVA

1831–?

P. T. Barnum worked with many Bearded Ladies through his career, but among the earliest and most famous was Madame Josephine Fortune Clofullia.

Born Josephine Boisdechene in 1831 in the Swiss village of Versoix, she had a beard by the age of two. The girl had apparently received a disproportionate share of her hirsute father's genes. When she was eight, Josephine's facial hair was more than two inches long. Doctors feared that cutting the fur would only make it grow in thicker. Her parents decided that if their daughter was going to be a freak, she would at least be an educated one—so they shipped her off to boarding school.

Josephine's whiskers extended six inches by the time she was sixteen. Naturally, the bearded teenager had become quite a curiosity. In 1849,

Madame Clofullia. *Becker Collection, Special Collections Research Center, Syracuse University Library*

to satisfy (and capitalize on) popular demand, her father began to exhibit his daughter's facial fleece in Geneva and later in France. Skeptical doctors examined the girl and confirmed she was indeed a biological woman.

While in France, Josephine met an artist, Fortune Clofullia—who was also bearded. Painting lessons blossomed into romance, and the shaggy couple was soon married. Now known as Madame Clofullia, Josephine reaffirmed the doctors' diagnosis by giving birth to a normal baby girl in 1851. The infant died after just eleven months. However, the couple had been busy working on a second child, and Clofullia gave birth once again shortly after their daughter's funeral. The baby boy, Albert, was said to look like his mother—beard and all.

In 1853, P. T. Barnum signed Madame Clofullia to appear at his American Museum in New York as the Bearded Lady of Geneva. To generate interest, the shrewd showman planted stories that Clofullia was actually a man. The controversy ended up in court, and Barnum's plan netted him a fortune in free publicity. To add to his profits, he also promoted the Bearded Lady's bearded son. Borrowing from the Bible's hairiest character, Barnum billed Albert as the "Infant Esau," a name that would later be used for young Annie Jones.

Madame Clofullia proved to be extremely popular and was seen by millions. She heightened her femininity with an elegant Victorian wardrobe and opulent jewelry. Her beard was styled after that of Napoleon III, who was so flattered to find out that he sent her a large diamond. The glittery stone, fittingly, adorned her beard.

James W. Coffey, in formal suit, with an unidentified man. *Becker Collection, Special Collections Research Center, Syracuse University Library*

JAMES W. COFFEY, THE SKELETON DUDE

1852–?

James W. Coffey's flesh and bones were introduced to the world on March 11, 1852, in Ohio. Although he grew up with a hearty appetite, he failed to put on weight. He was otherwise healthy. By 1884, Coffey, as the Ohio Skeleton, began profiting off his fragile five-foot-six-inch, seventy-pound frame in Chicago dime museums.

Coffey subsequently traveled the United States and Europe with various circuses. Fancy tights emphasized his slight appearance, but the outfit didn't defend his body from cold weather. So Coffey had a tight-fitting warm formal suit tailored. To add to his more dapper appearance, Coffey began wearing a monocle and carrying a cane. He even gave himself a doctorate, calling himself Dr. J. W. Coffey. Yet he became known by a not-so-medical moniker, Skeleton Dude. The distinguished bachelor flirted with women in the audience, though he didn't expect much reciprocation, joking that "most women don't like their Coffey thin."

Apparently his theory was wrong. An ossified girl from Louisiana named Emma Scholler fell in love with him and married him. This happened twenty-two times, in every city and town they traveled to. Local papers printed announcements of the unusual nuptials, and the price would double for museumgoers to witness the happy couple. Publicity stunts aside, Coffey married Mary Eveline Curtright in the late 1890s, and they had a normal child shortly after. Coffey was quite proud of this, believing it demonstrated that abnormal people could produce healthy offspring.

At the turn of the century, Coffey was featured at Huber's 14th Street Museum in New York City. But his success did not last long. He moved to Burlington, New Jersey, and attempted to earn a living at palmistry. This proved to be not nearly as fruitful as the Skeleton Dude career. Coffey, who had once been a barber in Cedar Rapids, Iowa, evidently didn't want to pick up the scissors again. Penniless, he was cared for by the city of Burlington.

✶

CAPTAIN GEORGE CONSTENTENUS, THE TATTOOED GREEK PRINCE

1836–?

✶ Captain George Constentenus (or Constantinus, or Djordgi Konstantinus) gained fame as one of the first Tattooed Men shown in America. The Tattooed Greek Prince flaunted 388 Burmese patterns covering nearly his entire body, including scalp, genitals, and the crevices between his fingers. Only his nose, ears, and the soles of his feet were

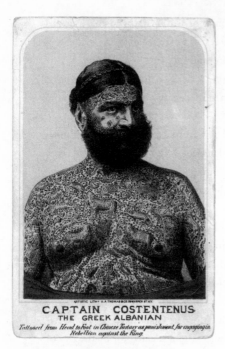

CAPTAIN COSTENTENUS
THE GREEK ALBANIAN

Tattooed from Head to Foot in Chinese Fantasy as punishment for engaging in Rebellion against the King

Captain Constentenus, 1882. This photograph was part of P. T. Barnum's family archives.
Ken Harck archives / Bros. Grim Side Shows

spared. The dark blue and red markings were symmetrically arranged in patterns of snakes, elephants, storks, gazelles, dragons, plants, flowers, and various other life forms.

Legend claims that he was born in 1836 in Albania. By the early 1870s he was in the United States, where he was exhibited by both the Great Farini and P. T. Barnum. Adorned in nothing more than a loincloth, Constentenus exposed his gallery of art for all to see. Audiences were told that he had been on a military expedition in Cochin China, when he and two others were taken prisoner by natives. The three soldiers were sentenced to a choice of horrible deaths: by starvation, wasps, tigers, fire, impalement, or by being cut to pieces from the toes up. But there was another option: receiving full-body tattoos and their liberty, if they lived through the torturous needling. "Tattooed? Why, of course we will choose that," Constentenus told his captors. While his fellow prisoners died from punishment, and while he suffered raging fevers and intense pain, Constentenus survived the three-month ordeal. The crowds who heard this tale were probably too busy staring at his shocking and exotic designs to pay any attention to its outlandish details.

The Captain's markings were the most elaborate ever exhibited in Europe or America. Doctors were fascinated with him; a skin specialist from the University of Vienna studied him extensively.

Constentenus earned a fortune during his days with Barnum, reportedly taking home $1,000 a week. He willed half his wealth to the Greek Church of London and the other half to freak friends in financial need.

Tattoo-happy sailors, Harley-Davidson enthusiasts, and self-made illustrated freaks have all benefited from the Captain's breakthrough success.

MYRTLE CORBIN,
THE FOUR-LEGGED WOMAN
1868–?

Myrtle Corbin, circa 1870s.
*Becker Collection, Special Collections Research Center,
Syracuse University Library*

Born in Cleburne, Texas, Myrtle Corbin (sometimes referred to as Josephine Myrtle Corbin) had a normal body, with the exception of her dipygus twin growing from between her legs. The small twin was developed from the waist down and was believed to be sexually functional. Each foot had three toes. In addition to the awkward legs dangling amid her own, Corbin had a clubfoot to make walking an even greater challenge.

The Four-Legged Woman was a popular attraction with P. T. Barnum, Ringling Bros., and in New York at Huber's 14th Street Museum and Coney Island. When exhibiting herself, Corbin dressed the superfluous pair of legs in shoes and socks matching her own. Thanks to her partial sister, she was able to earn as much as $450 a week. Her proud parents had several more children, hoping to give birth to another gold mine.

As one might expect, the extra body often got in the way. On one occasion, the helpless twin was accidentally burned while Corbin ironed her clothes. Fortunately, the extra limbs didn't interfere in her love life. She married a Kentucky man she met during her travels. Apparently her husband took advantage of the whole package, as she had five children—three born from her own body, and two from her twin's. Whether this was true or simply what audiences were told is not known; if Corbin possessed two sets of reproductive organs, it is medically possible.

MADAME BARONESS SIDONIA DE BARCSY
and BARON NICU DE BARCSY

Sidonia: 1866–1925

Nicu: 1885–1976

★ Born on March 1, 1866, in Hungary, Sidonia de Barcsy was normal in every way—until the age of nineteen. Shortly after she became a mother, on February 28, 1885, everything took a turn for the freakish.

Her son, Nicu, was a midget, weighing only one pound, twelve ounces at birth. Two weeks after his birth, Sidonia began to sprout hairs from her chin, though she somehow didn't realize it. Doctors examining her saw the growth and chose not to tell her, apparently thinking she wouldn't detect the growth by feeling it. "The doctor ordered that all mirrors be taken down from the walls of my home, as he was afraid that if I discovered what had happened to me it would have a serious result, owing to my delicate condition," de Barcsy once told a *New York Times* reporter, through her translator. When she later discovered the development under her chin, she was not too fond of it. She

Baroness Sidonia de Barcsy
HUNGARIAN LADY WITH NATURAL FULL BEARD. RECEIVED THE CROSS OF HONOR FROM THE PROFESSORS OF THE UNIVERSITIES AS THE QUEEN OF FREAKS.
BEARD GREW AFTER BIRTH OF SON

Madame Baroness Sidonia de Barcsy, circa 1900. *Collection of James G. Mundie*

cried often. Her husband, Antonio, was supportive and even claimed he would divorce her if she cut the hairs. He understood that her beard could be exhibited, which meant good money and plenty of traveling—who wouldn't want to see the bearded woman and her midget son? If Antonio could grow himself a third leg, they'd really be set.

In 1907 the family traveled to the United States. Mother and son worked in various circuses and sideshows, including those at Coney Island. Nicu, who had grown to twenty-eight inches, was called Baron. His mother became the Baroness (claiming descent from a noble Hungarian family). And Antonio was their manager. Baroness de Barcsy's beard had grown to a full six inches. Over the years she grew to enjoy the business and being a true attraction. The Baron also seemed to like entertaining. He embellished his act with magic, adopting the name "The Original Colibri" (hummingbird). Nicu escaped from handcuffs and stocks, and was, his postcard advertised, "undoubtedly the world's smallest Handcuff King." He found great joy in cigar smoking, and once boasted that he puffed twenty-five a day.

Baroness de Barcsy's career ended after a feud with a fire-eating co-worker. The origin of the feud is unknown, but the fire eater seems to have been intent on driving the bearded woman crazy. During the season they often were seated next to each other. On one occasion the fire eater whispered his evil intentions to the Baroness, then blew fire right at her beard. She moved just in time, but her beard was singed. In following shows the fire eater continued to taunt her with his flames and threatened to destroy her livelihood. At the end of the season she left the circus, and eventually settled with her family in Drummond, Oklahoma, and appeared with Campbell Brothers Circus.

On October 19, 1925, at the age of fifty-nine, Baroness de Barcsy died. Nicu retired from the business in 1932, and by the mid-1950s was in a rest home. He died there on July 31, 1976, at age ninety-one.

Madame Devere, 1891.
Author's collection

MADAME DEVERE

1842–?

As a Bearded Lady, Madame Devere held the honorable distinction of having a longer beard than any of her bewhiskered counterparts. Her fourteen-inch growth still holds a place in the *Guinness Book of World Records* as the longest on record for a female.

Jane Devere was born in Brooksville, Kentucky, and began to

sprout fuzz on her chin as a girl. By adulthood she had enough facial hair to make a living off it.

She began exhibiting her abundant beard in 1884 in dime museums across the country, including Huber's 14th Street Museum in New York City. She also paraded her shaggy jowl with the Sells Brothers and Campbell Brothers circuses, and in 1908, the Yankee Robinson Show.

Devere married, but her husband couldn't compete with her furry façade. With the exception of his moustache, he was clean-shaven.

✷

WILLIAM DOSS,
THE HUMAN TELESCOPE
Circa 1860s–?

✷ The unique William Doss was able to expand and contract his body to extraordinary degrees. Newspaper reports claimed he could increase his height by two feet within the span of two minutes. Doss's arms were said to stretch nearly eight inches in length. His gift appropriately earned him the name Human Telescope (as in the kind with expanding sections). Doss normally stood six feet, two inches. After his demonstration in expansion, he warranted a second billing as a giant. He was also able to contract his anatomy to the same extent in which he could expand it.

Doss had a hump between his shoulders, which straightened out when he elongated. The hump could be thrust forward, removing the appearance of a slouch and creating what looked like a massive chest. Scientists and physicians were baffled. Spectators were allowed to examine him and found no signs of illegitimacy.

The Human Telescope amazed audiences in the late 1800s through the early 1900s. He expanded and contracted in twenty countries and performed for royalty throughout Europe. In America, Doss appeared in opera houses and on vaudeville stages, and stretched for the Barnum & Bailey show for fourteen years.

ADMIRAL DOT
1864–1918

ADMIRAL DOT.
Thirteen years old   Twenty-five inches high.
Weighs only Fifteen pounds.

Admiral Dot, circa 1873. *Author's collection*

★ Thanks to a diminutive child named Leopold Kahn, a recently retired P. T. Barnum (whose museum had just burned down for the second time) made his inevitable return to show business. Born in 1864 in San Francisco, Leopold got his start in entertainment eight years later, after his parents introduced him to the celebrated showman. The well-proportioned boy was a mere twenty-five inches tall. Barnum took a shining to the young fellow, who reminded him of Tom Thumb. Unable to resist the temptation to show little Leopold to the world, Barnum went back into business. He dubbed his new star "The Eldorado Elf," but soon changed the name to the more prestigious-sounding "Admiral Dot."

The Admiral became a main performer in the newly organized Greatest Show on Earth. The talented Dot sang, danced, played instruments, and stood in the palms of the various giants who performed with the traveling circus. He spent two decades entertaining audiences, earning as much as $700 a week. While working with the Locke & Davis Royal Lilliputian Opera Company, Admiral Dot fell in love with another little performer, Lottie Swartwood, whom he married in 1892. By the end of his career, having reached a height of four feet, he had perhaps outgrown his role. Yet his wife stood taller, at fifty inches.

The miniature couple had two normal-size children, defying the Kahn family gene that was believed to produce one little person in every generation. Instead the gene was passed along to Admiral Dot's nephew, a midget called Major Atom.

Once retired, Dot and his wife moved to White Plains, New York, and opened the

Admiral Dot Hotel. The Admiral became active in the community, joining the Elks club and becoming honorary fire chief. His former employer's bad luck with fires seems to have passed along to the Admiral. His hotel burned to the ground in 1911.

In 1918, at the age of fifty-four, Admiral Dot fell victim to a fatal flu. His wife lived to be eighty-one, dying in 1950.

ELLA EWING, THE MISSOURI GIANTESS
1872–1913

Ella Ewing was born on March 9, 1872, in Lewis County, Missouri. A year later her family moved to the town of Gorin, which would become home to the Missouri Giantess. Little Ella grew normally until the age of seven. Her pituitary gland went haywire, and by the time she was sixteen, she stood seven feet tall. She peaked at a height of eight feet, four and a half inches.

Ewing did not immediately embrace her unusual height. Her first public appearance, it is said, was an emotional nightmare. She was selected to read the Declaration of Independence at a Fourth of July celebration, but she broke down in tears at the crowd's gawking. Ewing stayed home, out of the public eye, so as not to be viewed as a freak. Her parents sheltered her

Ella Ewing with unidentified man and woman, likely her parents, 1890. *Becker Collection, Special Collections Research Center, Syracuse University Library* from the inevitable stares, turning down offers from circuses and carnivals, but eventually they gave in. For $250 a week, plus expenses for her parents to accompany, Ewing would be exhibited out of state for the first time at the 1893 World's Columbian Exposition in Chicago.

The exposure made Ewing a star. The big girl from the little town soon found herself a main attraction in the Barnum & Bailey Circus. The shy giantess embarked on her new career, comforted by her parents' company. For once, among circus folk, Ewing was surrounded by people who didn't find her strange at all. They were all bizarre in their own ways, and this made her enjoy circus life. One thing that she still didn't enjoy was her large feet. She had a special canvas set up to block audiences' view of her size 24 shoes—even as she walked off the platform.

> ✱ Possibly the largest man to ever walk the earth was North Carolina's Miles Darden, who reportedly stood seven feet, six inches and weighed more than 1,000 pounds. He lived from 1798 to 1857.

Ewing later performed with Buffalo Bill's Wild West Show, with the Sells-Floto and Ringling Bros. circuses, and at the 1904 St. Louis World's Fair. Her career provided her with enough money to buy her parents a 120-acre farm near Gorin and build a home suitable for a giantess.

Unfortunately for Ewing, she had no husband with whom to share her roomy home. Men of her size were very few and far between, and as her mother explained, few normal-size men were brave enough to woo her. Although Ewing claimed to have had offers of marriage, they were refused, as the offers were most likely in pursuit of her fortune.

In the first week of 1913, pneumonia forced the giantess off her tour. She returned home to Missouri, where she died on January 10. Ewing had wished for her body to be cremated so that no one could dig it up. But her father couldn't go through with it. Instead, he had a special steel casket made and lined the grave with concrete.

In 1969, the Missouri Department of Conservation built a fifteen-acre lake near Gorin. It was named for Ella Ewing and has become a fishing attraction in the area. The Downing House Museum in Memphis, Missouri, features a room with Ewing's belongings, including her nine-foot iron bed.

GRACE GILBERT

1876–1924

Grace Gilbert was born in 1876 near Leetsville, Michigan. She spent her childhood on her parents' farm, slowly growing hair where it didn't belong.

Gilbert's beard settled in at six inches long when she was an adult. She made the most of it by exhibiting her furry chin from 1900 through 1923, primarily with the Barnum & Bailey Circus. She was also featured at Huber's 14th Street Museum in New York City. While Gilbert's beard was natural, its color was not. She used peroxide to bleach it, and had herself billed as Princess Gracie, the Girl with the Golden Whiskers. She was also known as the Female Esau.

Grace Gilbert, circa 1914.
Kobel collection

The bearded woman became a bearded bride on October 26, 1910, marrying her cousin Giles E. Calvin, a farmer from Kalkaska County, Michigan. At fifty-three, Calvin was nineteen years his bride's senior. It was his second marriage, but his first within the family. Although he did not have a beard, he did have a moustache. The bearded lady left the sideshow to live on her new husband's farm, and wore a veil when she was in public thereafter. But in the summer of 1923 she resumed exhibiting her beard, appearing at Coney Island.

Grace Gilbert died suddenly in her Kalkaska home the following January.

OTHER HAIRY ATTRACTIONS

Excessive hair has always produced popular sideshow attractions. But exhibits weren't limited to bearded women and hirsute wonders. There was plenty of room for long-haired ladies, Circassian girls, and people with furry features.

The Seven Sutherland Sisters were the most famous of the long-haired women. Hailing from upstate New York, the sisters boasted manes from three to seven feet long. They exhibited their luxurious locks with Barnum in the mid-1880s, but found greater wealth by selling a tonic guaranteed to help clean the scalp, grow hair, and prevent hair loss for sufferers of the Spanish influenza. The Sutherlands made millions over the course of several decades.

An example of a Circassian beauty, circa 1870.
Collection of James G. Mundie

"Circassian" beauties were common attractions. Sporting big, bushy afros, they were said to represent the purest stock of the Caucasian race, found in the Russian region of Circassia, on the Black Sea. Barnum exhibited his first Circassian in 1864, claiming she was the daughter of a prince and would otherwise have been doomed to bare her beauty in a Turkish harem. Of course, she, like others who followed, was just a local lady who grew her hair long and soaked it in stale beer for the frizzy, bushy effect. Some of these so-called Circassians were very young; one, Millie Zulu, was only eight years old when exhibited. Circassian stars adopted exotic-sounding names, often containing the letter *z*: Zula Zulick, Zaluma Agara, Zulida Hanover, Zoe Meleke, and Zula Zingara (meaning "Gypsy").

A more freakish attraction was hair sprouting from the center of the back. In the late 1800s, Kentucky-born Belle Carter wore a dress parted in the back to display the long tresses that sprang from her back like a misplaced ponytail. In the 1930s, Colon T. Updike exhibited a hairy thicket emanating from his lower back. It measured approximately eighteen inches long.

COL. RUTH GOSHON.
Age 43 years.   Weight 620 lbs.   Height, 7 feet 11 inches.
J. Baptiste, Photo   872 Broadway, cor 18th St.

Colonel Goshen. Note the military hat
that adds a foot or so to his height.
Kobel collection

★ Colonel Ruth Goshen was known as the Palestine Giant, billed as a Jerusalem-born Arab brought to the United States to be exhibited in P. T. Barnum's first American Museum. This was only one origin given for him, however. The circus manager W. C. Coup claimed he was an African-American from Kentucky. *The New York Times* wrote that he was a Prussian by birth. Another report called him Turkish. To add to the confusion, depending on the source, his name appeared as Ruth, Routh, Deruth, and Rutherford; his height varied from seven feet to eight feet, six inches; and his weight ranged from 400 pounds to 600.

Barnum reportedly found Goshen unemployed, hanging around the Bowery in New York, and hired him immediately. Understandably, the showman went with the eight feet, six inches, although another giant on the circuit maintained that the Colonel was more likely closer to the seven-foot mark. Captain Martin Van Buren Bates, who claimed to be seven feet, eleven inches, once said he could "lick the salt off the head of Col. Goshen." Goshen would have agreed; he once admitted Bates was the taller giant.

In addition to being tall, Goshen was strong. He could move a 1,700-pound cannon, it was said, and he once crushed the head of a grizzly bear with a giant rock. That these claims were unsubstantiated certainly didn't stop Barnum from adding the Strongman title to Goshen's billing.

Barnum paired his brawny giant with his direct opposite, Tom Thumb, to exaggerate their extremes. Goshen worked with other midgets as well; Admiral Dot often appeared standing in the giant's palm. Goshen stayed with Barnum for a number of years and toured with him as part of the Greatest Show on Earth, earning as much as $75 a week.

The giant also performed with little people outside Barnum's museum. In 1876 he worked alongside Commodore Nutt and a group of "Lilliputians" in a production of *Jack the Giant Killer*. The press was fond of the show, describing Goshen as "a monster who, beside the little ones, most forcibly illustrates the experiences of Gulliver among the Lilliputians."

Goshen didn't limit his company to the small. He considered himself an oversize Adonis, and some women seemed to agree. The narcissistic giant was married three times and had one daughter.

Aside from womanizing, the Colonel spent his leisure time telling tall tales—and not just about his height. There was the one about Thomas Edison's theft of his invention, the phonograph. And one about the flying machine Goshen had invented, which flew him around the country at night. He also claimed to have fought in the Crimean War.

Goshen retired in the late 1880s to Middlebush, New Jersey, where he became known as the Middlebush Giant. He lived on a farm, which he converted into a local attraction by filling its barn with curiosities collected during his travels. The farm remained his home until he died, in bed, on February 12, 1889. Just before he died, Goshen confessed a great sin to a priest. All the stories told about him concerning his age (which was also disputed) and origin were lies and exaggerations. The Colonel was not Arab, African-American, Turkish, or Prussian. His name was Arthur Crowley (later said to be Caley), and he hailed from the Isle of Man. It is believed that he was born in the village of Sulby in 1824. He was exhibited in London in 1852 and later in Paris, and joined Barnum in America shortly thereafter. His name may have been changed to Goshen for several reasons: Goshen was an area not far from Sulby; it was also a town in Connecticut, not far from Barnum's hometown; and it was a biblical land. Perhaps these three facts together led Barnum to package him as the more exotic Palestine Giant.

Burying the Colonel proved difficult, as no hearse in Middlebush could contain him. Eight struggling pallbearers pushed a large wagon with his coffin. Goshen's grave was said to be the largest ever dug in New Jersey. The former sideshow star left an estate worth $10,000.

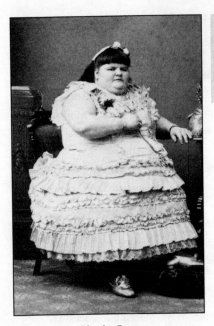

Blanche Gray.
Becker Collection, Special Collections Research Center,
Syracuse University Library

BLANCHE GRAY
1866–1883

★ Blanche Gray wasted no time putting on weight—starting in her mother's womb. Detroit's baby Blanche weighed twenty-five pounds at birth in November 1866. The event proved too much for her mother, who died days later. By age twelve, Gray had grown up to four feet, eight inches and out to 250 pounds. She had reached her peak height, but hadn't come close to her peak weight.

Gray's girth was exhibited first in New York's Bowery Hall and later at Coney Island. The young heavyweight soon fell in love with a twenty-one-year-old, 125-pound lightweight named David Moses, and they were married in October 1883 at Bowery Hall. The wedding caused a great hoopla and the big bride became a minor celebrity. A showman, quick to take advantage, planned to take her on tour across the country. But first Gray was due for a showing in a Baltimore dime museum. Tragically, it would prove to be her last.

Blanche Gray died, in bed, just weeks into her marriage. Her doctor claimed the cause was "a fatty degeneration of the heart." She also suffered from bronchitis, and had been feeling ill for a few weeks. The titanic teenager was only seventeen, but had tipped the scales at 517 pounds. "She had a heart as big as her body," claimed a groomsman from the wedding.

More than a thousand people attended Gray's funeral and watched as the six-foot-long, four-foot-wide casket was carried away in a large covered wagon.

ELLA HARPER,
THE CAMEL GIRL
1873–?

Ella Harper was born in Hendersonville, Tennessee, with an unusual orthopedic condition in her legs. Her knees bent in the opposite direction from normal and stuck out behind her like a camel's. This and her walking on all fours earned her her moniker. At times during her sideshow career she was exhibited alongside other quadripeds, including a den of performing lions and an elephant.

Ella Harper, circa 1886.
Becker Collection, Special Collections Research Center, Syracuse University Library

The Camel Girl was a star attraction in 1886 with W. H. Harris's Nickel Plate Circus. Newspapers hyped her arrival when the circus rolled into town. According to one paper, she was "pronounced by scientists the most wonderful freak of nature ever seen since the creation of the world, a beautiful young lady with the classic features of a woman but the body of a camel. It is said by those who have seen her that there is nothing like her today on earth, and that her counterpart never did exist." The paper later reported its disappointment in the Camel Girl, for she was "nothing more than a pleasant-faced young woman whose knees turned backward instead of forward." Perhaps the disenchanted reporter expected a couple of humps, or caught one too many glimpses of the Camel Girl drinking water.

Harper claimed to have exhibited herself in the four years prior to 1886. That was enough for her. She hoped to quit, go to school, and find a better job. At a salary of $200 a week, she most likely earned enough to leave the business and pursue another.

NORA HILDEBRANDT

Circa 1850s–?

Nora Hildebrandt displaying her tattoos, circa 1880s. *Johnny Fox's Freakatorium*

★ Nora Hildebrandt had the bizarre luck of being born to America's first professional tattoo artist, Martin Hildebrandt. The German-born maestro set up his tattoo shop in New York City in 1846. Though he had plenty of customers to needle, including sailors and soldiers from both sides of the Civil War, he eventually re-created his daughter with tattoos from head to foot.

The new Nora became the first Tattooed Lady to exhibit herself, in 1882. She and her 365 designs toured with the Barnum & Bailey Circus through the 1890s. Hildebrandt explained her father's work to audiences, but spiced up the story by adding that it was done forcibly after they were captured by Indians out West. The imprisonment lasted a year, over which time she was tied to a tree and tattooed daily. Her ludicrous tale recalls that of another Barnum tattooed attraction, Captain Constentenus. Although the fantastic fable and marvelous markings entertained the crowds, Hildebrandt may have been especially popular among male spectators simply because of the skimpy outfits worn to exhibit her flesh.

THE RINGLING BROTHERS

There were five Ringling brothers: Albert, Otto, Alfred, Charles, and John. But it was Charles, born on December 2, 1863, who proved to be the great showman. The brothers entered the circus world in 1884, with a small nine-wagon show in their hometown of

Baraboo, Wisconsin. It would develop into a major railroad show that toured most of the United States and parts of Canada. The Ringlings acquired other shows, including the Barnum & Bailey Circus in 1907 after James Bailey's death. The merger formed the Ringling Bros. and Barnum & Bailey Circus—the Greatest Show on Earth. By 1919, after Albert, Alfred, and Otto had died, Charles was left in charge. John had little involvement until 1926, when Charles died and he took over the reins. Three years later, for $2 million, John bought the American Circus Corporation, which consisted of the Sells-Floto, Hagenbeck-Wallace, John Robinson, Sparks, and Al G. Barnes circuses. Having absorbed his competition, Ringling became the Circus King. After the Depression, however, he was voted out of his seat of power. He died on December 2, 1936.

Other early showmen of note:

★ W. W. Cole, born in New York in 1846, began W. W. Cole's New York and New Orleans Circus and Menagerie in the early 1870s. He sold the show in 1886. The new owners renamed it Cole Bros. Circus, and combined it with the Clyde Beatty Circus in 1958. Cole died on March 10, 1915.

★ Adam Forepaugh, born Adam Forbach on February 28, 1831, in Philadelphia, opened an indoor show in his hometown in 1866 and took it on the road as the Great Adam Forepaugh Circus and Menagerie. Complete with sixty-five train cars, it proved a formidable rival to Barnum. Forepaugh managed the show until his death, on January 22, 1890. In 1896, James Bailey purchased the show and merged it with Sells Brothers Circus as Forepaugh-Sells.

★ John Robinson was born in Little Falls, New York, on July 22, 1807. Together with an English clown, Gil N. Eldred, he launched the Robinson & Eldred Great Southern Circus in 1840. Robinson went solo in 1857 with the John Robinson Circus. He died on August 4, 1888.

★ William Cameron (W. C.) Coup, born in Mount Pleasant, Indiana, on August 4, 1836, entered circus and sideshow management in 1861. In April 1871, along with the clown Dan Castello, he teamed with P. T. Barnum to create the P. T. Barnum's Grand Traveling Museum, Menagerie, Caravan and Circus. It was billed as the

(continued)

Greatest Show on Earth. Coup conceived the second ring in 1872, and perfected and popularized a system for putting the entire show on the railroad. After parting with Barnum, he went on to propose the Hippodrome, precursor to the first Madison Square Garden in New York. Coup, who died on March 4, 1895, is considered one of the greatest circus managers and organizers ever.

★ James Bailey, born James McGinness in Detroit on July 4, 1847, ran away from home at age fourteen. By 1872, he was part owner of Cooper & Bailey's Circus. He competed fiercely with Barnum, but merged with him in 1881 to form the Barnum & Bailey Circus. After Barnum's death in 1891, he became sole owner of the show. Bailey died on April 11, 1906, at his home near Mount Vernon, New York.

WILLIAM HENRY JOHNSON, or ZIP, THE WHAT IS IT?
Circa 1842–1926

★ Physically, William Henry Johnson was one of the least freakish in the freak shows. He was a pinhead, but his head wasn't as small as that of other microcephalics. Regardless, he was one of the most popular sideshow figures and had a longer career than any other exhibited attraction, pinhead or otherwise. Over the years he was best known as Zip, but was also called the Man-Monkey, the Missing Link, the Nondescript, and the What Is It?

Johnson was born around 1842, reportedly in Bound Brook, New Jersey. But anyone who saw him onstage would have heard that he came from a different race of humans found during a gorilla-hunting expedition near the Gambia River in western Africa. This race was said to range naked in its habitat, traveling about by climbing on tree branches. Very little is known about Johnson's true origins.

P. T. Barnum recruited him in 1860 and transformed him into Zip. He had his head shaved—except for a small tuft of hair on top—and dressed him in a furry suit to promote the Missing Link concept. Zip was even displayed in a cage for a time. Yet unlike other Missing Links, such as Krao, Zip wasn't hairy.

Zip would never speak to the public; he would only grunt. Legend has it that Barnum paid him a dollar a day to keep quiet and remain in character. Zip essentially acted like a wild man. Charles Dickens visited him in 1867 and asked, "What is it?" Later reports claimed this was the origin of one of his nicknames. But Barnum had coined the name for Zip in earlier years. Whatever it was about the What Is It?, it made Barnum a fortune. Such wealth allowed him to pay Zip $100 a week (in addition to the dollar a day for his silence), some of which was used to support Zip's sister. Barnum also bought his star attraction a home in Connecticut.

Zip, the What Is It? From an Ex.Sup.Co. (Exhibit Supply Co.) arcade card sold at Coney Island.
The Doghouse Collection / showhistory.com

Zip outlasted Barnum, but continued to work with the Ringling Bros. and Barnum & Bailey shows. The What Is It? brought his antics to Coney Island and was featured in various dime museums. His character changed through the years, though he never uttered actual sentences. He took to carrying a pop gun, which he fired if other freaks threatened his popularity, and later the violin. He couldn't play it, but like any enthusiastic bad musician, he could make a whole lot of noise. Being paid to stop playing was another source of income.

The playful pinhead was said to be good-natured all the time. His manager of thirty-five years, Captain O. K. White, claimed he never saw Zip unhappy, except when he wasn't on exhibition. "He amuses the crowd and the crowd amuses him," White once said. Zip even amused his co-workers. In 1919, someone gave him a toy badge, which he proudly wore with the belief that he now owned the circus. Zip would walk around backstage and bark orders to the staff, who humored him by agreeing to do as he asked.

As he grew older, Zip became known as the Dean of Freaks. He continued performing into his eighties, but succumbed to bronchitis on April 24, 1926, at New York's Bellevue Hospital. He had contracted the illness the previous summer while working as an extra in a Broadway show, *Sunny*, at the New Amsterdam Theatre. Many fellow performers attended his funeral. Captain White was so distraught that he collapsed soon after the funeral; he died two months later.

The What Is It? is now more of a What Was It? Many have speculated as to his true intelligence. Was he a complete idiot who was exploited for sixty-six years? Or was he in on it for all those years, maintaining his act 24/7? Perhaps he understood how to market himself. During the Scopes trial in 1925, Zip, as the Missing Link, offered himself as an exhibit. Not a bad way to generate publicity. Zip also proved, surprisingly, to be a hero late in his life. In 1925, while strolling about Coney Island during a break, he rescued a girl who had swum too far out in the water.

Captain White had helped him save his money, leaving him a wealthy man who could have retired long before his passing. In addition to the home purchased for him by Barnum, Zip owned property in New Jersey. What has left people most curious, though, is a statement he supposedly made to his sister on his deathbed: "Well, we fooled 'em for a long time." If that's true, he fooled more than 100 million of 'em.

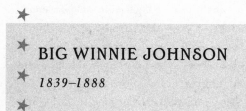

BIG WINNIE JOHNSON
1839–1888

Big Winnie Johnson didn't garner as much fame as her portly peers, but she did outweigh them. Tipping the scales at 849 pounds, she may have been the heaviest woman ever exhibited.

Johnson was born in 1839 in Henry County, Kentucky. She maintained a normal weight through her childhood and teen years. By age fifteen she was married, and soon afterward a mother; she would have ten children in total. The weight began piling on.

After Johnson's husband died, in 1882, she made use of her staggering heft by signing with a showman to go on exhibition. Traveling the country was no easy task for her. With great effort, she was put in a railroad boxcar, which would serve as both her transportation and her stage. Rather than take her out and hoist her in again at each tour stop, the showman simply opened the sliding doors for people to see Big Winnie.

In 1888, Johnson was scheduled to exhibit herself at Johnson's Dime Museum (no relation) in Baltimore. But her heart, afflicted by fatty degeneration, wasn't up to it. Johnson died on September 14. Her body was rolled off a bed into her coffin. It took twenty pallbearers to lift it.

JO-JO
THE DOG-FACED BOY
1868–1903

Jo-Jo the Dog Faced Boy. *Becker Collection, Special Collections Research Center, Syracuse University Library*

In a true case of "like father, like son," Fedor Jeftichew, a native of St. Petersburg, Russia, inherited hypertrichosis from his dog-faced dad. His entire face and body were covered in hair. Where his hair was excessive, however, his teeth were not. Jo-Jo had only five; two in the upper jaw and three in the lower.

The sixteen-year-old Jeftichew was brought to the United States by P. T. Barnum in 1884 and given the stage name Jo-Jo. Barnum advertised him as "the most prodigious paragon of all prodigies secured by P. T. Barnum in fifty years. The Human Skye Terrier, the crowning mystery of nature's contradictions." His literature on Jo-Jo explained the great difficulty in capturing him, and having to battle his ferocious and savage father in the forests of central Russia. In reality, the elder Jeftichew, who was said to resemble a poodle, had toured Russia with his son until he died at age fifty-nine.

Jo-Jo dressed like a Russian cavalryman, and looked quite distinguished with his abundant long, silky hair. Playing up to his description, the Dog-Faced Boy would bark and growl at the audience. Besides dog, he spoke Russian, German, and a little English. Jo-Jo was an immensely popular attraction, sometimes performing up to twenty-three times a day. By 1886 he was raking in $500 a week. Other promoters claimed to be exhibiting Jo-Jo, but were in fact using masked impostors.

In dog years, Jo-Jo lived only to age five. In 1903 the thirty-five-year-old Human Skye Terrier fell victim to pneumonia in Turkey.

Annie Jones raising a glass of wine, circa 1890. *Johnny Fox's Freakatorium*

ANNIE JONES, THE ESAU LADY

1865–1902

The career of Annie Jones began just a year into her life. She was born in Virginia on July 14, 1865—hairier than her father. Her mother was shocked by her daughter's furry appearance. Annie eventually had seven brothers and sisters, all of whom were normal (hair-wise, at least). Word of the bearded newborn traveled and caught P. T. Barnum's attention. A letter from the famous showman excited her parents, who thought they had hit the jackpot.

Young Annie was quickly brought to New York City to be featured by Barnum in his new museum (his first had recently burned) as the Infant Esau. Annie's mother signed a three-year contract, allowing her daughter to be exhibited for the princely sum of $150 a week. Mrs. Jones initially stayed in New York to care for her star attraction, but a family emergency summoned her back to Virginia.

The Infant Esau became hot property. Literally, in fact. The young attraction was stolen by a corrupt phrenologist who wanted a piece of the action. Annie was soon found in upstate New York. After a court battle, her mother gained custody from the kidnapper and the Joneses resumed working with Barnum.

As Annie grew, her stage name evolved with her. She became the Esau Child and later the Esau Lady. Jones was a hit not only for her ample facial hair, but also for the hair atop her head, which was six feet long.

Jones traveled with Barnum's Greatest Show on Earth and worked numerous dime museums in the off-season. Like many Bearded Ladies, she covered her face with a scarf in public. Her travels turned her into a cultured woman. She was also musically gifted, and strummed the mandolin with grace and beauty.

At sixteen, Jones married the resident sideshow talker, Richard Elliot. The marriage ended in divorce fifteen years later. She then married another talker, William Donovan, and the two left the sideshow and ventured into Europe to tour on their own. This plan was interrupted by Donovan's death. Jones quickly rejoined the Greatest Show on Earth.

In 1902, the Esau Lady fell ill. On October 22, while visiting her mother in Brooklyn, Jones died. For thirty-six of her thirty-seven years, Jones was one of the most celebrated bearded women—and children—of the era.

KRAO, DARWIN'S MISSING LINK
1876–1926

Born in Siam (Thailand), Krao was covered from head to foot in jet-black hair. The hair between her shoulder blades resembled a horse's mane. The promoter known as the Great Farini (born William Leonard Hunt) took Krao from her homeland when she was six years old and exhibited her in Europe. She later adopted the Farini name, but was better known simply as Krao.

The bearded wonder soon crossed the Atlantic to appear in the United States. Krao's career in this country began in a Philadelphia dime museum and later jumped to the big leagues with the Ringling Bros. and Barnum & Bailey Circus. She was very popular with audiences, and with other freaks as well.

Krao with an unidentified man, circa 1885.
Note the hair on her arms and legs.
Ken Harck archives/Bros. Grim Side Shows

Sometimes known as the Ape Woman, Krao was marketed as Darwin's Missing Link to reflect on current events. Charles Darwin's theory of man's descendance from apes was controversial at the time. Promoters capitalized on the debate, offering Krao as proof of Darwin's ideas—a middle ground between man and ape. Ads hailed Krao as belonging to a race of people who lived in trees and subsisted on "roots, nuts, grass, etc." She was said to have "pouches inside her cheeks wherein she stores food away like apes." Some scientists took this "missing link" claim seriously and actually focused papers on Krao. The 1896 book *Anomalies and Curiosities of Medicine* even discussed her "extraordinary prehensile powers of feet and lips." In truth, the supposed tree dweller was well-read, multilingual, and probably more intelligent than many of the gawkers who paid to see her.

Krao spent the last twenty years of her life living on Manhattan's Upper East Side with a German couple. She had her own floor and enjoyed cooking and entertaining guests. Barry Gray, a friend of hers, once told a newspaper: "She would have made an excellent wife. But she never married. She was a sensitive soul." Influenza claimed Krao's life on April 16, 1926.

LALOO

1874–1905

Laloo was born in Oudh, India, along with part of a brother. He was the second of four children, the others all normal. Laloo's partial sibling was a small, headless parasitic twin attached to his lower breastbone. They shared bloodstreams, and if the twin was touched, Laloo could sense it; if the weather was hot, both sweated. The dangling twin had two arms and legs, and a functioning penis complete with a urinary system; though lacking testicles, the twin was said to be capable of an erection. Unfortunately, when the twin had to urinate, Laloo became aware of the need only after it was too late; luckily, the twin was not able—and did not need—to defecate.

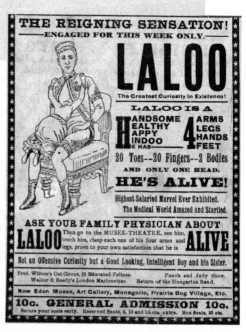

Newspaper ad for Laloo.
Author's collection

Laloo, who was exhibited in nearly every big European and American sideshow, was advertised as a "handsome, healthy, happy Hindoo." To add further interest to his shows (as if that were necessary), the twin would occasionally be dressed as a sister. Clothing concealed the twin when Laloo wasn't onstage.

Laloo was married in Philadelphia in 1894. Financially, he and his wife were in great shape. Laloo commanded a high salary, and even earned money from physicians who wished to give him personal examinations. He was known to spend his wealth quite lavishly.

Laloo died an early death, in a train wreck while exhibiting with the Norris & Rowe show in Mexico. He was buried in the state of Aguascalientes.

HOW DOES A TWIN BECOME PARASITIC?

Lazarus–Joannes Baptista Colloredo.
From Gould and Pyle, Anomalies and Curiosities of Medicine

Parasitic twins occur when an embryo begins to split, but fails to complete the process. One sibling stops growing normally, early in gestation, and may consist of anything from a single limb to an entire body that depends wholly on the fully formed twin's vital functions. Thus the name "parasitic."

Parasitic twins have always been spectacular attractions. Sideshows allowed people like Laloo, Jean Libbera, and Betty Lou Williams to earn healthy livings. An earlier celebrated case was that of a seventeenth-century Italian, Lazarus–Joannes Baptista Colloredo, who had a twin jutting from his chest. The head was visible and actually grew whiskers. The eyes were always closed and the mouth was always open, though it never made a noise. Colloredo exhibited himself across Europe.

In the early 1900s, doctors described the case of a buttock and a lower left extremity protruding from the left eye of an otherwise well-formed child. An additional tumor projected from the same vicinity.

More recently, an Egyptian baby, Manar Maged, was born with a second head attached to her skull. This condition is called craniopagus parasiticus. Manar's second head was capable of smiling and blinking, until February 2005, when doctors successfully removed it.

ANN E. LEAK

1839–?

Ann E. Leak was born armless on December 23, 1839, in Georgia. As with many freaks, publicity pieces explained her condition as the result of a maternal impression: Her alcoholic father came home one day with his coat thrown over his shoulders, hiding his arms. The seemingly casual sight apparently frightened her mother and affected her pregnancy.

Leak used her feet like hands. She mastered the use of scissors, knives, forks, and other instruments. She was also able to write, sew, crochet, and embroider. Most important, she could eat and dress herself. Her clothing was specially made with drawstrings as fasteners, and she used her feet and her teeth to put on her outfits. When signing cards for sideshow visitors, she often wrote, "Of hands deprived, of toes derived." Her marvelous penmanship and accomplishment of basic tasks demonstrated very fancy footwork.

In the 1870s and 1880s, Leak traveled with Barnum as well as Cooper & Bailey's Circus. After being wooed by several suitors, she married a man named Thomson and performed as Ann Leak Thomson.

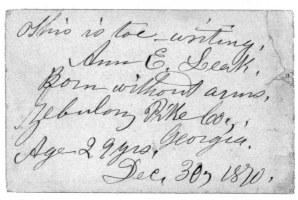

A *carte de visite* of Ann E. Leak, 1870. Her feet hold a writing instrument, and an example of her "toe writing" appears on the reverse. *Author's collection*

Lionel the Lion-Faced Man puffing a cigarette, circa 1920. *Collection of Marie A. Roberts*

LIONEL
THE LION-FACED MAN
1890–1932

Lionel the Lion-Faced Man began life as Stefan Bibrowski, in 1890 in a suburb of Warsaw. His appearance, it was claimed, resulted from his pregnant mother's having watched his father being torn to shreds by a lion. Even if the story had been true, it would have merely been a convenient coincidence, since the hairiness was actually a case of hypertrichosis. The six-inch locks covered Stefan's entire body, except for his palms and the soles of his feet.

A German showman discovered the hairy boy as a four-year-old and, with his parents' blessing (evidently his father hadn't been torn to shreds as was reported), began to exhibit him. The name Stefan Bibrowski wouldn't do for the stage; it was hardly catchy, or compatible with his incredible leonine looks. "Lionel the Lion-Faced Boy" fit him much better.

Lionel traveled throughout Europe and came to the United States several times, touring with Barnum & Bailey shows and performing at the Coney Island Dreamland Circus. Bibrowski grew into a lion-faced man, but at a mere five feet, three inches, he wasn't nearly as intimidating as his feline counterparts. His vocabulary extended far beyond a lion's roar, though; he spoke intelligently in five languages.

Not only did the long hair make him a rarity; it was truly his livelihood. Consequently, he was very protective of it. In 1904, while he was in New York, the hotel where he was staying caught fire, and Lionel apparently was the first out. "I couldn't afford to have my face singed," he said. "In that case I wouldn't be lion-faced any longer and would have to leave the circus and be just an ordinary citizen."

Lionel eventually became a German citizen, and is believed to have died in Germany in 1932. Other reports have him dying in Italy that same year.

Lester Roberts, a sideshow lecturer and friend of Lionel's, related that Bibrowski had actually wanted to be a dentist, but realized he would earn more as a freak. He must have realized also that few people would be willing to go to a dentist who looked like the king of the jungle.

GEORGE LIPPERT
1844–1906

Born in Germany, George Lippert was forever burdened with the task of carrying portions of an unborn brother. Lippert had two functioning hearts, and a third leg sprouting from his right side. The extra limb was well formed, but thinner than the other two. In total, Lippert had sixteen toes.

The three-legged man worked as a curiosity for nearly fifty years, many of them spent with P. T. Barnum. He was said to speak five languages and was known to be quite personable.

Lippert's career in show business came to an end after an illness; he then found himself homeless in Oregon. He was saved by a friendly florist who gave him aid and shelter.

In 1906, one of Lippert's hearts gave out. He lived for two more weeks, and died on July 28.

George Lippert. *Becker Collection, Special Collections Research Center, Syracuse University Library*

LEOPARD BOYS

An unidentified Leopard Boy.
*Becker Collection, Special Collections
Research Center, Syracuse University Library*

Among the various human oddities P. T. Barnum exhibited, there was usually a Leopard Boy (sometimes called a Piebald Boy). This was nothing but an African-American with the skin disorder leucoderma, or vitiligo. The National Vitiligo Foundation defines the syndrome as "spontaneous irregular depigmentation of skin which can occur at any stage in life." It leaves the skin spotted with white patches, and can occur in all races and in both sexes. Leopard Girls were also exhibited, as were white people turning black.

Barnum employed several piebald attractions. In the 1880s, their spots earned them a salary of $25 per week. One of Barnum's prodigies was known as Joe the Leopard Boy, who Barnum professed was discovered in Africa. Such curiosities were often billed as natives of African jungles, like their feline namesakes. It certainly sounded more exotic than hailing from plain old American civilization. Joe, who was born in 1869, was actually named A. E. Bishell. After his exhibitions with Barnum, he displayed his body in five-cent theaters. His career as a Leopard Boy ended in November 1909, when he was killed after falling through a trapdoor. It was believed to be an accident, not the work of a poacher.

People with vitiligo were attractions long before Barnum. In the 1790s, a man named Henry Moss exhibited and lectured on his own body in a Philadelphia museum. The showing was so popular that even George Washington took the time and paid to see the show.

COUNT PRIMO MAGRI
and BARON ERNESTO MAGRI,
COUNT ROSEBUD *and* BARON LITTLEFINGER

Primo: 1849–1920

Ernesto: 1850–?

COUNT MAGRI.   COUNTESS MAGRI,   BARON MAGRI.

SWORDS BRO'S, PROFESSIONAL PHOTOGRAPHERS. YORK, PA.

Count and Baron Magri with
Countess Magri, 1894. *Author's collection*

Primo and Ernesto Magri hailed from Bologna, Italy, where they were born about a year apart. Both were midgets, each standing just over three feet tall. They had nine normal-size siblings.

The brothers first exhibited themselves and displayed their musical talents on the piano and piccolo in 1865. Pope Pius IX was so enchanted after a performance that he bestowed titles on them; Primo became a count, Ernesto a baron.

The Count and the Baron soon came to the United States, where they were also known as Count Rosebud and Baron Littlefinger. In 1879 they toured with another sensation, Millie-Christine, the Two-Headed Nightingale. The Count and the Baron fenced, danced, and sang, to audiences' delight. The Magris later joined with the most famous little people of all, General Tom Thumb and his wife, Lavinia Warren. "They were far more cultured and intelligent than most of the little people we had met, and the social relations between us were very pleasant," Mrs. Tom Thumb commented.

The social relations between the Count and Lavinia became particularly pleasant. In 1883, when Tom Thumb died, Rosebud was poised to make his move. But he was a gentleman, and knew to allow the widow time to grieve. Once he did propose, Lavinia accepted, and the two were married on April 6, 1885 at the Church of the Holy Trinity in New York. Baron Magri, always by his brother's side, served as best man. Another midget, Miss Lucy Adams, was the bridesmaid. After the wedding, Count Magri was frequently referred to as "Mrs. Tom Thumb's husband."

The Baron set his sights a little higher than his brother's: he married a much taller woman. Littlefinger and his towering, five-foot-two-inch wife had three children, all of whom grew to normal heights.

The brothers and the new Countess Magri formed the Lilliputian Opera Company, and began touring dime museums and performing with vaudeville companies. Other midgets often joined the show, which featured such appropriate sketches as "Gulliver Among the Lilliputians." The acts combined music, comedy, dancing, and pantomime. Although the Opera's popularity eventually waned, the brothers and the Countess continued performing for many years. Their travels led to a meeting with President Taft in 1911.

The Count and Countess lived lavishly, and thus, despite healthy earnings, they needed to exhibit themselves as they advanced in age. In 1919, the seventy-eight-year-old Countess passed away. Over the next year the Count lost both his wealth and his health. He was forced to have many of Lavinia's belongings auctioned off, and hoped to spend the earnings on a trip home to Italy. On October 31, 1920, Count Primo Magri died in a Middleborough, Massachusetts, hospital. Perhaps he found it difficult living without his dear wife. His death came on her birthday, nearly one year after her passing. What ultimately became of the Baron is unknown.

THE LILLIPUTIAN OPERA COMPANIES

One or another Lilliputian Opera Company is mentioned in this book, and it should be noted that more than one such group used the popular diminutive term. These traveling troupes often featured singing, recitation, specialty acts, and short pieces of theater written especially for the little players. The performances were often geared toward children, but as a reviewer of the Count and Countess Magri's Lilliputian Opera Company wrote, "The entertainment is quite as amusing to the grown people as it is to the children."

An earlier company than the Magris', Deakin's Lilliputian Comic Opera, was run by a savvy theater producer named Harry Deakin. There were also the American Lilliputian, the Locke & Davis Royal Lilliputian, and the Pollard Lilliputian opera companies. The Pollard actually included children, who, unlike the other Lilliputians, would eventually outgrow the role.

MAY-JOE

1905–?

According to the story on the back of May-Joe's pitch card, he was born on October 16, 1905, on a farm in Ashland County, Ohio. His real name was Georgie Francis Ethinger. An undeveloped twin left him with a third leg and a second stomach. Georgie was his parents' fifth child, and the only one stricken with an abnormality.

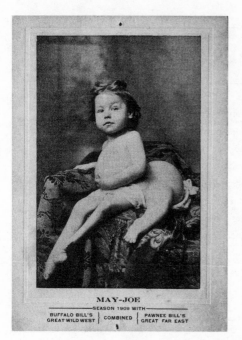

MAY-JOE

SEASON 1909 WITH

| BUFFALO BILL'S GREAT WILD WEST | COMBINED | PAWNEE BILL'S GREAT FAR EAST |

May-Joe, 1909.
Johnny Fox's Freakatorium

It seems the Ethingers felt blessed enough with their other children and decided to make the freakish Georgie profitable. In 1906, they turned the infant over to a team of managers, Bolus and Startzel, for public exhibition. The showmen dubbed him May-Joe and claimed that the baby was both male and female, admitting, however, that the male traits were dominant. According to their pitch card: "The peculiar anatomical construction of the child is such as to have excited the interest of scientific men all over the country, and many of these have requested permission to make careful examination of one of Nature's strangest freaks." A careful examination surely would have shown that the child could not possess both sets of genitalia. Parasitic twins are always the same gender, although, as in the cases of Laloo and of Piramel and Sami, showmen loved to contradict nature and bill the sibling as being the opposite gender. Perhaps May-Joe's genitalia suffered a deformity because of the positioning of the twin.

In 1908, May-Joe toured with Cummings Big Twelve Shows United, and the next year was exhibited with Buffalo Bill's Great Wild West and Pawnee Bill's Great Far East combined show. As time passed, May-Joe ultimately shifted toward his supposed female side. As such, he was later dressed as a girl and billed as Joe Pearl and Josephine Pearl.

MILLIE-CHRISTINE, THE TWO-HEADED NIGHTINGALE

1851–1912

$\bigstar$ Any set of conjoined twins would be expected to endure a more difficult childhood than normal children. But from day one, Millie-Christine had it even rougher than the average set of such twins. She (they always referred to themselves in the singular, though the census counted her as two) was born into slavery. The girls came into the world, connected at the lower spine, on July 11, 1851, in Welches Creek, North Carolina, at a farm owned by a blacksmith named Jabez McKay. Their mother already had seven children and was said to have a large pelvis. So she had plenty of practice and was well equipped to give birth to the seventeen-pound twins.

Millie-Christine.
Reference Handbook of the Medical Sciences, *vol.* 7

Not sure what to do with such a curiosity, McKay sold them for $1,000 to a South Carolinian named John C. Pervis, who planned to exhibit his newly acquired sensation. Before they turned four, the twins would be sold again, to a Mr. Brower, who was backed financially by Joseph Pearson Smith (who also purchased their mother), for $10,000 (though some reports claim as much as $30,000), and stolen twice. The kidnappers, knowing they couldn't exhibit the twins publicly, did so privately in the Philadelphia area. Smith and the twins' mother searched for three years before discovering that the girls were now on exhibit in Birmingham, England. Finally the law got involved. Since slavery was illegal in England, the court awarded Millie-Christine to their mother. She stuck with Smith and toured with the twins.

Though Millie-Christine treated herself as one, she occasionally functioned as two.

The twins ate separately. One was a soprano, the other a contralto. And Christine was the stronger of the two physically, while Millie was said to have the more dominating spirit.

By 1860, Smith had died and Millie-Christine was willed to his son. Joseph Pearson Smith, Jr., saw the potential to earn a fortune and exhibited his new inheritance all over the world, billing her as the Two-Headed Girl. Since the girls considered themselves one, why couldn't the showman do so as well? A girl with two heads, four arms, and four legs would draw immense crowds. Advertisements promised more than a physical sensation: "Her mental faculties are of a superior order, and double, thereby enabling her to converse with two persons at one time." Over the years Millie-Christine, as one, was also called the Eighth Wonder of the World, the United African Twins, and the Two-Headed Nightingale.

Millie-Christine was a phenomenon onstage, even performing for royalty, including the Prince of Wales and Queen Victoria. A typical show required Millie-Christine to do much more than simply stand there to be marveled at. She entertained audiences with her musical skill on piano and guitar. She sang duets and danced the waltz and polka with ease. She even composed her own verses, which her two voices recited in unison:

> I'm happy, quite, because content,
> For some wise purpose I was sent;
> My maker knows what he has done,
> Whether I'm created two or one.

An impressed reporter from the Liverpool *Daily Post* remarked: "The spectator is rewarded not by one smile, as in the case of ordinary young ladies, but by two distinct smiles, winked at you by two pairs of sparkling and roguish eyes, and thrown at you by two different sets of the purest ivory that ever adorned the mouth of an Indian Sultana."

The two-headed wonder worked in fairs and sideshows for years, and did a brief stint with Barnum. At one time she reportedly earned $25,000 a season working the county-fair circuit. She was believed to have earned more than $250,000 during the span of her career.

Millie-Christine continued performing until age fifty-eight. Sometime after emancipation, she changed her last name to McKoy. Once retired, the Two-Headed Nightingale built a home in Columbus County, North Carolina. Millie died of tuberculosis on October 8, 1912, at age sixty-one. Christine died seventeen hours later.

FANNY MILLS, THE OHIO BIG FOOT GIRL

1860–1899

Shortly after her birth in England, Fanny Mills and her family immigrated to the United States and settled in Sandusky, Ohio. There, her father ran a dairy farm. But Fanny Mills wasn't your average farmer's daughter. As if being called Fanny weren't bad enough, the poor girl suffered from the disfigurement of Milroy's disease.

This disease, similar to elephantiasis, caused her feet to dwarf those of your average Sasquatch. The syndrome, which prefers to afflict women (seventy to eighty percent of victims are women), also turns the enlarged, overlying skin a reddish hue.

Mills covered her feet with size 30 shoes—said to be made from the skins of three goats—and was pitched as the Ohio Big Foot Girl, with the biggest feet on earth. Each foot measured nineteen inches long and nearly ten inches wide. Pillowcases served as socks. Despite the enormous feet, Mills weighed only 115 pounds—a statistic almost as amazing as her shoe size.

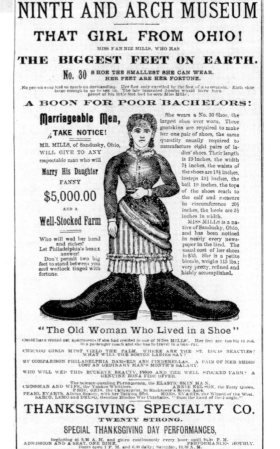

Ad promoting Fanny Mills.
Otterbein College, Courtright Memorial Library

Fanny Mills. Note her one bare foot.
*Becker Collection, Special Collections Research Center,
Syracuse University Library*

A reporter who visited Mills's home described her deformity: "Her feet look like two immense hams. The toes are irregular, and the little toes are represented by two little knobs. There are no toenails, although the places where they should be are clearly defined."

In 1885, Mills realized her gargantuan feet were worth a fortune. Accompanied by an attendant from Sandusky, she began exhibiting them in dime museums along the East Coast. The aide, Mary Brown, stayed at Mills's side to help her walk and change her massive shoes. Showmen claimed that her father would offer $5,000 and a well-stocked farm to any man who would marry his daughter. The deal was advertised as "a boon for poor bachelors!" Eligible men were told not to permit "two big feet to stand between you and wedlock tinged with fortune." The enormous extremities were exaggerated by claims that "'the old woman who lived in a shoe' would have rented out apartments if she had resided in one of Miss Mills'." The ad was effective to a certain extent, eliciting many letters from potential husbands. But Fanny Mills's father was already dead. And the bachelorette had in fact already married. William Brown, her aide's brother,

made Mills his bride, free of charge. She is believed to have had a stillborn child in 1887.

At the height of Mills's career she was earning up to $150 a week. Her employment was cut short by illness in 1892, and she returned home with her husband to live on the farm in Sandusky. Mills's life was also cut short; she died at age thirty-nine.

★ In 1880, an eleven-year-old boy from Canton, Ohio, identified only as Taylor, was reported to have feet measuring thirty-six inches long. "They were whoppers," a journalist remarked.

GENERAL MITE

1864–?

General Mite, standing next to a chair, circa 1880. Little people were often posed next to furniture to emphasize their small size. *Courtesy Tom Hernandez*

Francis Joseph Flynn was born in 1864 in Greene, New York. He got off to a very small start, weighing only two and a half pounds at birth. Little Francis took care of most of his growing in his first year, reaching an eventual height of twenty-two inches. By the time he was fourteen, showmen had dubbed him General Mite, "a human miracle!" He weighed all of nine pounds—though his general's uniform surely added enough weight to protect him from a sudden gust of wind. His specially made gloves measured only three inches long. Flynn was advertised as "remarkably handsome and perfect in form and feature." And like most sideshow attractions of the time, he was "no doubt the Greatest Wonder of the Nineteenth Century."

The tiny general often traveled with another lightweight star, Lucia Zarate. The two were quite the spectacle—together earning $500 a week. The miniature couple seemed to be made for each other, and in 1885 planned a marriage in Philadelphia. Their engagement was made official at a dime museum after a fierce lover's quarrel; Zarate had become jealous when a visiting woman gave General Mite a caramel. Zarate and the General kissed and made up, and he popped the question with a diamond ring small enough to fit her finger. It's likely the marriage was a mere publicity stunt. General Mite was reported to have married another midget, Milly Edwards, in Manchester, England, a year earlier.

INDIAN'S FAT BOY.
CHAUNCEY MORLAN.
—AGE, 19 YEARS; WEIGHT; 513½ POUNDS.—
Harrie Rose, Photographer, INDIANAPOLIS, IND.

Chauncey Morlan and his mother, 1888.
Ken Harck archives/Bros. Grim Side Shows

CHAUNCEY MORLAN
1869–1912

Described by the press as a human freight car, Chauncey Morlan enjoyed a lucrative career as a Fat Man in the late 1800s. Born in Indiana on April 27, 1869, he weighed more than 400 pounds by age fourteen. At fifteen, the fat boy turned pro and became a featured attraction with showman Adam Forepaugh. In the early 1890s, a beefed-up Morlan fell in love with something other than his next meal—six-foot-two-inch, 490-pound Annie Bell, the Ohio Giantess. Though he was shorter, Morlan's 748 pounds made him much wider than his sweetheart. The corpulent couple was exhibited at Huber's 14th Street Museum in New York, where they were married on November 30, 1892. The newlyweds spent the next six weeks celebrating their nuptials and exhibiting their girth at the museum. They welcomed many wedding gifts from spectators.

After Huber's, the Morlans worked in various dime museums around the country. They earned enough money to purchase an estate in Indiana and retire from show business. Mrs. Morlan grew ill from diabetes and died on March 30, 1904. She weighed 420 pounds at her death.

By 1909, Morlan had slimmed down to 490 pounds and found a second wife. His bride, Stella Banning, weighed only 100 pounds, about as much as his first wife's thigh. The couple lived in Indiana for the next three years, until Morlan's death.

JAMES MORRIS

1859–?

James Morris wasn't a typical attraction. He wasn't excessively short, tall, fat, thin, or hairy; he wasn't missing a single limb. Morris was a handsome, healthy, well-educated man. He just happened to have the ability to stretch his skin as much as eighteen inches from his body painlessly. This was most likely due to the condition called Ehlers-Danlos syndrome.

Morris, born in Copenhagen, New York, waited awhile to decide to turn a profit on his gifted skin. He first worked in a cotton mill, where he would pull his epidermis to amuse co-workers. When he later joined the military, he again enter-

James Morris. *Becker Collection, Special Collections Research Center, Syracuse University Library*

tained with his elasticity. Officers invited friends and journalists to see Morris's talent. Word traveled and he was recruited by the Westminster Museum. By the early 1880s, he had launched his career as the India Rubber Man and the Elastic Skin Wonder.

The India Rubber Man traveled with the Barnum & Bailey Circus for years, exhibiting himself around the United States, Canada, and Europe. One of his favorite stunts was to pull the skin of his neck up to cover his nose. And his nose was another fun toy. In 1898, *Scientific American* reported his stretching "the skin of his nose, which, according to the picturesque language of a spectator, then takes on the aspect of an elephant's trunk."

Morris earned $300 a week in his first season. His salary was halved in the years that followed. Morris spent much of his money on drinking and gambling, and thus had to continue performing for many years to fund his vices.

In addition to stretching his skin like Silly Putty, Morris earned extra money as a barber. When traveling with the circus he often styled the tresses of employees, and he even had his own shop in New York City.

Although the India Rubber Man was called a "matchless marvel," he had at least one fellow skin-stretcher. A man named Felix Wehrle shared this capability.

THE MURRAY MIDGETS

Circa 1860s–?

The Murray Midgets with their mother.
Author's collection

The Murray Midgets were billed as triplets (John, Joseph, and James) when exhibited at Barnum's American Museum or when touring the country in the late 1800s. According to an 1880 newspaper report, they were brothers, but not triplets, born in New York between 1860 and 1870. The three were all little, but stood at different heights. The smallest brother was thirty-seven inches tall. The largest was the most intelligent, and according to another newspaper story, he was "a cross triplet" who was prone to bully his "smaller and duller brethren." Even a midget can be a typical big brother.

The Murrays were always accompanied by their mother. Showing either a knack for business or blatant favoritism, she would place a child's bank on the platform in front of the most handsome son's feet. If a young woman approached, mother Murray would suggest she put a dime in the bank. Many dimes were donated.

PAULINE MUSTERS

1876–1895

In the *Guinness Book of World Records,* Pauline Musters has the honor of being the shortest mature female ever recorded. She was just a little bigger than a hardcover edition of the aforementioned book.

Musters was born on February 26, 1876, in Ossendrecht in the Netherlands. At birth she was a petite twelve inches. Those nine months in her mother's womb represented her greatest growth spurt. Through her nineteen years of life, she never reached two feet in height, peaking at just over twenty-three inches. At age nine she weighed only three pounds, five ounces; eventually she beefed up to nine pounds. Given measurements of 18½-19-17, the featherweight was actually overweight for her size.

LADY DOT,
THE MIDGET MITE.

PERMANENT PHOTOGRAPH.   BROWN, BÂHNES & BELL.

Pauline Musters with an unidentified woman, circa 1890s. *Author's collection*

Onstage, Musters was known as Princess Pauline and Lady Dot, the Midget Mite. (No relation to Admiral Dot, General Mite, or Major Mite.) Besides being marveled at for her diminutive dimensions, she entertained as a talented acrobat and dancer. Musters toured Belgium, France, Germany, and Britain before being invited to the United States in 1894. Her debut performance on New Year's Eve astounded audiences at New York City's Proctor's Theatre. Doctors were amazed at the tiny star's size and agility during special receptions she held.

Perhaps the little princess would have grown a few more inches had she lived longer, but pneumonia and meningitis dashed any such hopes. Pauline Musters succumbed to the illnesses on March 1, 1895, in New York City.

SANDERS K. G. NELLIS

1817–?

Of the many Armless Wonders to demonstrate their deft feet to the public, the first to hold such a title in America is believed to be Sanders K. G. Nellis, who was born on March 12, 1817, in Johnstown, New York. Not only did he lack arms, but he would not grow very tall, either. Nellis was technically a midget, peaking at four feet, six inches and 116 pounds.

The Armless Wonder was exhibited at Peale's Museum and Scudder's American Museum in New York City by his teenage years. In 1836, he traveled north and appeared at Washington Hall in Salem, Massachusetts. For a twenty-five-cent admission, astonished audiences watched him fold origami designs, cut shapes of valentines and people, draw animals, wind a watch, and shoot a bow and arrow with remarkable accuracy, and listened to him play the cello and accordion, and sing patriotic songs. The crowds got their money's worth.

Nellis later joined up with P. T. Barnum. The showman's June 1, 1851, circus bill for the Great Asiatic Caravan, Museum and Menagerie announced: "Mr. Nellis, the man without arms, will load and fire a pistol, and do other feats with his toes!" Over the years, Nellis traveled throughout North and South America, the West Indies, the British empire, and Europe.

What became of Nellis is unknown. Variations of his extraordinary act were performed by the many Armless Wonders who followed in his versatile footsteps.

CHARLES *and* ELIZA NESTEL,
COMMODORE FOOTE *and* THE FAIRY QUEEN

Charles: 1849–1937

Eliza: 1857–1937

Charles W. and Eliza Nestel were midget siblings, born in Fort Wayne, Indiana. They had a brother and a sister of normal size.

In 1861, the two began performing in the theater, starring, appropriately, in a show called *The Little People.* Naturally, they billed themselves as the Smallest People in the World. Charles stood an inch over three feet, Eliza an inch under. Both stopped growing by the age of six.

Charles became known as Commodore Foote, while Eliza was called the Fairy Queen. Charles in fact wanted to be a commodore, and he often wore a military uniform onstage.

In the 1880s, the Commodore and the Queen toured the world with P. T. Barnum, from dime museums in Chicago and New York to the court of the full-size Queen Victoria in England. The talented twosome also performed with the American Lilliputian Opera Company.

Charles and Eliza Nestel.
Author's collection

Foote was known to speak three languages and was quite the ladies' man. "Wherever he turns he leaves many an aching heart behind him," one newspaper reported. "He goes in for booty and beauty, without the slightest compunction, and is chivalrous to a high degree." Yet he stuck by his sister. They almost always appeared in public together, and were separated only once, when little Charles accidentally slipped through a stage door in Washington during a meeting with President Lincoln. Eliza did not follow her brother through the hole.

The curious couple performed for many years, both living to quite an old age. Charles died on April 15, 1937. Eliza, blind and crippled, was so grief-stricken she stopped speaking. Her silence lasted ten days; she died April 25, at age eighty.

NICHOLI, THE LITTLE RUSSIAN PRINCE

Circa 1870s–?

Looking more like a toy than a boy, at sixteen pounds and a mere twenty-two and a half inches tall, Nicholi may have actually lived up to his billing as the Smallest Man in the World.

According to "A Sketch of the Life of the Russian Prince," Nicholi said he was born in Siberia, where his father was a prison laborer in the mines. Nicholi's minuscule appearance supposedly earned him a trip to the czar, and with a little begging on his knees, he convinced His Majesty that his father was innocent. The czar investigated and found the claim to be true. Thus, Nicholi saved his father from the freezing mines of Siberia, proving "that every person born in the world is created for a purpose; and God in His

"THE LITTLE RUSSIAN PRINCE,"
The Smallest Man in the World. Weight 16 lbs., Height 22½ inches Age 32 Years. Native of Russia.
Speaks German, Russian and English.
FRANK WENDT, Photo, Boonton, N. J.

Prince Nicholi with an unidentified man. *Author's col*

wisdom may have created diminutive Prince Nicholi to prove the innocence of his father."

The story is likely filled with ballyhoo. The documentary *Freaks Uncensored!* suggests that Nicholi suffered from the extremely rare disease progeria, which causes very rapid premature aging. He was billed as being in his thirties when he was most likely around eleven years old. A 1908 Trenton, New Jersey, newspaper article states that Nicholi was a member of the Elks club and spoke Russian, Hebrew, English, and German. All of which would have been quite impressive for an eleven-year-old. Perhaps he was neither a prince nor a progerian, but rather just a very little Russian man.

COMMODORE NUTT

1844–1881

George Washington Morrison Nutt was born in Manchester, New Hampshire, on April Fool's Day, 1844. His size may have been nature's practical joke, but Nutt would laugh along and make the most of it.

In 1862, P. T. Barnum spent $30,000 to add the twenty-nine-inch-tall Nutt to his stable of attractions. He was known as "The $30,000 Nutt." Nutt received the same make-over treatment as Tom Thumb. He was deemed a commodore, trained to perform, and had appropriate costumes prepared for him. Barnum first exhibited him in his American Museum, and like so many after a New York debut, Nutt soon became rich and famous.

The Commodore frequently toured with the General—fellow little man Tom Thumb. Barnum had miniature carriages built for both, drawn by Shetland ponies. Nutt's carriage was designed to look like a nutshell, with small windows for the Commodore to peer outside. Although he attained a great deal of fame, he would never be quite the household name Tom Thumb was. But the two men would be forever linked. The Commodore served as Tom Thumb's best man at his wedding to Lavinia Warren in 1863. The wedding party was immortalized in a photo of the "Fairy Wedding Group," featuring the aforementioned three and Minnie Warren, Lavinia's sister.

Commodore Nutt with Minnie Warren.
Author's collection

Nutt, along with General Tom Thumb and the Warren sisters, toured Europe from 1869 to 1872, dazzling royalty across the continent with their petite stature, and their duets, dances, orations, pantomimes, and military exercises. Upon returning to the States, the four repeated their success entertaining American audiences.

Nutt eventually grew slightly taller and fatter, becoming more like a walnut than a peanut. Ultimately he reached a height of forty-three inches and weighed a little less than seventy pounds. The enlarged Nutt later performed on the West Coast with Rodnia (Major Nutt), his brother, who was also a midget.

Offstage, the Commodore attempted to run saloons in Oregon and San Francisco, but he had little success. At just over three and a half feet, it was no easy task for him to keep order in a room full of drinkers. Nutt returned to New York City, where he bought another saloon. After he was caught selling liquor without a license, the courts put an end to his saloon-keeping ventures. Bright's disease put an end to his life, on May 25, 1881.

COUNT ORLOFF, THE ONLY LIVING TRANSPARENT *and* OSSIFIED MAN

1864–1904

One of the more bizarre and unbelievable human oddities exhibited was Ivannow Wladislaus Von Dziarski-Orloff. In addition to being ossified, he was transparent.

Born in 1864 in Budapest, Orloff began losing his strength by age fourteen. Within four years, his limbs became so weak he was unable to stand. His condition worsened: as his bones and muscles softened, his limbs curved like overgrown fingernails. Whether he had a luxurious recliner or a bland wooden chair to sit in, Orloff suffered great pain. He was known to smoke opium to help with his physical anguish.

The ossified man could have earned a living from his unusual shape alone. But it was his extraordinary transparency that made him unique. Doctors, or any spectators for that matter, could witness his blood circulating through his body. A light shining on his chest allowed people standing in front of him to read a newspaper held up to his back.

Orloff capitalized on his afflictions by exhibiting at the Royal College of Medicine in Berlin for three years. He became known as Count Orloff, the Only Living Transparent and Ossified Man. By 1893 the Count was seen, and seen through, in America. The 1896 book *Anomalies and Curiosities of Medicine* explained that his transparency was "due to porosity of the bones and deficiency of the overlying tissues."

He eventually moved into the management side of curiosities with the launch of Count Orloff's International Agency. The Count died in 1904.

NOAH ORR, THE UNION COUNTY GIANT
1836–1882

Colonel Noah Orr was much like fellow giant Colonel Ruth Goshen. Both were billed as around eight feet tall, packed with muscle, and they shared the same faux military rank. But unlike Goshen, Orr didn't have a confusion of names and nationalities in his biography. He was born in Darby Township, Ohio, on September 19, 1836. The oversize boy grew up to be a farmhand and was known locally as the Union County Giant. Word of his size traveled, and P. T. Barnum soon beckoned. While Orr was initially reluctant, his farmer boss persuaded him to accept the showman's invitation. With his

Noah Orr, in full military regalia,
with an unidentified little person.
Union County, Ohio, Historical Society

immense height, handsome looks, and friendly personality, Orr was certain to be a successful attraction.

By 1865, Orr was featured in Barnum's American Museum. He later traveled with the famous impresario before joining the Adam Forepaugh and John Robinson circuses. Like many giants, Orr performed with the Lilliputian Opera Company, starring with Admiral Dot in its production of *Jack the Giant Killer*. Orr also portrayed Powhatan in a theatrical presentation of *Pocahontas*.

The giant was never weighed in a conventional manner. It was approximated, however, by some friends who had Orr stand on scales set at 550 pounds. He easily tipped the scales, indicating he weighed even more (his death certificate would specify 774 pounds). With such size came great power. Orr often demonstrated his remarkable strength by lifting a barrel of cider and drinking straight from its bunghole.

Aside from circus life, Orr kept busy in Marysville, Ohio, as a member of the Masons, the Knights of Pythias, and the Order of Red Men. He was also a family man, the father of six normal-size children.

In 1882, the big man grew ill with a softening spinal cord. On the evening of July 1, his lower limbs completely paralyzed, he died in Marysville. The Knights of Pythias buried him in a casket seven feet, eight inches long. Either Orr exaggerated, as most giants did, his claim of eight feet, or his soft spine had made him shrink. Regardless, his coffin was too big for the hearse and was carried to the cemetery on a farm wagon. Thousands attended the service. Orr died a poor man, and for decades his grave remained unmarked. In the 1940s the local historical society raised money to give the legendary giant a proper tombstone.

JULIA PASTRANA,
THE UGLIEST WOMAN IN THE WORLD

1834–1860

In 1834, in Mexico, the world was introduced to a baby girl destined to grow into one of its ugliest residents. Julia Pastrana, who was part Mexican Indian, was spotted with shiny black hair all over her body. Her ears were big. Her nose was unusually wide and flattened, with large nostrils. A moustache helped hide her bulky lips. And her teeth were abundant, as each jaw was reportedly equipped with a double row. Pastrana was beyond hairy. Showmen would later describe her as the link between mankind and the orangutan.

Julia Pastrana. *From Gould and Pyle,*
Anomalies and Curiosities of Medicine

Pastrana's mother died when she was a girl. An American known only as M. Rates later discovered her in Mexico. She was four and a half feet tall, had a good figure, and a face that would command attention. Rates brought his repulsive find to the United States to be exhibited. Her unusual appearance, combined with a gentle singing voice, made Pastrana one of the greatest living curiosities. In 1854, when exhibited at New York City's Stuyvesant Institute, she was called "the Hybrid, or semi-human Indian from Mexico." Advertisements claimed that "Christmas holidays cannot be more agreeably passed than in attending the Levees of Julia Pastrana, whose dulcet voice enchants the ladies."

After a few years of touring with Rates, Pastrana found a new manager, Theodore Lent. He taught his prized oddity Spanish dances and popular songs, enhancing her act. He also instructed her to hide. She was not allowed out during the day, as any appearances in public would give away the show. Despite her sheltered existence, Pastrana was a bright woman. She learned three languages and loved to read, and she had a strong sense of spirituality. Yet to the public she was simply Julia Pastrana, the Ugliest Woman in the World. Or the Baboon Lady. Even the Nondescript.

Lent took Pastrana around the world, exhibiting her in England, Germany, Poland, and Russia. Along the way, there wasn't a single challenger to her title of Ugliest Woman (though later Grace McDaniels, the Mule-Faced Woman, would certainly have been a contender). Lent and Pastrana earned a fortune, and the manager proclaimed his love to his simian star. The greedy showman attempted to prove affection by marrying Pastrana, though most likely he was trying to assure his main source of income. The marriage was consummated at least once, as evidenced by Pastrana's pregnancy in 1859 and the birth, in March 1860, of a baby boy, in Russia. Much to Pastrana's dismay, the newborn didn't have his father's desired normal looks; he looked like her. The baby was covered in hair and shared her deformities. Pastrana was distraught, but Lent must have been giddy at the prospects the infant suggested. The boy died a day and a half later, and five days later, in St. Petersburg, Pastrana died. This marked the beginning of her second career in the sideshow.

Always an opportunist, Lent sold the bodies to a Russian professor named Sukolov. He embalmed the bodies and displayed his work in the anatomical museum at the University of Moscow. When Lent saw what an attraction they were, and realized he could keep profiting from his deceased family, he quickly bought them back from Sukolov. Russia wouldn't allow the bodies to be exhibited on tour, so Lent brought them to London, and then to the land where capitalism reigned supreme. Pastrana was shown in the United States as the Embalmed Female Nondescript. By 1864, Lent had milked the dead of their last drop. He loaned them to a traveling English museum of curiosities, and his wife and son continued their posthumous tour of the world. In the meantime, Lent needed a new attraction, so he married another hairy woman and exhibited her as Zenora Pastrana, Julia's sister.

Over the years, the mummies were passed around, still earning money. The ongoing exhibition lasted more than a hundred years. In 1973, Pastrana and son were seen in a Swedish amusement park. Three years later they were brought to Oslo and stored at a fairgrounds. Vandals stole the bodies and left them in a ditch. Mice ate the baby. Pastrana lost an arm, which was recovered and replaced. By 1990, she was safe inside the Institute of Forensic Medicine in Oslo. Doctors later examined the mummy and determined she suffered from "generalized hypertrichosis terminalis with gingival hyperplasia" (basically, overgrown hair, overgrown gums). A radiographic examination showed that her teeth were normal, not excessive as had been reported. Finally a description Pastrana might have been happy to hear.

The now accurately described Nondescript remains in Oslo, with one arm detached, half her face torn open, a naked body, and an appearance uglier than ever. Fortunately, she will never be billed as the Ugliest Woman again: her sideshow career came to an end in Norway, and she is no longer exhibited to the public. But her story lived on in a 2003 theatrical production, *The True History of the Tragic Life and Triumphant Death of Julia Pastrana, the Ugliest Woman in the World*. The play was performed in complete darkness, eliminating the need for any actress to replicate Pastrana's unparalleled looks.

PIRAMEL *and* SAMI, THE DOUBLE-BODIED HINDU ENIGMA

Circa 1888–?

Piramel and his parasitic twin brother, called Sami, were born in Madras, India. Many sources claim they were born in 1888; Ellis Island records state 1892. Sami's body and limbs jutted out from Piramel just below the chest.

The Indian boy and his partial twin were an instant attraction. Piramel began exhibiting himself at an early age and often appeared with his cousin, a dwarf named Soopromanien. As with Laloo, another Indian with a parasitic twin, the curiosity surrounding Piramel was enhanced by claims that his brother was a sister. Such a combination, a male with a female parasitic twin, is genetically impossible. Nevertheless, Piramel and Sami were billed as "Brother and Sister, Double-Bodied

"PIRAMEL"
The Double Body Boy.

SOOPROMANIEN
British Indian Midget

Piramel (and Sami) and Soopromanien.
Author's collection

Hindoo Enigma." Sami was dressed accordingly, in further degradation of the poor parasitic brother.

Piramel and Sami came to the United States and traveled with Ringling Bros. Daniel Mannix, author of *Freaks: We Who Are Not As Others*, maintains that Piramel didn't trust American food and would eat only food prepared by his own Indian cooks. His (and his brother's) final tour was in 1915, after which he retired to his homeland.

MISS JENNIE QUIGLEY,
19 Years Old—Height, 28 Inches—Weight, 32 lbs.

HUGHES & CO., PHOTOGRAPHERS, ST. LOUIS.

Jennie Quigley with an unidentified woman, 1870.
Author's collection

JENNIE QUIGLEY, THE SCOTTISH QUEEN

1851–1936

In 1864, standing well under two feet, thirteen-year-old Jennie Quigley left Scotland for America. She became a protégée of P. T. Barnum, who bestowed on her the name "The Scottish Queen." The title stuck throughout her career, which lasted nearly fifty years.

Quigley traveled the world, entertaining royalty and commoners alike. Through the decades, she performed with various other little people, including Commodore Foote and his sister the Fairy Queen, a fellow midget monarch. In the mid-1870s, Quigley starred with Commodore Nutt and the giant Colonel Goshen in a production of *Jack the Giant Killer*. Billed as the Smallest Woman in the World, Quigley won rave reviews as a "charming little mite of femininity who captured the hearts of everybody by the perfection of her acting, as well as by her personal beauty and naturalness of character."

The Scottish Queen retired from show business in 1917. Perhaps, like other midgets, she outgrew her novelty. She eventually grew to a height of forty-one inches. She never married, although it was rumored that Commodore Nutt was "sweet" on her. Jennie Quigley lived to the ripe old age of eighty-four. She died on March 11, 1936, at her normal-size nephew's home in Chicago.

THE SACRED HAIRY FAMILY OF BURMA, MAHPHOON and MOUNG PHOSET

Mahphoon: 1822–?
Moung Phoset: 1856–?

The Sacred Hairy Family of Burma was both sacred and hairy for generations before ever being exhibited to a mass audience. In the late 1880s, the family belonged to King Theebaw of Burma, who believed that having them around him would bring good fortune. They were treated as mascots, showered with jewels, and shown to visitors only on important occasions.

Theebaw had two members of the family residing at his court—Mahphoon and her son, Moung Phoset. Both were covered in long, silky hair from head to foot, with locks sprouting from their cheeks, chins, foreheads, the corners of their eyes and the insides of their ears. The auburn-colored tresses reached fourteen inches

Moung Phoset and Mahphoon of the Sacred Hairy Family of Burma, circa 1887. *Becker Collection, Special Collections Research Center, Syracuse University Library* on some portions of their bodies. Only the palms of their hands and the soles of their feet were spared from hair.

The family's hypertrichosis ran through five generations. In the first four, each hairy member married a normal spouse and had seven children. In each case, there were four normal and three hairy offspring. Moung Phoset's six siblings all died, leaving him the sole representative in his immediate family. With Theebaw's help, he attempted to pass his genes to a sixth generation by marrying a maid at the court. The young bride was not attracted to the woolly bachelor, but Theebaw promised her a snazzy silver-handled umbrella if she went through with the matrimony. The offer was too good to resist. Unfortunately for him, Moung Phoset's materialistic new wife did not produce the traditional seven children.

In 1885, King Theebaw was overthrown by the British, and the liberated Sacred Hairy Family was forced to give up the lavish palace lifestyle. Legend has it that a Captain Papierno discovered them in the woods, "where they lived much like beasts of the forest, on what roots they could gather." Papierno fed and comforted them, all toward preparing them for exhibition.

Two years after they gained their freedom from Theebaw, P. T. Barnum secured the furry family for his Barnum & London Greatest Show on Earth production. Advertisements proclaimed that $100,000 was being paid for the privilege of exhibiting the attraction for one season, and Barnum billed his latest prize as "a new and most prodigious race of unearthly beings." These "unearthly beings" were accompanied by Moung Phoset's clearly terrestrial wife and Mahphoon's normal nephew. Together, they were an instant sensation at London's Egyptian Hall. The four simply sat onstage, smiling at admiring crowds. This new lifestyle was particularly easy for Mahphoon, who was now blind, and thus endured the many wide-eyed stares with ease.

Barnum's tour soon brought the family to the United States. In conjunction with showman Adam Forepaugh, he briefly exhibited them at New York's Madison Square Garden, beginning on March 14, 1887. *The New York Times* reported that "the Siamese twins, the double-headed nightingale, the tattooed man, Tom Thumb, and Chang, all rolled into one, could not compare with them in point of attractiveness."

The family's magnificent appearance had no encore. After Barnum's one-year contract, no further mention is made of any Sacred Hairy exploits.

THE SHIELDS BROTHERS, THE TEXAS GIANTS

Circa 1850s/1860s–?

In 1880, one of P. T. Barnum's talent scouts heard about four giant brothers living on a farm in Hunt County, Texas. Upon visiting the curious quartet, the scout easily persuaded them to leave the fledgling farm and travel the country as entertainers. Thus began the career of Gus, Frank, Shadrack, and Jack Shields.

The Texas Giants were billed as towering just over eight feet tall. Documentation from the 1880s listed Gus at seven-foot-ten; Frank and Jack at seven feet, eleven and three-quarter inches; and Shadrack at seven-foot-eight. A perhaps more realistic report from 1880 had Jack, the youngest and tallest of the brothers, as only seven feet (though still growing).

The Shields Brothers, circa 1880s.
Author's collection

The Shields Brothers traveled with P. T. Barnum through the 1880s across America, and then overseas in England. At a salary of $100 a week, the mighty foursome found standing around onstage, clad in military uniforms, to be much more sensible than toiling endlessly on the farm.

The giants also toured with the Forepaugh-Sells and the John Robinson circuses, in addition to exhibiting themselves at various dime museums. Occasionally they branched out on their own. Shadrack found a new giant to team with, or more precisely, a giantess. On Christmas Day, 1890, he married a seven-foot-ten immigrant named Emma Anna O'Brien. They toured together as the Tallest Married Couple on Earth.

In the 1890s, Frank, Gus, and Jack returned to Texas, where two of them opened a saloon. Shadrack, the last to leave show business, reportedly became a Missouri Giant. The vertically gifted newcomer enjoyed great popularity in his adopted home state, and was elected mayor of his town and appointed justice of the peace. Who better to establish a longer arm of the law?

ISAAC W. SPRAGUE, THE ORIGINAL THIN MAN
1841–1887

Isaac Sprague with his wife
and child, circa 1880.
Johnny Fox's Freakatorium

Isaac W. Sprague was born in East Bridgewater, Massachusetts, on May 21, 1841. According to his autobiographical pamphlet, aside from being "an expert in the art of swimming," he was a normal, active child. At age twelve he began to lose weight rapidly. Some believed he was swimming too much. Had Sprague discovered the key to weight loss? Doctors shot down the theory, but were stumped as to why the boy was withering away. His appetite seemingly remained healthy.

As an adult, Sprague worked with his father, who ran a shoemaking business and later opened a grocery. But the more emaciated Sprague became, the weaker he grew. After his parents died, it became too difficult for him to continue working and earning a living. He gave up his job at the grocery and looked for a new line of work. In 1865 he found his answer, on a visit to a sideshow passing through town. Upon seeing Sprague, the proprietor promptly offered him a job. He initially refused, but ultimately ended up accepting the position. It was time to capitalize on his looks, by appearing as a Living Skeleton.

Soon after, he became even more ambitious. Sprague went straight to P. T. Barnum in New York and showed off his thin frame. In a promotional booklet, he described the audition: "Mr. Barnum stood very near me, and I overheard him say to his agent, 'Pretty lean man, where did you scare him up?'" The job was his, at $80 a week. But his career with the master showman ended abruptly when the American Museum burned down for a second time in 1868. The skeletal Sprague managed to slip out and escape the flames. With Barnum busy mired in the aftermath, it was time for the Thin Man to offer himself to someone else, namely a wife. Sprague married Miss Tamar Moore, and they had three healthy sons. His family gave him a renewed passion for life. "Life, that had at times seemed so little worth preserving, now seemed more precious," he wrote. Sprague later resumed touring with Barnum's circus and others. His weight may have varied over the years, but at age forty-four, and at a height of five feet, six inches, he weighed a wispy forty-three pounds. After numerous medical exams as an adult, physicians determined that Sprague suffered from an extreme case of progressive muscular atrophy. He was known to walk around with a can of milk to help keep himself alive.

Isaac Sprague's life ended in poverty. The Living Skeleton became a dead one on January 5, 1887, in Chicago.

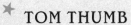

TOM THUMB

1838–1883

History's most famous little person was born Charles Sherwood Stratton, on January 4, 1838, in Bridgeport, Connecticut. He weighed an impressive nine and a half pounds at birth but stopped growing at eighteen months. By 1842 local showman P. T. Barnum had heard about the tiny child. Having had recent success in showcasing the

Tom Thumb dressed as Napoleon, circa 1845.
This image was part of P. T. Barnum's family archives.
Ken Harck archives/Bros. Grim Side Shows

unusual, Barnum envisioned Charles as his next star. He met with the boy's parents, and persuaded them to allow their son to be exhibited for three dollars a week. He was twenty-five inches tall and weighed just sixteen pounds.

Barnum molded the boy into a singer, dancer, and all-around entertainer. Inspired by the thumb-size knight of Arthurian legend, he gave him the name Tom Thumb. But instead of knighthood, Barnum's Tom Thumb gained the rank of general. General Tom Thumb's age was bumped up from four to eleven to convince audiences that he was truly a dwarf and not just a very small toddler. Barnum's genius deceit worked, and Tom Thumb was a sensation. The showman had created a true gentleman in miniature—his star was drinking wine at dinner by the age of five and smoking cigars by age seven.

General Tom Thumb and Barnum set off to tour Britain and Europe in 1844. They began in London at the Princess Theatre. Barnum, the master of showmanship, had four Shetland ponies cart Thumb to performances in a tiny, custom-built carriage. After a few successful engagements about town, he was invited to appear before Queen Victoria at Buckingham Palace. The talented Stratton performed as Frederick the Great and Napoleon, and in Scottish costume and elegant court dress. Her Majesty, rather small herself at just under five feet, was quite taken by the little general. He and Barnum were invited to perform again for the Queen and the Prince of Wales. Tom Thumb was in demand. Exhibitions at Egyptian Hall earned an amazing $500 a day. He even starred in a play written for him, *Hop o' My Thumb*. He and Barnum later graced France and Belgium with their presence before returning to London. With all the success, the boy Thumb had become quite the ladies' man and enjoyed numerous opportunities to kiss adoring women.

In 1847, the showman and the General returned to America as millionaires. The two made each other famous. Tom Thumb took his earnings and purchased a mansion in his hometown. He and Barnum compounded their riches with tours around the United States, including a visit to President Polk. In 1849, Barnum and Thumb's father formed the Great Asiatic Caravan, Museum and Menagerie, which starred Thumb until his father's death, in 1855. Thumb soon resumed touring, but without Barnum.

Tom Thumb and Barnum remained close. When Barnum ran into financial difficulties, the General helped him by touring Europe again.

During a visit to the American Museum in 1862, Tom Thumb met a new little person in Barnum's stable of oddities, a young lady named Lavinia Warren. Romance blossomed between the two Lilliputians, and an engagement was soon announced. Barnum made the union a true event, arranging for 2,000 wedding guests, including Commodore Nutt as best man and Minnie, Warren's sister, as bridesmaid. Charles Stratton and Lavinia Warren were married on February 10, 1863, at Grace Church in New York. Now Thumb had everything: fame, fortune, and a suitably sized sweetheart.

The General and Mrs. Thumb were a popular attraction for years and earned a great deal. Along with their mansion, they owned a yacht and several horses. As the years passed, Thumb began to age quickly. His skin became wrinkled and yellowish, and he fattened up to seventy pounds. A newspaper reported that he looked "like an orange that had been sat upon." He even grew, soaring to a full three feet, four inches. Despite the changes, he continued performing.

Tom Thumb in his miniature carriage pulled by Shetland ponies.
Ken Harck archives / Bros. Grim Side Shows

Tom Thumb and Lavinia Warren.
Author's collection

"People seem to have an idea I have retired, but the truth is I can't do without the excitement of public life," he said in 1880. A year later, Thumb and Warren joined their old friend Barnum in his new venture, the Barnum & London Circus. To add further interest to the act, Barnum exhibited them with their baby. Of course, the infant was not actually theirs. The real mother, a nurse, was never far away.

Tom Thumb's illustrious career came to an end in 1883. On July 15, the General suffered a fatal stroke. More than 10,000 people attended his funeral. Thumb was only forty-five, but in those years he lived larger than most normal-size men: he had seen the world, amassed a fortune, and perhaps kissed more women than any man alive.

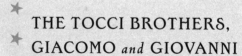

THE TOCCI BROTHERS, GIACOMO *and* GIOVANNI
1875–1912

It would seem a cruel joke for conjoined twins to be born on Independence Day. Of course, in Turin, Italy, where Giacomo and Giovanni Tocci were born on July 4, 1875, no holiday was celebrated. The day was made extraordinary, though, by the arrival of these amazing twins. Joined from the sixth rib downward, sharing one abdomen and one pair of legs, they appeared to be a two-headed boy. The Toccis made other Siamese twins run-of-the-mill in comparison. Despite being conjoined, the brothers did enjoy some independence from each other. Each had his own two arms, heart, lungs, and stomach. Their heartbeats and breathing patterns differed, and their sensations were separate. One could sleep while the other played a game. One could suffer from a cold while the other remained healthy. In personality, they were clearly individuals. Giovanni was known to enjoy drinking beer and sketching. Giacomo preferred mineral water and had a more volatile disposition, sometimes even kicking his brother's drawings off their lap. Unfortunately, they also displayed independence in the one area in which they depended on each other most—walking. Each brother controlled one leg, so walking was impossible. They were able to stand, but nothing more.

When their father first saw his sons he was quite saddened. But then he realized the fortunes that could be made from exhibiting them. Their sideshow career began when they were only a month old. Giacomo and Giovanni would travel throughout Europe and eventually tour the United States. In America they were touted as "the greatest human phenomenon ever seen alive," a claim few could argue. It was reported that they earned as much as $1,000 a week (not a bad living even today). But the brothers were not happy. Fame and fortune didn't exactly compensate for the fact they were forever connected. They returned to Italy when they were sixteen, and retired from touring. They refused to be exhibited again, and went into seclusion.

Years later, when they were adults, the French press reported that each had married. This must have been an interesting arrangement, particularly because the brothers possessed only one set of genitals. Little else is known about the Toccis. They reportedly died in 1912, but they do live on in another form. The extraordinary twins were an inspiration for Mark Twain's classic *Pudd'nhead Wilson*; indeed, his original title for the work was "Those Extraordinary Twins."

The Tocci Brothers, circa 1880s. *Author's collection*

WHAT CAUSES CONJOINED TWINS?

In short, conjoined twins occur when a fertilized egg procrastinates a division. If an egg splits in the first twelve days after conception, identical separate twins are created. If it waits till the thirteenth day or later, the embryos do not divide completely. This leaves the twins conjoined. They can be connected by a ligament, as were the original Siamese twins, Chang and Eng Bunker, or attached even closer—at the head, chest, rear end, or lower body.

It's estimated that only one in 200,000 live births will result in conjoined twins. Seventy-five percent of cases are stillborn or die within twenty-four hours after birth. Approximately seventy percent of conjoined twins are female, though it is not known why. Conjoined twins are always the same sex, never mixed (life isn't quite that cruel).

The term "Siamese twins" began with Chang and Eng, who were born in Siam (modern Thailand) in 1811. They were the most famous conjoined twins, and they toured the world. They were also the first case whose medical history was documented. There were recorded cases of conjoined twins before them, including brothers in Constantinople in the year 945 (the earliest recorded pair) and a set of sisters in England, Mary and Eliza Chulkhurst, known as the Biddenden Maids, for the village where they were born around 1100. They were joined at the shoulders and hips.

Had Chang and Eng, and some of history's other conjoined twins, lived today, they might have been separated as infants. Separation surgeries became common in the 1950s. About 200 sets of conjoined twins have been divided since. Surgeries performed on adults, however, are rare and risky. The attempt made in July 2003 to separate the Iranian twins Ladan and Laleh Bijani, who were joined at their heads, for example, proved unsuccessful. Neither sister survived.

CHARLES TRIPP
1855–1930

Charles Tripp holding a knife and fork with his feet, circa 1880. On the floor are a paper doll, writing instruments, and photos of him. *Becker Collection, Special Collections Research Center, Syracuse University Library*

Born without arms on July 6, 1855, in Woodstock, Canada, Charles Tripp became one of the most well known Armless Wonders to be exhibited. As a boy he quickly learned to use his feet to compensate for his lack of arms. He was a local sensation. The seventeen-year-old Tripp heard about the famous P. T. Barnum and his museum, so he packed up his belongings and went to New York, determined to earn a living with the showman. He marched into Barnum's office, took off his shoes, and demonstrated his dexterous feet. He was hired on the spot.

Tripp's career would last more than fifty years. During this time, his performances displayed acts that were ordinary to him, but extraordinary to audiences. His many feats with his feet included elegant penmanship, shaving, woodcarving, paper cutting, painting, and photography. He spent most of his career traveling the world with Barnum and with Ringling Bros. and Barnum & Bailey shows. Many promotional photos were taken of him, perhaps the most famous the one pairing him with the legless acrobat Eli Bowen on a tandem bicycle, one pedaling, the other steering—an example of teamwork even the fully limbed could learn from (see page 282). Tripp's talented toes commanded as much as $200 a week.

The Armless Wonder married later in life. He settled down, and limited his touring schedule to North American carnivals only. His wife put her hands to good use by selling tickets to the shows. Her position was short-lived, however. Tripp died of asthma in Salisbury, North Carolina, in January 1930, at the age of seventy-four.

UNZIE

1868–?

The Land Down Under's greatest sideshow export was an albino known as the Hirsute Wonder and the Aboriginal Beauty from Australia. Unzie's true origins are somewhat mysterious. According to his biography, he was an Aborigine born in 1868 in Tarrabandra, New South Wales. Young Unzie was supposedly worshipped by his people as a "special dispensation from Heaven," until he was kidnapped by an Englishman and taken to Melbourne. In 1886, Unzie was exhibited in public for the first time.

Unzie with a hat resting neatly atop his fluffy hair, 1899. *Author's collection*

It's unlikely that Unzie was an Aborigine. The Fort Wayne, Indiana, *Gazette* explained in 1895: "It has hitherto been believed that the lower specimen of the human race was the Australian aborigine. A curious contradiction of this theory is found in the presence of an intelligent, well-educated Australian native in this country. Except in the contour of his features, he resembles his race in nothing." Not only did Unzie entertain audiences, he was a respectable ambassador for his supposed people.

Unzie was the most famous of the sideshow albinos. He evidently traveled the world exhibiting his pure white skin and mighty mass of hair, and in 1890 arrived in the United States, landing in San Francisco. He made his way across the country, appearing in dime museums, such as Huber's 14th Street Museum in New York City, where he was referred to as the "Australian with the remarkable head." His biography described his great white shocks of hair as "elastic, crispy, and electric." Unzie's snow-white afro was trimmed twice a week to maintain its six-foot circumference. Tuxedos and top hats complemented his look, helping him maintain a distinguished and dapper appearance.

What became of the Hirsute Wonder is not known. One can only hope for his sake that he wasn't a victim of male pattern baldness.

LAVINIA WARREN
1841–1919

✶ Born on Halloween in 1841, the tiny Mercy Lavinia Warren Bump was nature's trick *and* treat. She was six pounds at birth and stopped growing by age ten, when she stood thirty-two inches and weighed just under thirty pounds. Thanks to her short stature, she would become almost as famous as an ancestor she claimed, William the Conqueror.

Lavinia didn't exhibit herself for the public until she was seventeen. Before that she spent a year teaching elementary school in her hometown, Middleborough, Massachusetts. The petite teacher managed to keep her classroom orderly—quite a feat when even the youngest students were taller than she.

Lavinia Warren and Tom Thumb with their wedding party of Commodore Nutt and Minnie Warren, along with P. T. Barnum, 1863. This photo was part of Barnum's family archives. *Ken Harck archives/Bros. Grim Side Shows*

But then Lavinia made a major career change. An entrepreneurial cousin invited her to appear in his "floating palace of curiosities" along the Ohio and Mississippi rivers. Lavinia was no longer a teacher, she was an entertainer. Soon P. T. Barnum heard of the budding star. He wrote a letter requesting to meet with her, and she accepted his offer to appear at his American Museum. Barnum trimmed her name to Lavinia Warren and provided her with elegant dresses and luxurious jewelry.

Warren's real ticket to fame and wealth came in the form of General Tom Thumb (Charles S. Stratton). Barnum's old friend visited the museum and met the diminutive damsel. The two hit it off, perhaps with a little help from Barnum. On February 10, 1863, Thumb and Warren were married at Grace Church in New York. Naturally, Barnum made a huge spectacle of the event, which was attended by 2,000 guests. Commodore Nutt and Minnie, Lavinia's equally tiny sister, served as the wedding party.

The elfin quartet toured the continents, and Mrs. Thumb became the world's most renowned female midget. The Thumbs later toured with a baby, as proof that the marriage was prosperous. In fact, they never had any children—the baby was merely a Barnum publicity stunt.

On July 15, 1883, General Tom Thumb, who had been looking older than his forty-five years, suffered a fatal stroke. Despite her resolution to remain a widow after his death, the ever-popular Warren soon changed her mind. "The excitement of public appearances, to which I have been used all my life, was too seductive," she explained. When another small man, Count Primo Magri, proposed, she accepted. In April 1885 they tied the knot, at the Church of the Holy Trinity in New York. She and the slightly taller Italian count had met while performing with the Tom Thumb Company. Though remarried, Warren continued to exploit her first husband's fame. The new couple was initially exhibited as "Mrs. General Tom Thumb and her husband." She later relinquished her former name and adopted the noble title of her second husband, becoming Countess Magri.

Together, the Count and Countess traveled the country with their Lilliputian Opera Company. In 1904 they settled in Lilliputia, the new "Midget City" at Coney Island. The hardest-working little people in show business even ran a store in Middleborough, Massachusetts, selling general goods and autographed photos. In spite of their efforts and lingering popularity, Lavinia Warren never earned the riches she had made with Tom Thumb.

Warren spent nearly sixty years appearing before the public. "I have shaken hands with more human beings, royal and plebein, rich and poor, great and small, old and young, native and foreign, than any other woman in existence," she wrote in her autobiography. After meeting President Taft in 1911, she observed that she had met every U.S. president since Lincoln. The long, brilliant life of Countess Mercy Lavinia Warren Bump Stratton Magri ended on November 25, 1919. She was seventy-eight years old.

THE WILD MEN OF BORNEO, WAINO *and* PLUTANO (HIRAM *and* BARNEY DAVIS)

Hiram: 1825–1905
Barney: 1827–1912

The Wild Men of Borneo with (probably) Hanford Warner. *Author's collection*

The Wild Men of Borneo were neither wild nor from Borneo. Hiram and Barney Davis were brothers, both midgets who were mentally slow but physically extraordinarily strong.

Hiram was born in 1825 in England. His brother was born two years later in Long Island, New York, where the Davis family had relocated. Both reached a height of three and a half feet and each weighed about forty pounds. In 1852 a showman, Lyman Warner, discovered them and offered to purchase the boys from their widowed mother. She couldn't resist the prospect of a handsome payment.

Warner added an exotic element to their small stature by renaming them Waino and Plutano, and claiming they were from faraway Borneo. Waino's name signified "good," for his calm demeanor when captured. Plutano's, in contrast, indicated "bad," for his fierce resistance. An 1893 promotional booklet, "What We Know About Waino and Plutano, Wild Men of Borneo," described their capture, which allegedly took place in 1848. "When first brought before the public," it went on to say, "Waino and Plutano were hardly more elevated in social standing than ourang-outangs of a like size; but no ourang-outang could climb a tree with more agility than they displayed."

Few if any spectators had met anyone from Borneo or knew any better. Although Hiram and Barney actually had gentle dispositions, they played their roles and acted wild onstage. They spoke in their "native tongue," which was pure gibberish, the universal language of the wild. Yet they flexed their English-speaking skills by reciting poems they had been taught. They would also demonstrate their mighty muscles by lifting dumbbells and members of the audience. Their exhibitions progressed over the years from rented rooms to dime museums to sideshows.

After Warner died, in 1871, his son Hanford took over the care and exhibition of the Wild Men. By 1903, Hiram had become ill, and their days on the sideshow circuit came to an end. They settled in Massachusetts with Hanford Warner. Hiram died in March 1905. Barney lived another seven years, dying in March 1912 at age eighty-five. The two are buried together in Mount Vernon, Ohio.

GEORGE WILLIAMS, THE TURTLE BOY
1859–?

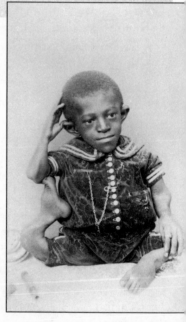

Arkansas-born George Williams seems to have suffered from parastremmatic dysplasia, a severe form of dwarfism that twists and deforms the limbs. The deformity left him standing only eighteen inches tall and weighing thirty-nine pounds as an adult. A 1902 Ohio newspaper article exaggerated his physical nature: "Where the legs ought to be there are what may by courtesy be called feet, but which [resemble] more the flippers of a turtle than the feet of a human being. The hands are also fashioned after the flippers of a turtle. The chest is flat and the back curved like that of a turtle, but from the angle of the jaws upward George is a perfect man, far above the average intelligence." While no hard shell developed on the Turtle Boy's back, a lively advertising banner depicted him with one.

During the late 1800s and the early 1900s,

George Williams. *Becker Collection, Special Collection Research Center, Syracuse University Library*

Williams was a sensation at carnivals, dime museums, and even a YMCA event. His popularity earned him a multiyear tenure in New York at Huber's 14th Street Museum. Unlike his reptilian counterpart, the Turtle Boy wasn't one to just sit around. Williams was able to entertain guests not just by showing his misshapen limbs, but by using them as well. He overcame his deformity and grew into an accomplished musician on harmonica and flute. And despite his small size, he possessed a full, rich baritone voice.

When not performing, Williams enjoyed shooting craps and playing pool. One of his pool pals was a fellow freak.

> ✴ Although there have been a number of Turtle Boys and Girls, a late-nineteenth-century man named Samuel Keene best fit the description. The four-foot-tall Turtle Man of Battle Creek, Michigan, had stunted limbs and layers of bony cuticle hardening on his back, webbed fingers, and a mouth said to stretch from ear to ear.

Laloo (and his parasitic twin) consented to Williams's ground rules, allowing him to walk along the edge of the table—a feat as impressive as his skills with the cue. Games between the two would likely have drawn larger crowds than many exhibits at dime museums.

In the mid-1880s, the Turtle Boy was earning $75 a week, less than the fortunes other freaks were making but still a decent wage. Williams missed out on a big payday when he lost a suit against the City of New York in 1910. He had suffered injuries after being thrown from his "go-cart" as he was wheeled over a defect in the sidewalk. If he had won the $10,000 he sought, the Turtle Boy probably could have retired his herpetological name.

✴

✴ LUCIA ZARATE, THE MEXICAN LILLIPUTIAN

✴ 1863–1889

✴

✴ Lucia Zarate was born in San Carlos, Mexico, on January 2, 1863. She measured a mere seven inches and weighed a feathery two and a half pounds. Lucia suffered from ateliotic dwarfism, more descriptively known as infantile dwarfism. The Mexican Lilliputian

Lucia Zarate, circa 1880s.
Courtesy Tom Hernandez

was of course exhibited as the smallest person in the world, which was fairly accurate. Only the younger Pauline Musters, at just over twenty-three inches, rivaled her. Of the tiny pair, Zarate earned the Guinness record for the lightest recorded human adult. At age seventeen, she weighed only about four pounds, eleven ounces. Zarate eventually cracked the two-foot mark, standing twenty-six and a half inches tall. She was so small that she could wear a normal ring as a bracelet and her hat was the size of a teacup.

Other than her size, Zarate was normal in every way. She was said to be friendly and intelligent. Little Lucia came to the United States at the age of twelve and became one of the best-paid midgets ever. Her tiny stature commanded a giant salary of $20 an hour. She was believed to have earned up to $200,000 through her fifteen-year career.

Zarate died in October 1889, when a blizzard struck while she was traveling with a circus in the Rocky Mountains. She was only twenty-six.

A BRIEF GLOSSARY OF CIRCUS AND SIDESHOW LINGO

Bally or *Ballyhoo.* A free show set up outside a sideshow to attract a crowd. The term dates back to the 1893 World's Columbian Exposition in Chicago. The word is said to derive from *dehalla hoon,* an ostensibly Arabic expression used to call Middle Eastern fakirs and dancers to the stage. It mutated into "ballyhoo" and was cemented into the sideshow lexicon.

Blow-off. An extra act or exhibit at the end of a show, costing an additional fee.

Dime museum. A museum that flourished in the latter half of the nineteenth century, featuring cabinets of curiosities, paintings, wax figures, freaks, theatrical performances, and more. Admission, as the name suggests, cost a dime.

Ding. As in "ding 'em," meaning to get more money from a crowd. The term is onomatopoetic in origin: a metal bucket would be passed around to collect money and when the coins hit the bottom—*ding.*

Fakir. Often used for a Middle Eastern (or supposedly so) street performer who swallowed swords, ate fire, lay on beds of nails, or performed other stunts. The word is Arabic for "poor person" or "someone who has nothing." A fakir does not have to be poor; the term relates to a spiritual belief that all things in life are temporary.

Gaff. A fake.

Glomming geek. A geek show performer who bites the heads off chickens or other creatures.

Making the nut. Making money. Back in the day, a show employee would arrive in town early to square everything with the sheriff, in order to run illegal games and get away with it. When a carnival showed up in horse-drawn wagons, the sheriff would send his deputy to remove the nuts from the wagon wheels. Once you paid the sheriff, you got your nuts back and you could move on to the next town.

Midway. The area in a circus between the entrance and the big top, where concessions, shows, and rides would be found.

Single-O. A show featuring one attraction.

Ten-in-one (10-in-1). A show featuring ten attractions.

Tip. The crowd a talker gathers in front of an attraction.

With it. A phrase many people use without realizing its origin. Saying you were "with it" meant you were with the show.

PART TWO

Who's going to support these people, if they can't support themselves? For the
past thirty years I have been able to give employment to scores of them, give
them financial independence, and companionship. You realize this when you
see a mule-faced girl, a guy with three legs[,] and a girl weighing 500 pounds
playing poker with a guy who shuffles and deals with his toes. In a crowd
like that nobody sits around feeling sorry for himself or anybody else.
You could be accepted there if you had nine arms and ten heads.

DICK BEST, *on the hiring and exhibiting of freaks, 1959*

~ *The* ~

SILVER AGE

From the FORMATION *of the* RINGLING BROS.
AND BARNUM & BAILEY COMBINED SHOWS
to the DECLINE *of the* AMERICAN SIDESHOW
(circa 1919 *to* 1970s)

Banner line for the Al G. Barnes & Sells-Floto circus sideshow, circa 1920s. One banner promotes "Mr. and Mrs. Tom Thum III." *Ken Harck archives/Bros. Grim Side Shows*

★ ★ ★ ★ ★ ★ ★ ★ ★ ★ ★ ★ ★ ★ ★ ★ ★ ★ ★

W hat if you had been born with no limbs? No arms to hold things, hug loved ones, reach food, or even wave hello. And no legs to take you places. But your mind is perfectly functional and capable. Would you be using your disadvantages for financial gain?

Whether limbless or otherwise deformed, freaks continued to earn a living in sideshows through the Roaring Twenties and after the Great Depression. Americans were even entertained by conjoined twins singing and dancing in vaudeville theaters and by little people sneaking and scurrying in movies like *The Unholy Three* and *The Wizard of Oz*. But as the years progressed, the collective American attitude shifted, giving rise to that cultural beast we call political correctness. Some sectors of the public took it upon themselves to decide what was right for freaks and what wasn't. It raises the question of what's scarier: having no limbs or having no choice?

★ ★ ★ ★ ★ ★ ★ ★ ★ ★ ★ ★ ★ ★ ★ ★ ★ ★ ★

John Aasen and an unidentified man.
Eddy County Museum

JOHN AASEN
1890–1938

★ When John Aasen was a baby, there were no indications he would grow up to be one of the world's tallest men. He was born in Minneapolis, and his family soon moved to Sheyenne, North Dakota. John's parents died when he was very young, before his great growth spurt began. When he was about ten, a disorder in his pituitary gland sparked a sudden surge. He eventually stood out over the rest of the townspeople, allegedly at eight feet, nine inches, and weighed 503 pounds; more realistic reports have him as only seven feet, four inches. While he was a local anomaly, Aasen wasn't the only curious figure in town. His best friend there was a three-foot midget named Lawrence Buck.

In 1917 and 1918, Aasen worked for Midway Chemical of St. Paul, selling products in the Huron, South Dakota, area. But unless he was demonstrating chemicals that caused physical enlargement, this was not the job for a man of his stature.

Aasen soon realized this. He took advantage of nature's gift and made a living off his height. Known as Johnny the Gent, Aasen traveled the world with the Al G. Barnes Circus, Barnum & Bailey, C. A. Wortham's World's Best Shows, and Foley & Burk Shows. The promoters claimed he came from Norway, the son of giant parents, descended from a race of giants. To set off his height, Aasen frequently appeared with his childhood friend Buck.

Aasen was the beneficiary of a colleague's misfortune. In 1922, the giant George Auger died the day before he was to leave to film Harold Lloyd's *Why Worry?* in Hollywood, and Aasen stepped into the role. He continued his Hollywood career appearing with W. C. Fields in *Two Flaming Youths* (1927), and with Laurel and Hardy in *Should*

Married Men Go Home? (1928), and starring in *Growing Pains* (1928). Not surprisingly, he played a giant in all four movies.

Just as Aasen broke into Hollywood with a bit of luck, it was bad luck that forced him out. His acting career and circus career both came to an end in 1933, when he was hospitalized with a brain tumor. He lost weight and began withering away. In 1936 he was arrested on charges of drunkenness. He weighed 330 pounds at the time. That night in jail he drank two gallons of coffee and requested food to help regain some lost weight.

By 1938, Aasen was a patient at Mendocino State Mental Hospital in California. On August 1, having dwindled down to 247 pounds, less than half his normal weight, he died.

John Aasen earned a fortune as a giant, but died with very little money. He gave much of his wealth to his aunt and a grandmother, and lost a great deal during the Depression.

ALBERT-ALBERTA
1899–1963

Albert-Alberta was born simply as Alberta, on November 4, 1899, in France. Eventually half of her body developed male characteristics, thus forming Albert. Or so audiences were led to believe—and they frequently did. In truth, like most sideshow hermaphrodites, Albert-Alberta was a female impersonator, in this case really named Harry Caro. His left half, from head to toe, was shaved and soft-looking, while his right was hairy and muscular. Albert's foot purportedly wore a size 8½ man's shoe, and Alberta's modeled a size 4½ woman's high heel.

The half man, half woman enjoyed a long career of gender bending, having worked at Coney Island, Hubert's Museum in Times Square, and on the Loew's theater circuit. At Hubert's, a curtain was opened to reveal Albert-Alberta sitting on a small stool wearing one fake breast (filled with birdseed). The performer would stand and announce in a

Albert-Alberta and his "younger brother," circa 1930s. Note Albert-Alberta's male and female sides with corresponding underwear and footwear. Interestingly, the Albert half wears an earring. *The collection of Bobby Reynolds*

silly French accent: "Ladies and gentlemen, you look upon the stage, you say to yourself, 'That looks like a man.' I don't claim to be a man, because I'm not a man. I don't claim to be a woman, because I'm not a woman. I do claim to be a real and true hermaphrodite."

Albert-Alberta also performed with a "younger brother" as the Alberta Sex Family. This brother had two breasts and was billed as a boy turning into a girl—the opposite of Albert's supposed origin. In their souvenir pitch book, the little brother was described as "the only boy able to nurse a baby boy." According to showman Bobby Reynolds, who as a teenager worked with the "family," this boy's breasts didn't need to be filled with birdseed, as they were real.

Love didn't come easy for the dual-sexed being. Albert-Alberta's literature described the difficulties: "I might not be what a young lady might expect; at the same time I would be a terrible disappointment to a young man. Therefore I cannot marry." Fittingly, his one love in life was neither man nor woman. Albert-Alberta channeled his passion into raising Pomeranian dogs. The man-woman's best friends were often spoiled with beef kidney treats.

Albert-Alberta maintained his sexual duality until his dying day, which came in September 1963. The half man, half woman suffered a fatal heart attack after being mugged one night while walking home in New York City. He was buried in full makeup and costume.

HALF MEN, HALF WOMEN

Attractions billing themselves as half man, half woman (or half-and-halfs) were a dime a dozen from the 1920s through the 1960s. Very few of them, however, were actual hermaphrodites (born with both male and female sex organs). Some may have had deformed genitalia, for instance a prolonged clitoris or a misshapen penis, which created the illusion of a double sex, but generally the "hermaphrodites" were female impersonators. Many of them even owned the sideshows they starred in.

The half-and-half act was initially popular and profitable as a sex show. Sex has sold since the beginning of humanity, so naturally it sold well in the sideshow. Curious crowds were enticed by gender-bending fellows in drag—all dolled up—and hoped to catch a glimpse of skin. Usually the half-and-half act would work the blow-off: spectators would have to pay an additional fee to witness the supposed hermaphrodite. Once inside, the half man, half woman would lecture about him/herself, then charge yet another fee to be seen disrobing. Clearly, female impersonators couldn't strip entirely. Some wore rubber torsos with fake breasts. The torsos ran from the neckline to the waist, the edges hidden with strategically placed necklaces and G-strings. Somehow this often fooled the audience.

Many show owners claimed that a female impersonator was preferable to a true hermaphrodite. This was because men in drag had to work hard at looking beautiful and glamorous, whereas the real things might neglect themselves and lack the showmanship needed for the exhibition.

By the 1950s and 1960s, many towns had local establishments offering sex shows. This put an end to the half-and-half act in the sideshows. In Ward Hall's words, "Carnivals at one time brought a sense of wonderful wickedness to town—games of chance, half-and-halfs, girl shows, tattoo artists, fortune-tellers—but by the end of the fifties, the wonderful wickedness was already in town." It's possible that the new strip clubs, which stayed open year-round, rather than being in town for only a few weeks, were paying off the police whom carnival owners had once paid off.

The half-and-halfs adapted by altering their acts to be more literal renderings of the

(continued)

name—one half of the body developed as a man, the other as a woman. In addition to those featured in this book, the roster of half-and-halfs has included: Anna-John Budd, Bobby Kork, Elsie-John, Esther Lester, Flo-Floyd, Henri-Etta, Jean-Jeanette, Joe-Ann, Josephine Joseph, Leo-Leola, Lu Verne, Mlle. Za Za Frazee, and Roberta-Robert.

SAM ALEXANDER, THE MAN WITH TWO FACES

Circa 1920s–1997

The Man with Two Faces didn't always carry that distinction. Sam Alexander was born with only one face, but as a young man he suffered a devastating, disfiguring accident. He had just been promoted at the Shubert Theatre in Chicago and decided to celebrate. On the way to a club, he and some friends walked past an establishment that steam-cleaned fifty-five-gallon metal drums that had held gasoline. Alexander, who already had had a bit too much to drink, unwisely threw a lit cigarette into a drum. The resulting explosion burned off his face and the bottom of his arm (which was, fortunately, covering his eyes).

Alexander spent a year in the hospital before being moved to a nursing home. The bones in his face were visible, so a mask was made to allow him to go out in public—should he ever wish to. Alexander may not have had a face, but he still had ambition. He found an ad for a Pete Kortes sideshow playing near the nursing home. This would be his salvation. Alexander introduced himself to Kortes, and wasted no time in taking off his mask to show him what he had to offer. He was hired on the spot as the Man with Two Faces. Onstage, the masked Alexander would tell his story, then turn around and unmask himself, before facing the audience again. It was a shocking image. Kortes later made Alexander the blow-off for the show.

The two-faced marvel went on to join the Ringling Bros. and Barnum & Bailey show. Ward Hall, who worked with him from 1960 to 1967, recalls an episode at Madison Square Garden in which Alexander proved simply too shocking. Circus director John Ringling North, who had never visited his own sideshow, finally did during the year Alexander was working. "Some social ladies who were in his party that evening saw Sam and were offended," Hall remembers. "So he told the sideshow manager [to] take Sam off the stage." Alexander was actually paid *not* to perform at the Garden.

After Ringling, Alexander worked with the Clyde Beatty Circus. He eventually ran his own sideshow, and was responsible for rescuing the pinhead Schlitzie from being institutionalized.

Over the years, Alexander underwent seventy-two operations on his face. It was restored, and he was able to retire the mask. "It was still like looking at a patchwork quilt, the colors of the flesh . . . on his face didn't match entirely," Hall says. "If there was anyone in the world who had the right to be bitter, it was Sam. He didn't have a bitter bone in his body."

Sam Alexander passed away in 1997.

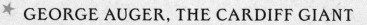

✴ GEORGE AUGER, THE CARDIFF GIANT
✴ *1882–1922*

✴ **K**nown as the Cardiff Giant, George Auger was born in Wales in 1882. As a teenager, he quickly dwarfed his classmates, reaching six feet by age fourteen. According to a newspaper report, he had to leave school because "so much fun was poked at him, and he didn't dare get into a fight for fear of killing someone." He ultimately grew to an advertised eight feet, four inches, though Ellis Island records claimed a more conservative seven-foot-ten.

Auger served on the police force in Wales, and with his intimidating height he must

CAPT GEO. AUGER.

CARDIFF GIANT.

TALLEST MAN ON EARTH. 23 YEARS OF AGE.
WEIGHS 320 POUNDS.
BORN IN CARDIFF, WALES.
SIZE OF HAT, 7 3-4; COLLAR, 18; SHOE, 16.

Captain George Auger, circa 1905. Giants
commonly demonstrated their height with their arms
extended over the heads of normal-size people.
Collection of James G. Mundie

have been quite effective at his job. In London, he occasionally served as a member of Queen Victoria's police escort. She called him Captain because of his unusual size, and the name remained.

After a few trips to the United States around the turn of the century, Auger immigrated with a sister, Lucy, in 1909. The Captain crossed the pond to perform as the Tallest Man on Earth with the Barnum & Bailey Circus. He augmented his height with high-heeled boots and a plumed hat. He was often shown with the Doll Family midgets, whom he held in his hand. The gig provided steady employment for roughly twelve years.

In addition to standing tall for the circus, the Captain was recruited by the U.S. Army to encourage shorter but, one hoped, equally formidable men to enlist for service in World War I. But Auger himself was an entertainer, not a fighter. After retiring from circus life, he wrote short stories and starred in a vaudeville production of *Jack the Giant Killer.* He nearly took vaudeville to the next step with a career in Hollywood, when he was cast for the role of Colosso in the Harold Lloyd film *Why Worry?* An excited Auger was set to earn $350 a week in his new career in moving pictures, but this bright future was not to be. On November 30, 1922, the day before he was scheduled to leave for California, Auger died suddenly, of indigestion, while at a friend's home in New York.

HUGH BAILY, THE PRETZEL MAN

Born 1935

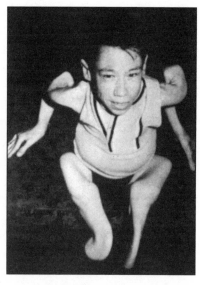

Hugh Baily. *Ward Hall collection*

The Pretzel Man, known also as Spider Boy and Crawfish Boy, was born with horribly deformed and twisted limbs. Most likely he suffered from the same parastremmatic dwarfism as the similarly malformed George Williams, the Turtle Boy, before him. Both of Baily's shins were bent at nearly ninety degrees. His arms were curved and twisted in several places. He looked like a used Bendy Toy, only he didn't unbend. Unable to stand, he was measured sitting; he reached a height of about eighteen inches.

The Pretzel Man spent his career working with showmen Dick Best and Walter Wanous. One performance was captured in the 1973 movie *The Mutations*. "I don't sing or dance, do flip-flops or anything else like that," Baily announces as he's wheeled before the crowd. He simply describes his condition and lets the audience stare in amazement.

JANE BARNELL, LADY OLGA

1871–?

Jane Barnell started her career not as a Bearded Lady, but as a bearded baby. Little Jane was born in Wilmington, North Carolina, to a Russian Jewish father and a part-Catawba Indian mother. Her beard began to grow shortly after she was born. Jane's mother, upset by the unusual facial hair, believed someone had cursed her child. Jane's father was more accepting. When she was four years old, the Great Orient Family Circus and Menagerie came to town. Jane's father was in Baltimore on business. Her mother wanted to rid herself of the freakish girl, so she took advantage of her husband's absence and sold her daughter to the circus showman.

Little hairy Jane toured with the circus in Europe until she became ill in Germany in 1876. Somehow the hospital where she was placed contacted her father, who came and rescued her from exhibition. He brought his daughter home and left her to be raised by her Indian grandmother on a farm. When Jane was seventeen she returned to Wilmington and took a job as a hospital nurse. The job didn't last long; apparently the sight of a bearded nurse wasn't helping anyone feel better.

In 1892, a neighbor who worked in the circus convinced Barnell she could make a fortune exhibiting her whiskers in a traveling show. Thus she started a second career in the sideshow with the John Robinson Circus. She became known as Princess Olga, and later Madame Olga. When "Madame" became too common with other performers, she switched to Lady Olga. She boasted the longest beard of the Bearded Ladies, thirteen inches. Every year it was styled in whatever manner was popular at the time.

Lady Olga performed in many dime museums and circuses, including Ringling Bros. and Barnum & Bailey, Royal American Shows, Forepaugh-Sells, and Coney Island Dreamland. She was also the Bearded Lady in the movie *Freaks;* she subsequently found the film insulting and regretted doing it. Later in her career she was featured at Hubert's Museum in Times Square in New York City, where she was occasionally presented thus: "It gives me the greatest pleasure at this time to introduce a little woman who comes to us from an aristocratic plantation in the Old South and who is recognized by our finest doctors, physicians, and medical men as the foremost unquestioned and authentic female bearded lady in medical history. Ladies and gentlemen, Lady Olga!"

Although Lady Olga was proud of her extraordinary beard, she wasn't always a lady when addressed by the crowd. She did not enjoy being asked personal questions or receiving pity, and on occasion would tell off obnoxious onlookers. Lady Olga also went through periods of depression. Yet as she told *New Yorker* writer Joseph Mitchell, "My beard has been my meal ticket."

Despite her bushy chin, Lady Olga was still feminine. She landed four husbands and gave birth to two children with her second, a German musician. Unfortunately, neither survived infancy. It is not known when Lady Olga died, though she was known to be living in New York in the late 1940s with her fourth husband, a circus clown and talker. She no longer exhibited her beard, preferring to be a housekeeper instead.

✶

PERCILLA *and* EMMITT BEJANO, THE MONKEY GIRL *and* THE ALLIGATOR-SKINNED MAN

Percilla: 1918–2001
Emmitt: 1918–1995

Percilla was born in 1918 in San Juan, Puerto Rico, with hypertrichosis, a condition that causes excessive hairiness all over the face and body. The affliction gave her a full, black beard, even as a baby. Knowing she could be exhibited for profit, her parents brought her to the United States. They met a sideshow promoter name Karl Lauther, who fell in love with Percilla and adopted her. First he billed her as the Little Hairy Girl, but later changed that to the Monkey Girl. He even bought her a chimpanzee, Josephine, to appear in her act.

The Monkey Girl spent her childhood in the sideshow. But when she was twenty, she discovered that there was more to life than performing. A man named Emmitt Bejano, who worked for Lauther as the Alligator-Skinned Man, would become the love of her life.

The Alligator-Skinned Man was born in Florida in 1918, afflicted with ichthyosis. The condition made his skin hard and scaly; only

Percilla and Emmitt Bejano, the World's Strangest Married Couple, circa 1940s. *Collection of Bob Blackmar*

his face and hands were smooth. Emmitt had received his surname from the showman Johnny J. Bejano, who adopted Emmitt when he was a young boy. By age twenty, Emmitt had left Bejano's show for Lauther's.

Percilla and Emmitt eloped and were married in 1938. Percilla later gave birth to a baby girl, who died of pneumonia shortly thereafter. The two tried to have other children, but were unsuccessful, and later adopted a son, Tony.

The Bejanos eventually ran their own sideshow and exhibited themselves as the World's Strangest Married Couple. The two truly loved each other. Percilla once teased Emmitt, saying, "I think I'll shave and dye my hair blond and have a new look." He responded, "You do and I'm gonna walk out on you. I love you as you are."

In the 1950s the Monkey Girl and the Alligator-Skinned Man dropped their monikers and retired near Tampa, as Percilla and Emmitt Bejano. People who knew Percilla say she was always very friendly, but she shied away from having her photo taken, fearing that others would exploit her image. She always wore a veil to cover her beard when in public—after all, she didn't want to offer any free shows. Percilla and Emmitt remained happily married for fifty-seven years, until he died, on May 14, 1995. The former Monkey Girl shaved her face for the last few years of life. She died in her sleep on February 5, 2001.

ANIMAL ODDITIES

Mother Nature doesn't discriminate in creating anomalies. Like humans, animals are occasionally born with extra limbs or heads. And the sideshow has always been there to exhibit them. Two-headed calves, five-legged cows, two-faced pigs, three-legged chickens, two-headed turtles, dwarf horses, and many other unusual creatures have all sold tickets for showmen.

The extraordinary creatures have often been presented alive. In 1923, an impresario known as Professor Gold even invited veterinarians to see his eighty-eight animal attractions free of charge.

A six-legged sheep called Lucia gained fame in the early 1930s. Dexter Fellows, a press agent for Ringling Bros. and Barnum & Bailey, purchased the woolly wonder from a farmer in Yorktown Heights, New York, and named her after the sextet in the opera *Lucia di Lammermoor.* The sheep was exhibited at Madison Square Garden and later sold to a showman at Coney Island. Lucia's many legs certainly helped her get around, as she was seen later at the Chicago World's Fair.

Moe Joe, one of Col. Hunsley's two-headed turtles, 2004.
© *Liz Steger*

Taxidermy has helped give many freakish beasts a longer exhibition life. Many can still be seen in Ripley's museums and other shows of oddities. Live animal anomalies still make occasional appearances. Fire eater, sword swallower, and showman John Strong tours state fairs with an eight-year-old two-headed tortoise, a six-year-old six-legged cow, a two-year-old six-footed pig, and other curious creatures. All are in good health. Strong has collected unusual animals since he was eleven. Col. Hunsley's Freaks and Oddities show features two living two-headed turtles and various stuffed animals. And Johnny Fox's Freakatorium was home to Frik and Frak, a living two-headed turtle billed as "the most anatomically sound two-headed turtle in zoological history."

BARBARA BENNETT

Circa 1940s–2000

Barbara Bennett was born in the 1940s to a wealthy family. As an adult, she wanted to maintain the financial comfort she had been accustomed to as a child. However, Bennett's limbs were shrunken and disfigured, as a result of osteogenesis imperfecta, and she was unable to stand. Her torso and head were normal, but her arms and legs developed like those of a child. Though physically deformed, she had an entrepreneurial spirit and eventually owned three places of business.

In the 1970s, Bennett's business sense shifted dramatically. While visiting the Hall & Christ sideshow she became acquainted with the showmen and told them she wanted to be in show business. Ward Hall offered her a position in the last show of the season to determine if it was really what she wanted. It was. She joined the sideshow, along with her similarly afflicted daughter and her husband, Ed. Bennett was billed as the World's Smallest Mother.

After her first full season, Bennett's capitalistic mindset brought her to request a Single-O show. In such an exhibit, performing alone, Bennett would earn a larger percentage of the take. "I told her it's much harder," Hall recalls. "In the big show, you're on five minutes, then you go relax. The Single-O, you're on all the time. She wanted to do that." Hall's partner, Chris Christ, built her a show space resembling a small house. In addition to the tiny mother and daughter exhibited inside, a model of the U.S. Capitol built from matchsticks served as an attraction. Crowds were told that Bennett had spent twenty years constructing it.

The World's Smallest Mother was occasionally accused by audiences of being none other than a man they had seen previously. The man they were referring to was Pete Moore, who was afflicted with the same condition and billed as the World's Smallest Man. According to Moore's widow, Adena Baker, Bennett was thrilled when she finally made his acquaintance. "Good to meet the person I get accused of being in drag!" she exclaimed.

The Bennetts worked the Hall & Christ show for nearly eight years. They then purchased the set so they could work fewer shows. Four years later, Barbara Bennett retired. She eventually had three more children to whom she was the World's Smallest Mother in the privacy of their home. Barbara Bennett passed away on Christmas Day, 2000.

MARY ANN BEVAN,
THE WORLD'S HOMELIEST WOMAN
1874–1933

The World's Homeliest Woman wasn't always the epitome of ugliness. Bevan was actually an attractive woman in her earlier years, before she suffered from acromegaly. The disfiguring ailment, a disorder in which the pituitary gland overproduces growth hormones, can cause adults to suddenly begin growing again. Hands and feet may swell, and the changing bone structure alters facial features. Bevan's pleasant face became grotesque, as her brow and lower jaw protruded and her nose expanded.

Bevan's more beautiful days began in London, where she was born as Mary Ann Webster. She became a nurse and by 1903 had married a farmer from Kent, Thomas Bevan. The happy couple had four healthy children. All was well with the Bevans until Thomas died unexpectedly, in 1914. It has been reported that his widow's acromegaly manifested itself after his death, though other sources claim the disease had already set in.

Mary Ann Bevan, the World's Homeliest Woman, circa 1920s. *Kobel collection*

Bevan decided to capitalize on her worsening appearance in order to help support her family. She entered a "Homeliest Woman" contest and bested 250 unsightly competitors. Blessed with such an unfortunate title, Bevan found work in the sideshow. The job seemed secure, as doctors promised she would continue to grow uglier.

In 1920, Bevan was in the cast of Coney Island's Dreamland Circus Side Show. She endured the disgusted looks of spectators for years, all to feed and educate her children. She occasionally treated visitors to photos of her beautiful family and boasted of her son's position in the British navy.

The World's Homeliest Woman also appeared with the Ringling Bros. and Barnum & Bailey show. In 1929, while performing at Madison Square Garden, Bevan fell in love with the show's giraffe keeper, known only as Andrew. The two were friendly with each other, and most important, the sideshow star didn't repulse the giraffe keeper. Nevertheless, Bevan chose to risk her career and get a makeover. A local beauty shop enlisted experts to work their magic on her. Some people held that the manicure, massage, permanent, and various other treatments improved her looks, while other people told a newspaper that "the rouge and powder and the rest were as out of place on Mary Ann's countenance as lace curtains on the portholes of a dreadnought." If only *Extreme Makeover* had been around to accept Bevan's challenge. After seeing the results for herself, the still-homely woman remarked, "I guess I'll be getting back to work." Her job was safe. There is no report on the giraffe keeper's reaction.

> In addition to managing scores of human oddities, Samuel Gumpertz, who managed Dreamland at Coney Island in the early 1900s, managed a young Harry Houdini.

Bevan continued exhibiting herself for the next several years, despite increasing pain and blindness from the disease. Her title as the World's Homeliest Woman was eventually relinquished upon her death in 1933.

ESTHER BLACKMON,
THE ALLIGATOR-SKINNED WOMAN
1926–2003

Esther Parnell was born on March 5, 1926, in Kenly, North Carolina. She had three brothers and one sister with normal skin, but like another brother, William, she was afflicted with a reptilian hide as a result of ichthyosis. (William performed as the

Alligator Boy; an alcoholic, he drank himself to death at an early age.)

Besides creating extremely dry skin, ichthyosis left Parnell bald. Not even an eyelash graced her body. Occasionally she treated herself to a wig.

Parnell married Thomas Blackmon at the age of twenty-two; she would be known in the sideshow business by her married name. At about the same time, the Alligator-Skinned Woman adopted the title of World's Strangest Mother. She gave birth to the first of her six children in 1948; all of them were born normal.

The alligator-skinned mother spent fifty-six years in the sideshow industry, mostly with Dick Best on Royal American Shows and his fellow showman Walter Wanous. Blackmon was also featured in two movies—*The Mutations* (1973) and *The Sentinel* (1977). She died on August 24, 2003, twelve days after her husband.

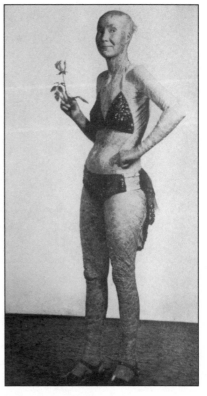

Esther Blackmon. *Author's collection*

EMMETT BLACKWELDER, THE TURTLE MAN
1923–1996

Emmett Blackwelder came into the world with a few pieces missing. Born in North Carolina on December 28, 1923, Blackwelder had stubs for arms and legs. His hands and feet were nowhere to be found.

Emmett Blackwelder. *Ward Hall collection*

Emmett's father made him learn to take care of himself as a boy. His brothers and sisters were instructed not to help him with basic tasks, such as dressing himself, no matter how much he cried or screamed. While young Emmett thought his father was cruel, he later realized how much it had helped him become independent, and he was grateful for the strict rules.

Blackwelder grew quite skilled with his stubs and was able to live self-sufficiently. Even without hands, he was a proficient handyman—wielding a screwdriver in his mouth, he was able to disassemble and repair various pieces of electronic equipment. He could even drive a vehicle. In the early 1950s, Blackwelder's nimble stumps helped him find work shining shoes. In 1953 he caught the attention of newspapers by shining the shoes of Marta Batista, wife of the Cuban president.

A better-paying job presented itself in the sideshow. Blackwelder demonstrated arresting dexterity by playing with a wooden paddleball. The act made for a terrific attraction. Blackwelder performed as Emmett the Turtle Man (his stubby limbs recalled a turtle's) with various shows, including Ward Hall and Chris Christ's sideshow, which occasionally joined with Ringling Bros. and Barnum & Bailey. He enjoyed his years with the sideshow and worked hard to please audiences. The only time he wouldn't take the stage was the last day of the season. According to Hall, he may have been left behind once as the show was taken down. After that, Blackwelder always went home after the second-to-last day.

The Turtle Man invested his earnings in real estate after each season. By 1984, he had retired from the sideshow business and married his high school sweetheart, and was living in comfort back home in North Carolina. Emmett Blackwelder died in 1996.

DICK BRISBEN, THE PENGUIN BOY
Born circa 1940s

Dick Brisben is somewhat like a Mr. Potato Head gone awry. His right arm is shortened, lacking the elbow, forearm, and hand. But it does have one finger. His left arm is merely a stub. Instead of legs, he has ankles connected directly to his hips.

Brisben was born in South Dakota and grew up just north of his birthplace, in Jamestown, North Dakota. The state welfare program gave him aid, and a special school for the handicapped educated him and even fitted him with a prosthetic arm. But Brisben never liked the arm and rarely wore it. He made do with what he had naturally. Despite his deformities, he learned to type and play the electric organ. He managed to supplement his meager welfare payment by working a popcorn stand in the summer and shining shoes and selling Christmas cards in the winter.

In 1960, Brisben found his ticket off welfare—Ward Hall's sideshow. The two met after a show, and Hall asked Brisben if he'd like to join up. Brisben was ready to, but since he was a dependent of the state, his caretaker had to give her blessing. Hall explained his intentions to make money with Brisben. It was his honesty that earned the caretaker's approval, as did the condition that Brisben could return home if he disliked the sideshow. This never became an issue.

With his new career came a new name. Brisben waddled, so he was called the Penguin Boy. During his act he waddled across the stage—"like a penguin across the polar ice caps of Antarctica"—and lit a cigarette with his limited appendages. Brisben stayed with Hall's sideshow for twenty-seven years, never bound to a contract. His successful career allowed him to purchase a home in southern California. Brisben enjoyed his performing years, knowing the sideshow was a sure place he could have a job.

> The Porcupine Man, an Englishman, grew quills on his body. His successful sideshow career ended in 1920 after a case of smallpox made his quills disappear. The condition had afflicted his ancestors, who were exhibited as Porcupine Men in the early 1700s.

Left to right: Ward Hall, Bruce Snowdon with a two-headed chicken, and Pete Terhurne, 2003. © *Liz Steger*

If P. T. Barnum were alive today, he would be either a dear friend or a bitter rival of Ward Hall. Blessed with a gift of gab and a flair for entertaining, Hall is one of the last showmen from a bygone era. His successful career in the business began in the 1940s and lasted until his retirement at the end of 2003. It was supposed to last only a couple of weeks. Or so his father thought when he let him join the circus in 1946.

Hall was born in the early 1930s in a small town in western Nebraska. "It was 120 degrees in the summer, forty below in the winter. I wanted to get the hell out of there as soon as I was old enough to know there was another place," he recalls. An urge to join the circus led him to the library, where he studied books on fire eating and magic. At fifteen, he dropped out of school and joined Dailey Bros. Circus, earning $30 a week. Although he performed magic, he soon gave it up for ventriloquism because, as he explains: "I am primarily a lazy person, and I objected to having to reload all that magic stuff for each performance." The dummy was one simple prop.

Yet Hall had some ambition, and by 1948 he teamed up with showman and knife thrower Harry Leonard and joined Rogers Bros. Circus in Texas. When the resident sword swallower and sideshow manager continued to miss shows, Hall took over. From then on, he managed various sideshows until he owned his own production.

When Leonard passed away in the 1960s, Hall joined an aspiring showman, Chris Christ. By 1967, the partnership yielded the Hall & Christ sideshow, which was later rechristened Christ & Hall—Hall couldn't put his name before Christ. The pair produced sideshows for Circus Vargas, Ringling Bros. and Barnum & Bailey, and countless state fairs over the decades. In addition to their live shows, the two men were involved in producing sideshow documentaries, including *Last Great American Sideshow* and *Being Different*.

Having worked with hundreds of performers throughout his career, Hall became known as the King of the Sideshows. His favorite attractions were Schlitzie the Pinhead and Percilla the Monkey Girl. But it wasn't the unusual freaks who made the most money. "People love giants, midgets, and fat people," Hall says. "Because this is the fairy tale. Jack Sprat ate no fat, his wife would eat no lean, Jack and the Beanstalk, the little people of *Gulliver's Travels.* These are stories people have been told when they were small children. It's much easier to sell an attraction that you can paint the pretty picture about, rather than something gruesome. We're going to have a man drive nails into his head with a hammer, we're going to have someone put their face down in broken glass. Or we're going to see these wonderful little people. The world's smallest married couple. Why, they're so tiny, so cute, you'd want to hold them in the palm of your hand. It's much easier to sell the pretty picture." Of course, while it was the freaks who brought in the crowd, it was the working acts that entertained the people. The giants were not as tall as promised, the midgets not as small, and the fat people not as fat.

Though he's most renowned as a showman, Hall has also enjoyed a writing career, which has included several theater musicals. He retired in the winter of 2003, but continues to write and lecture. However, that retirement turned out to be more like a vacation. In May 2005, he and Chris Christ took to the road once again, opening the World of Wonders show at the Pennsylvania State Fair—the first of many stops along the East Coast. "I've got twenty-five more years to work," Hall says. "Then I'm going to retire."

★ Betty Broadbent was one of the world's most famous Tattooed Ladies. Her illustrious career as a sideshow attraction was rooted in rebellion. Broadbent, who came from a wealthy and prominent Philadelphia family, got her first tattoo in Atlantic City when she was just sixteen. Her mother was furious. This made the independent-minded Betty equally furious. In defiance, she went back to Atlantic City the next weekend and got more tattoos. Her enraged mother kicked her out of the house and disowned her. This only made Betty angrier. She responded by spending the next six years having her entire body tattooed, leaving only her face clean of markings. By 1927, even before finishing her body art, she was primed to join the circus.

Broadbent's finished gallery featured 465 designs in four colors, including roses, eagles, pirates, gypsies, the American flag, and Charles Lindbergh, Queen Victoria, and other famous people. "It is a woman's privilege to change her mind, but I am the one woman who no longer has that privilege," she once stated.

The beautiful but unusual Broadbent was featured in the Sells-Floto sideshow in 1930. As the decade wore on, the tattooed wonder became a big attraction and her career boomed. In 1939, Broadbent starred in the Ringling Bros. and Barnum & Bailey sideshow and appeared at the New York World's Fair.

The Tattooed Lady continued exhibiting her picturesque flesh until 1968, at which time she became ill and retired to Riverview, Florida, with her husband. A year later her estranged mother died, and Betty's father was left with the family fortune. Broadbent reconciled with his daughter, and within a few years, after his death, she inherited a great deal of wealth. She and her husband purchased a farm and lived out their lives happily together.

Ward Hall, who once employed Broadbent, said of her: "When you say a Tattooed Lady, you put the emphasis on lady. She was always a lady."

MELVIN BURKHART,
THE ANATOMICAL WONDER
and THE HUMAN BLOCKHEAD

1907–2001

The performance bug bit Melvin Burkhart shortly after he was born in 1907 in Kentucky. As a kid he was always a show-off: "I couldn't sing. I couldn't dance. I couldn't tell funny stories. But I could catch attention by anatomical muscle control, which I didn't know I had at the time." Others had noticed Burkhart's unusual muscle skills and showed him off to friends. In the early 1920s he made an appearance in a vaudeville act that was visiting town, and this led to his developing the Anatomical Wonder act, also called the Anatomical Blunder. He was able to suck his stomach into his spine, contort his face into the Two-Faced Man (smiling on one

Melvin Burkhart performing his Human Blockhead routine, 2001. © *Liz Steger*

side, frowning on the other, "mad and glad all at the same time," in his words), elongate his neck, and pop his shoulder blades out from his back.

In his youth Burkhart had a stint as a professional boxer, which led to a broken nose that required many bits of bone to be removed. As he watched the doctors go in and out of his nose with their instruments, a lightbulb turned on in his head. Burkhart realized he could push things in and out of his nose himself, namely with a hammer and spike. Thus was born the Human Blockhead, and Burkhart's claim to fame that would last more than sixty years. "All you gotta do is get a good start, and then you pound like the devil," Burkhart would say as he hammered the spike into his nose. "Ooh, hit a bone. But what do you expect out of a bonehead?"

Burkhart spent thirty years with the James E. Strates sideshow. He also performed with Ringling Bros. and Ripley's, and later, as an octogenarian, at Coney Island. Besides delighting audiences with the Human Blockhead and Anatomical Wonder routines, he swallowed swords, ate fire, and threw knives. Burkhart, who was made an honorary member of several magic societies, would sometimes do five or six acts in a ten-act show.

> ✳ Arthur Loos, an attraction in the 1930s, was appropriately known as the Rubber-Skinned Man for his ability to pull his facial skin out eight inches. The skin beneath his chin hung loose, much like a basset hound's.

Burkhart officially retired in 1989 and moved near Gibsonton, Florida, to live with his wife, Joyce. He continued performing until just a month before he passed away, in November 2001, at the venerable age of ninety-four. One other achievement, perhaps as impressive as all his stunts, is worth noting: In his long life, Burkhart never cursed, smoked, or drank.

✳ WILLIE CAMPER
✳ 1924–1943

✳ Before Elvis, the biggest thing in Memphis was a fellow named Guicel "Willie" Camper. He was a normal-size child until the age of nine. He got big quick: reportedly eight feet, six inches big. He had a brother and a sister, both of normal size; his parents barely made it above the five-foot mark. When Willie was eleven, he had to leave school because he couldn't fit in his desk.

Camper, who ate two large meals a day, weighed 480 pounds and reached those eight and a half feet by the time he was eighteen. By then he had already been in show business for five years and traveled around the world. If there was any truth to the notion that a man's shoe size was indicative of other dimensions, women may have shuddered. Camper wore a size 32. Two dozen apples could rest inside those shoes. Each hand was said to be large enough to hold a dozen eggs. But as with others, his height was most likely exaggerated. The 1979 edition of the *Guinness Book of World Records* listed Camper as only seven-foot-two. He was still growing when a heart attack took his life during a sideshow performance on May 1, 1943. Had a freight train not blocked medical help from arriving in a timely fashion, he might have been saved. And perhaps his height would have gotten closer to the superior claim.

Willie Camper with an unidentified man, circa 1940. *Kobel collection*

EDDIE CARMEL, THE JEWISH GIANT
1936–1972

Known as the Happy Giant and the Jewish Giant, Eddie Carmel would've preferred just being happy and Jewish.

The sixteen-pound baby Carmel was born on March 16, 1936, in Tel Aviv, and came to the United States at the age of two. His father and mother stood only five feet, six inches, but Carmel's maternal grandfather was known as the world's tallest rabbi, at seven feet, five inches.

Carmel lived a normal life in New York City until age fifteen, when he was diagnosed with acromegaly. By seventeen he needed his clothes custom-made. Towering over awe-struck classmates, the seven-foot-plus Carmel graduated from high school and enrolled in City College to major in business.

A few years into his studies, Carmel realized that a giant was doomed to make a living based on his size. He dropped out of school and pursued a career in show business. In addition to his great height, Carmel possessed a strong, deep voice and a good sense of humor. With the total package, he hoped to be the world's tallest comedian. He also played with a rock-'n'-roll band, Frankenstein and the Brain Surgeons, and recorded a single, "The Good Monster." Carmel's big break in show business finally came with a role in the 1962 film *The Brain That Wouldn't Die*. Clearly, there was a monster theme for the giant. His large hands, prominent chin, and big feet made people think of Frankenstein. The giant was even said to walk like the nuts-and-bolts monster.

Carmel would have liked for one of these gigs to earn him a living, but he needed to supplement his income with a position in the sideshow. He never wanted to be thought of as a freak, but he couldn't deny that he was an attraction. He exhibited his enormous body and oversize features in the 1960s with Milt Levine's World of Mirth show and with Ringling Bros. and Barnum & Bailey during its Madison Square Garden appearances in New York. Levine's show billed the giant as eight-foot-one; Ringling hyped the Tallest Man on Earth as a greatly exaggerated nine feet, five-eighths of an inch and 500 pounds. Although he eventually stopped growing, most likely at about seven-foot-seven, Carmel's features enlarged as he grew older. Onstage he would raise his mighty hands and show his size 24 shoe (claimed to be a 35) for spectators to gaze at in wonderment.

Carmel was paid twice what other performers earned, yet he didn't enjoy his time as a feature attraction. He disliked being asked to stand and disliked having to compare his hands with those of normal-size people. By the late 1960s, his condition had worsened and was causing him great pain. In 1969 he was forced to end his sideshow career, as he could no longer climb up to the platform. Arthritis set in and Carmel needed two canes to walk. Soon even the canes couldn't help him. The giant's heart could no longer support his massive body, and he died on July 30, 1972.

Eddie Carmel made the most of his condition, yet it's not his various entertainment roles for which he is best known. Rather, it is the photograph by Diane Arbus titled *A Jewish giant at home with his parents in the Bronx, N.Y. 1970* that has given him immortality. Standing next to the elder Carmels, probably in much discomfort, the giant maintained his sense of humor by remarking, "Isn't it awful to have midget parents?"

JEAN CARROLL

Born circa 1910

On some rare occasions, a performer may pose as a double attraction, such as a Fat Lady who also happens to be a dwarf. Even rarer is a person who is born with an anomaly, corrects it, then becomes a self-made freak. This was the case with Jean Carroll, born Jean Furella in Schenectady, New York.

Jean Carroll, with tattoos, and an unknown gentleman. The inset shows Carroll earlier, with a beard. *Collection of James G. Mundie*

Carroll had a beard as a young girl and joined the Hagenbeck-Wallace Circus by the age of ten. As a young woman, she fell in love with a contortionist and sideshow talker named John Carson. Though he loved her and wanted to marry her, he couldn't accept her facial hair. While Carroll was willing to remove her beard for love, she didn't want to lose her position in the show. Famed sword swallower Alec Linton suggested a solution for the dismayed couple: Carroll could lose the beard and become a tattooed lady. Apparently Carson felt he would be perfectly comfortable with an illustrated woman, so Carroll had her beard removed by electrolysis. "Only by falling for a guy would I have shed that silky foliage of mine," she once said. A well-known tattoo artist, Charlie Wagner, then etched Carroll's flesh with 700 designs, including the Holy Family on her back, the crown of thorns on her right leg, and the Rock of Ages on her left. The clean-shaven, fully illustrated Carroll wasn't content merely to exhibit her new image to the sideshow crowds, so she broadened her audience by working as a stripper.

In 1951, Carson died. Two years later, Carroll met another sideshow talker, Larry Rapp, while working at Coney Island. The two were married on April 30, 1953, and held a large reception at Hubert's Museum in Times Square. "My new hubby's one guy who'll never get bored," Carroll told a reporter. "When things get dull, I'll go into a shimmy, and what'll he see? Free motion pictures!"

CLICO, THE WILD DANCING SOUTH AFRICAN BUSHMAN

1857–1940

The Wild Man was a staple of the sideshows, whether it was in the form of Wild Men of Borneo (Waino and Plutano or their imitators); glomming geeks, who bit heads off chickens; or just men acting like savages. One of the most famous was none of the above. Clico, the Wild Dancing South African Bushman, was exactly that. Clico, whose real name was Franz Taaibosh, was an actual African Bushman, who loved to dance.

According to his "Life Story," Taaibosh was discovered in the Kalahari Desert by one Captain Hepston. While pursuing ostriches with a bow and arrow, the Bushman suffered a leg injury. Hepston came to his aid, then looked after him, and eventually "tamed" him. An essay by Neil Parsons in *Africans on Stage: Studies in Ethnological Show Business* postulates that Taaibosh was more likely born into

Clico the Wild Dancing South African Bushman a not-so-wild pose, 1928. *Johnny Fox's Freakatorium*

"captivity" on a farm. Hepston, who had been living as a farmer in South Africa, met the talented little Franz (he reportedly stood just over four feet tall) and decided to mold him into an entertainer. Managing the Bushman in show business appeared to be a much more lucrative line of work for Hepston.

Around 1913, Hepston took Taaibosh to the stages of England and France, where he performed his Khoisan style of step-dancing. He caught the attention of Coney

Island Dreamland manager Samuel Gumpertz, as well as scouts from Ringling Bros. and Barnum & Bailey. Taaibosh and Hepston crossed the Atlantic in 1917 to begin working at the Dreamland sideshow and shortly after with Ringling. Taaibosh was called Clico, for the Bushman "click" language. A Ringling agent named Frank Cook befriended Clico and asked to become his legal guardian. Since Hepston had no written contract with Clico, Ringling's lawyers were able to wrest the Bushman away.

In 1919, at a press conference at Madison Square Garden in New York, Clico proved he could speak beyond clicking. He announced that he had lived with apes for years and that he never felt at home unless he had a chimpanzee around his cage. Clearly, he had been prepared well in the art of ballyhoo. A newspaperman at the press conference put a damper on the story by claiming to recognize Clico from a livery stable in his Minnesota hometown. Either the journalist was mistaken or Clico had simply found some grunt work between gigs.

In addition to performing, Taaibosh once accepted a moonlighting position at the Field Museum in Chicago. He posed as a model for sculptors, representing his race, and thus became immortalized in the natural history museum's anthropological collection. Though Taaibosh was around sixty-eight at the time, he claimed to be one hundred. Museum personnel believed him.

Clico enjoyed a long career dancing as a Wild Man, even into his elder years. Like nonprofessional wild men, he was said to enjoy cigars, beer, and women. Taaibosh finally retired in 1939 and died in Hudson, New York, on August 31, 1940.

DIANE DE ELGAR
Born circa 1920s

Unlike Freda-Fred, Albert-Alberta, and other half-man, half-woman acts, Diane De Elgar didn't have a gimmicky show name. Nevertheless, De Elgar's act was extremely successful. Beginning in 1948, and lasting thirteen years on and off, De Elgar was the most profitable attraction working for showman Ward Hall.

She was a he, named George Searle. Hall built him a runway on the midway, complete with marquee lights and a spotlight shining from a tower erected nearby. At showtime, Hall would go through the usual bally before introducing the star at the end. De Elgar would swoop onto the runway in a tight-fitting gown with a six-foot ostrich feather boa. Hall recalls his pitch: "Diane De Elgar is the strangest living human being in the world, because Diane is truly a hermaphrodite. Not a half man or half woman. She is all man and all woman. Diane can legally dress as a man or woman. She can marry a man or woman, because she can become the father or mother of children. She is married, and is the mother of two children; a girl eight, a boy twelve. Today you are going to be invited in the sideshow for the adults only, where under bright lights you are going to see Diane expose her body without veils or nets, and you will see that indeed, she has both sexes of male and female." To entice the crowd further, De Elgar announced a guarantee: "If there is any member of the medical profession within the hearing of my voice, I invite you to come in free as my guest, and at your discretion, any doctor may step upon the stage with me and publicly examine any part of my body. And if you find any part of me a fraud, we will present that member of the medical profession a cash reward of ten thousand dollars."

De Elgar disrobed onstage during the performance, but not completely. After the show, for an extra quarter, people were admitted to an additional act, the blow-off, where they witnessed De Elgar's big, manly, size 13½ feet and her false breasts, which were nothing more than two stockings filled with birdseed. The birdseed allowed for gentle squeezing as she fondled herself. For another fifty cents, prurient onlookers could catch a glimpse of her G-string. These two extra fees made the blow-off quite lucrative.

Hall remembers one occasion when a diagnostician from Johns Hopkins University stayed after the show and introduced himself. De Elgar, in an attempt to honor her guarantee, guided his hand under her dress in an impromptu examination. The diagnostician swore she was real.

During the off-season, De Elgar reverted to her other self. Living as a male, George Searle took another job as an impersonator—this time in department stores around Christmas as the Jolly One himself, Santa Claus.

THE THREE DEL RIOS

Trinidad: 1915–?

Delores: 1916–?

Paul: 1920–?

The Three Del Rios, Trinidad, Delores, and Paul
Author's collection

Trinidad, Delores, and Paul Rodriguez were born in Madrid, all three of small stature. Their twelve brothers and sisters were of normal height, as were their parents.

By the 1930s the siblings were being exhibited in Mexico, where they became known as the Three Del Rios. The name certainly rolled off the tongue much easier than "the Three Rodriguezes." They next toured the eastern United States with George A. Hamid, an entrepreneur from Atlantic City. Trinidad found her way west, appearing under her real last name in the Midget Village at the 1935 California Pacific International Exposition in San Diego. Another promoter, Harry Leonard, exhibited the Three Del Rios in 1937. The following year they headed for Hollywood and landed roles in *The Wizard of Oz.*

It was 1938, and Paul had reached a height of nineteen inches and a weight of twelve pounds, about half as tall as Tom Thumb. His big sisters were indeed big, relatively speaking—Trinidad was thirty-three inches and Delores twenty-seven. Paul's tiny stature attracted press. He appeared life-size in a spread in the June 20, 1938, issue of *Life*—with room for an article. It recognized him as the Smallest Man in the World, but described how Hollywood hadn't noticed: "In that hive of eccentricity he was regarded simply as another midget. No one took the trouble to ascertain that he actually was the smallest living midget." Luckily, Paul didn't have big Hollywood aspirations. According to comments he made to journalists, his ambitions were to be a detective for the FBI, to drive a car, and to play major-league baseball. The latter was the most far-fetched, given that he was shorter than the bat.

In 1939 the Three Del Rios joined Johnny J. Bejano's sideshow. Bejano recruited them with the hope of exploiting their popularity from *The Wizard of Oz*. Expecting them to be a big attraction, Bejano paid them accordingly. When crowds didn't flock to the show as anticipated, Bejano upheld his contract nonetheless and ended the season broke.

The Three Del Rios later became three individual Del Rios, as the siblings split to pursue their own exhibition careers.

★

★ THE DOLL FAMILY

★ *Frieda (Grace): 1899–1980*
Kurt (Harry): 1902–1985
★ *Hilda (Daisy): 1907–1970*
★ *Elly (Tiny): 1914–2004*

★

★ Before these midget siblings became the aptly named Dolls, they were
Frieda, Kurt, Hilda, and Elly Schnei-
der, all born in Germany. They had
five other siblings, all of them of normal height.

The Doll Family with an unidentified woman.
Kobel collection

In 1913, Kurt and Frieda toured
German nightclubs as "Hans and Gretel," a dancing couple. During one of their appearances they met promoter Burt Earles and his wife. The Earleses became their managers
and one year later brought the two Schneiders to America.

Early in their career stateside they appeared at Coney Island's Dreamland Circus Side

Show, billed as "Hans and Gretel, the Smallest Dancing Couple on Earth," and "The Smallest Society Dancers." They later changed their first names to Harry and Grace and took their managers' surname. People often observed that the perfectly proportioned little people looked like dolls. So Harry and Grace adopted yet another name, Doll.

By 1921, Harry and Grace Doll were the smallest naturalized citizens of the United States. Twenty-two-year-old Grace stood three feet, nine inches and weighed forty pounds. Harry, nineteen, was three inches shorter and three pounds lighter.

The American Doll household soon grew, as Harry and Grace brought their two younger sisters to the States in 1925. Hilda became Daisy, while Elly was called Tiny. In the late 1920s and early 1930s the Dolls ventured into the movies, appearing in such films as *The Unholy Three* (1925), *Special Delivery* (1927), Laurel and Hardy's *"Sailors, Beware!"* (1927), and of course, *The Wizard of Oz* (1939). Daisy, Harry, and Tiny (in an uncredited role) also appeared in *Freaks* (1932). In fact, Harry was partly responsible for the existence of the movie. When he came across the short revenge story "Spurs," by Tod Robbins, he passed it along to director Tod Browning, with whom he had worked on *The Unholy Three.* Browning turned "Spurs" into *Freaks.*

While the Dolls enjoyed success on the big screen, their bread and butter was on the stage. The midget family spent decades starring with the Ringling Bros. and Barnum & Bailey show. "The circus is our home, and we wouldn't ever want to be anywhere else," Tiny Doll once said.

In 1942, Daisy became the first and only Doll to marry. Her husband was an usher for the Ringlings, and at five feet, five inches came in handy for the whole family when it came to driving.

Aside from show business, the Dolls devoted themselves to various hobbies while traveling with the circus. Grace was an avid reader of novels. Daisy loved tabloid newspapers, particularly for their easier-to-handle size. Tiny was a stamp collector and a seamstress, often sewing her own trousers. Harry enjoyed tinkering with mechanical devices, smoking cigars, and playing blackjack with his friend Jack Earle, the Texas Giant.

The Dolls performed with the Cristiani Brothers Circus in 1959 before retiring to Sarasota, Florida, after a long, fruitful career. Daisy died in November 1970. Grace followed on March 16, 1980, and Harry on May 14, 1985. Tiny Doll survived until age ninety, succumbing to heart failure on September 6, 2004.

TOD BROWNING AND *FREAKS*

Tod Browning is most famous for his controversial 1932 film, *Freaks*, as well as the first *Dracula*, starring Bela Lugosi. Charles Browning, Jr., born on July 12, 1880, in Louisville, Kentucky, was in the circus before he turned to film. In 1896, he ran away to join the Manhattan Fair & Carnival Company; he changed his name to Tod. His first gig was as a talker pitching a Wild Man of Borneo. Browning moved from the bally platform to a "Living Corpse" act, featuring his live burial. Patrons witnessing the event would return two days later to see him revived. Browning's sideshow career thrived, but he eventually landed with Ringling Bros. as a clown. He moved into vaudeville and comedy before trying his hand at directing.

Browning produced several hit movies in the 1920s and early 1930s, including *The Unholy Three, The Unknown*, and the aforementioned *Dracula*. In *Freaks*, an adaptation of Tod Robbins's story "Spurs," he created one of the most haunting movies ever. With the advent of political correctness and the decrease in human oddities, its cast of real sideshow performers will never be matched in cinema. Browning assembled Harry, Daisy, and Tiny Doll, the Hilton sisters, Lady Olga (bearded lady), Johnny Eck (half-boy), Schlitzie (pinhead), Jenny Lee and Elvira Snow (pinheads), Josephine Joseph (half man, half woman), Prince Randian (human torso), Pete Robinson (human skeleton), Frances O'Connor (armless girl), and other curiosities for the project. They were complemented by "normal" people, such as Wallace Ford as Phroso the clown, Leila Hyams as the in-génue, Olga Baclanova as Cleopatra the acrobat/villainess, and Henry Victor as Hercules.

The plot is a simple revenge story. The evil Cleopatra decides to marry the diminutive Hans (Harry Doll), who she discovered has inherited a fortune. Along with her lover, Hercules, she attempts to poison Hans and steal his money. When the freaks catch on to the dastardly plan, they exact their revenge and turn Cleopatra into something even more revolting than any naturally born freak.

When MGM released the movie, it was immediately banned in the United Kingdom, and remained so for some thirty years. In the United States, signs posted in theaters warned: "Children positively not admitted. Adults not in normal health are advised not to see this picture." The manager of a Paramount theater stated further: "When we say no children admitted, we mean it. And I wish I knew some way to classify the grown people so as to keep out those extra-imaginative or sensitive people who really shouldn't see this picture." Posters assured audiences that what they would see involved no makeup or trick photography.

Although people flocked to sideshows to see freaks in person, they didn't appreciate seeing them on the big screen. *Freaks* disgusted both critics and audiences. For Browning, it was a career ender. Though he made a few films afterward, he faded into obscurity during his lifetime.

Decades later, on October 6, 1962, Browning was found dead in the bathroom of a friend's apartment. The next year, *Freaks* was brought back to life in theaters; by the 1970s it had attained cult status.

DOLLY DIMPLES
1901–1982

Before there was a Dolly Dimples there was Celesta Herrmann. Born in Cincinnati on July 18, 1901, she weighed a normal seven pounds, eight ounces. In her first eight months she had a very small appetite. A family friend believed she needed to eat a lot of meat and often dangled offerings in front of her. Celesta learned to love it; in fact, her first words were, "Meat, meat, meat." Of course, she learned to love all food. Any allowance she earned was spent on snacks. She even bargained for deals, asking the clerk

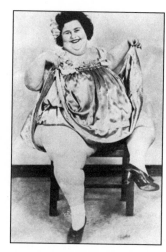

Dolly Dimples at 555 pounds.
Kobel collection

at the cookie stand for a penny's worth of broken cookies, rather than purchasing the whole ones.

Others had fun at her expense. Classmates teased her, calling her "Tubby" and "Fatso," and ostracizing her. She weighed 150 pounds in the fifth grade, and in several years nearly doubled herself. At 295 pounds she dropped out of high school.

Although she was hefty, she was also quite beautiful, and soon met the man who would be her husband, Frank Geyer. A trim 135 pounds, he didn't have quite the appetite of his supersize wife. Celesta would bake cakes and pies for him, but he would only eat a piece, leaving her the rest. She gained 100 pounds in a year.

In 1927 the couple attended the Happyland Carnival outside Detroit. Celesta's ample assets were spotted and she was offered a job as a Fat Lady. With that, Dolly Dimples, the World's Most Beautiful Fat Lady, was born. In an effort to

⭐ In 1924, Pete Robinson, a fifty-eight-pound Thin Man married the not-so-thin 467-pound Bunny Smith. The two met while working in the Ringling Bros. and Barnum & Bailey show.

make a big attraction even bigger, she included in her daily diet several pounds of meat and potatoes, multiple loaves of bread, a gallon of milk, and enough desserts to single-handedly keep Betty Crocker in business. Dolly Dimples successfully toured with Ringling Bros. through the 1930s and 1940s. Her four feet, eleven inches supported 555 pounds and a seventy-nine-inch bust. It took twelve yards of cloth to make a dress large enough to cover such a mass of flesh.

Dolly's passion for eating was not shared by her vital organs. In 1950 she suffered a near-fatal heart attack. Her doctors ordered her to diet, or she would die. She listened, and adhered to a strict diet limited to baby food. Over the next fourteen months, Dolly Dimples was shed and Celesta Geyer appeared, a svelte, 112-pound woman. She had lost 443 pounds. The *Guinness Book of World Records* recognized her achievement as the greatest weight loss in the shortest period of time.

Suddenly a skinny lady, Geyer would spend the rest of her life helping others to lose weight. She wrote *Diet or Die: The Dolly Dimples Weight Reducing Plan* and *The Greatest Diet in the World*, and diligently answered letters from around the world. "I feel it's my privilege and a God-given legacy to help prolong life," she said. "God gave me my chance, and I am sure it was to help others." Her daily lunch now consisted of a cup of chicken soup, a soda cracker, gelatin salad, and skim milk. When she wasn't preaching weight loss, she ran a small gallery of amateur art.

"My friends told me I'd kill myself if I went on a crash diet," Geyer told a reporter. "Well, if I do they don't have to bury me on a truck anyway, I'll fit in a hearse now." That she did, but not until February 1982.

WILLIAM DURKS, THE MAN WITH TWO NOSES AND THREE EYES
1913–1975

The saying "a face only a mother could love" was put to the test with William Durks. Promoter Ward Hall, who worked with him for one season, says that Durks looked as if "he had been hit in the face with an axe."

Durks was born on April 13, 1913, on a farm in northern Alabama, with two noses and a harelip. Even worse, his eyes were sealed and required an operation to be opened. The disfigured boy was deprived of an education. In Arthur Lewis's book *Carnival*, Durks explained, "None of the kids or teachers could ever look at me, and my mom and pop didn't have no money to give me a private education. So what could I do?"

At the age of fourteen, Durks left the farm and exhibited his flawed face in a Single-O show. He eventually became known as the Man with Two Noses and Three Eyes. The third eye was actually drawn on with an eyebrow pencil in an indentation between his eyes—as

William Durks, circa 1960. The indentation between his noses served as his third eye.
Collection of Bob Blackmar

though he didn't look bizarre enough already. Despite the claim of three eyes, Durks could see out of only one.

Public outings were few and far between, but when necessary, Durks typically pulled his hat down to cover his face. Slits cut near the brim helped him see. Although he was generally very peaceful and kind, Durks didn't appreciate it when strangers questioned his covered face. If they wanted to see it, he simply obliged. In *Carnival*, he described the reaction: "Many's the time I seen 'em faint dead away and hit their damned heads on the floor. I seen great big men turn around and puke. Serves 'em right!"

Despite his occasional boldness, Durks was shy onstage. His close friend Melvin Burkhart helped him overcome his timidity and taught him how to work the crowd. Eventually Durks would be the star of the show. Burkhart even played matchmaker for him, setting up a date with Mildred the Alligator-Skinned Woman. The date apparently went well. The Man with Two Noses found a wife, thus giving hope to lonely bachelors everywhere.

Durks spent most of his career with the Slim Kelly and Whitey Sutton sideshow on the James E. Strates shows. In the 1960s, he was earning as much as $100 a week plus a cash bonus at the end of the season to hold him over. Appearances at Hubert's Museum in New York City also supplemented his off-season income.

In 1968, Durks became a widower. He followed his beloved Mildred seven years later, in May 1975.

✷

✷ JACK EARLE, THE TEXAS GIANT
✷ *1906–1952*
✷

✷ Jacob Erlich weighed a mere three pounds, twelve ounces at birth, so his parents may have suspected their son would be a midget, but never a giant. Born in Denver, Erlich was off to a slow start, and until age seven was smaller than other kids. But then his days of being the little guy ended. A remarkable growth spurt would shoot him up to an advertised eight feet, six inches.

After moving with his family to El Paso, the teenage Erlich left the Lone Star State to use his height in Hollywood. Success came fast, and Jacob Erlich became Jack Earle. The giant of the silent screen starred in forty-eight films, including *Hansel and Gretel* (1923) and *Jack and the Beanstalk* (1924). An unfortunate accident ended his movie career. Earle fell off a truck and was blinded for four months. The injury affected his overactive pituitary and made him grow even more.

Back in El Paso, Earle attended a Ringling Bros. and Barnum & Bailey show. The featured Tallest Man in the World was Jim Tarver. Circus managers may have believed they really did have the world's tallest man until management noticed someone was actually loftier than Tarver. The circus hired Earle, with the title he deserved. He exaggerated his height by wearing cowboy boots and a cowboy hat. Earle spent fourteen years with the circus, befriending many midgets in the show.

By 1940, he had had enough of standing tall onstage. The one thing he disliked most was being

Jack Earle as a salesman, circa 1940s.
Kobel collection

asked, "How's the weather up there?" The joke got very tired; it was repeated to him too often. But when he met Robert Wadlow, Earle found himself asking the same annoying question. Wadlow was even taller than Earle—eight feet, eleven and a half inches. Earle shared his story with a newspaper reporter: "I was so flabbergasted, when I saw him the only thing I could think to ask was, 'How's the weather up there?'"

Earle left the circus for a career completely unrelated to his height—he sold wine in San Francisco. Then again, he probably could have sold anything. Everyone loved meeting with the world's tallest salesman. When not making sales, the giant merchant pursued other interests. He was a painter, a sculptor, a photographer, and a published poet with a book entitled *The Long Shadows*.

Earle retired in El Paso. He was having a $20,000 home built, oversize and complete with nine-foot-high ceilings, but died before occupying it. His kidneys failed him, and he died in a local hospital on July 19, 1952; Earle was forty-five years old.

Johnny Eck and his twin brother, Robert,
circa 1928. Note Johnny's gloves on the ground.
The collection of Jeffrey Pratt Gordon / johnnyeckmuseum.com

★ JOHNNY ECK,
★ THE LIVING HALF-BOY
★ *1911–1991*

★ Johnny Eck was born John Eckhardt, Jr., on August 27, 1911, in Baltimore. He entered the world without the lower portion of his abdomen, without legs. His mother did give birth to one pair of legs that day. They were attached to his normally limbed twin brother, Robert.

Johnny learned to walk on his hands after just one year of life. Using special gloves to serve as shoes, he was able to run around and keep his hands in pristine condition. He eventually reached a full height of about eighteen inches and a weight of fifty-seven pounds.

Eck's sideshow career had its beginnings, strangely enough, in a church, where the boy was attending a magic show along with other crippled children. The magician turned a large piece of paper into a lacelike tablecloth and invited anyone in the audience to come up to the stage and take it. Johnny, being one of the more agile in the crowd, swooped up to claim his trophy. The magician was amazed and immediately saw Johnny's potential to perform. After a little sweet-talking, he persuaded the Eck family to sign a contract. The magician's tricks carried over to the contract, transforming what was supposed to be a one-year engagement into ten years after Johnny's parents had already signed him away. The sneaky magician simply added a 0 to the 1 after the signing.

Shy at first, Johnny grew to love the stage. By age fourteen he was performing regularly, often with his twin. Together they carried out what has been called the most bizarre stunt ever seen. An illusionist, Rajah Raboid, would call a volunteer from the audience to be cut in half. The volunteer would walk up to the stage and climb inside the magician's box, where he was sawed in half, much to the audience's delight. Raboid then put the two halves of the box back together and the volunteer would stand and walk back to his seat. As he was walking, however, he would suddenly split in two at the waist, his torso crawling off to the right, his legs to the left.

The audience would scream, of course; some would faint, others would walk out. No one would have suspected that the "volunteer" had a twin brother like Johnny Eck to make such a stunt possible. Johnny took Robert's place in the magician's box, to become the head and torso, while a dwarf wearing pants pulled up over his head became the legs.

Johnny featured his talents on the big screen as well as the stage. He appeared in Tod Browning's 1932 classic *Freaks* and was featured in the first Tarzan movie ever made. Eck also appeared in various Ripley's Believe It or Not! Odditoriums around the country. Ripley called him "The Most Remarkable Man in the World." Surely many have agreed, including the founder of johnnyeckmuseum.com. Jeffrey Gordon, who owns an extensive collection of Eck memorabilia and personal items, says of the Living Half-Boy: "The most remarkable thing about Johnny Eck was not that he starred in *Freaks*, or worked with Robert Ripley or was part of the most amazing version of the sawing-the-man-in-half trick ever to this date. Nor was it the fact that by the age of four he was an accomplished artist, typist and letter writer. It wasn't that he was a Punch and Judy operator, expert model maker, train conductor and racecar driver, either. It was the fact that no matter where he was, Johnny was the center of attraction. He didn't need a stage to be a showman. Life was his stage and he was always smiling at it."

On January 5, 1991, when he was seventy-nine, the curtain closed on Eck's stage. It would have been easy for him to have spent those many years feeling sorry for himself, but as he once explained: "To ask me if I'm sorry I have no legs is like asking an Eskimo if he's sorry he never tasted an artichoke."

Happy Jack Eckert.
From the collection of
Milo Anthony and Cristina Boothe

HAPPY JACK ECKERT
1874–1937

Jack Eckert's career as a Fat Man began as a fat boy. He was born in Lafayette, Indiana, and entered show business when he was just ten. The youngster already weighed 265 pounds. Eventually his waist expanded to more than a hundred inches around, and his chest to eighty-four. His belly was said to hang down nearly to his knees. Eckert ballooned to a massive 739 pounds. Everything was big about Jack, except his feet—the huge man wore only a size 9 shoe.

Happy Jack Eckert, as his name suggests, was a jolly Fat Man. Though he would have argued with that claim. Not the jolly part, but the fat part. Eckert maintained he was merely built proportionally. He managed to keep his "proportional" body somewhat agile, getting around without terrible difficulty. But travel required special arrangements. When the main form of transportation was still the railroad, Eckert had to ride in the train's baggage car or boxcar. Later he had a special automobile made to accommodate his mass.

Eckert worked with sideshows, including Great American Shows, for fifty years. This was a considerably long career for a Fat Man, as health problems generally affect most people suffering from such obesity. Eckert somehow avoided such problems. Instead, his demise came after his car collided with a freight truck in Alabama. The 739-pound juggernaut was no match for the truck. Eckert died from accident-related injuries on March 11, 1937, at the age of sixty-three. His specially built casket was six times the size of a normal coffin.

EKO *and* IKO, THE AMBASSADORS FROM MARS (GEORGE *and* WILLIE MUSE)

George: 1890–1971

Willie: 1893–2001

✻ The Ambassadors from Mars were actually the brothers George and Willie Muse, born near Roanoke, Virginia. The African-American albinos wore dreadlocked hair and were said to have been found near the remains of their spaceship. Earlier in their career the dreadlocks led promoters to exhibit them as sheep-headed cannibals from Ecuador.

George and Willie claimed to have been kidnapped by the circus when they were children. Their mother, Harriet, searched for her sons desperately for twenty-eight years. When Ringling Bros. and Barnum & Bailey came to town in 1927, she finally found them. But they were now Eko and Iko, onstage, dressed up and playing music. Mrs. Muse confronted the circus manager and demanded he return her sons. That night they went home with her. George and Willie were happy to see their mother, but

Eko and Iko in full costume. *Johnny Fox's Freakatorium*

they had loved traveling and performing, despite the fact that they were not paid a cent for their work (undoubtedly because of the racism prevalent in that era). The Muse family sued the circus for $100,000 for payment due to the Ambassadors.

The case made the brothers local celebrities, but they didn't know what to do with themselves. So they went back to performing and found an adequate stage right on their front porch. The circus eventually settled with the family, and the brothers elected to return to the show. From then on they were paid, though less than white performers who worked less. Still, they did well for themselves, earning money during the Depression. In the off-season they continued to travel, even performing once for royalty in England. By 1939 they were able to buy their mother sixteen acres of land in Roanoke County. In the 1940s, Eko and Iko left Ringling and joined the Clyde Beatty Circus.

After nearly sixty years of performing, George and Willie retired in 1961. They had traveled extensively and enjoyed luxuries that would have never been possible without their peculiar albinism. Though they never married, they did like spending money on women.

The brothers purchased a home in Roanoke, near their family. George died of heart failure in 1971. Willie, however, wasn't ready to join his brother. He lived on. And on. He survived a stroke, pacemaker surgery, third-degree burns, and blindness. Under the meticulous care of his grandniece, he lived to the ripe old age of 108, passing away on April 13, 2001.

According to *The Roanoke Times*, when Willie was 107 he told his grandniece that after his next birthday he was going home to live with God. He did just that—a journey taking him much farther than Mars.

LAVONDA EVANS
1920–?

Lavonda Evans was best known as Tiny Lavonda and Little Lavonda. According to Daniel Mannix's *Freaks: We Who Are Not As Others*, she was tiny and little because she "was not only a dwarf but had no legs, her feet being directly attached to her body." Although photographs of her suggest she may have suffered from osteogenesis imperfecta, which would have caused her legs to be shrunken and twisted beneath her body, unable to extend fully, and her feet to look as if they came directly from her body.

By the age of twenty-eight, Lavonda was nearly two feet tall and weighed twenty-one pounds. The little lady married a dwarf twenty-eight years her senior, Alva Evans, who performed as a circus clown. Alva was blessed with functional legs, which propped him up to a height of four feet. When Alva wasn't busy clowning, he was pushing Lavonda around in her wheelchair.

Peaking at twenty-four inches, Lavonda was billed as the Smallest Woman in the World when she appeared with the Clyde Beatty Circus. In 1951 she hoped to add a second title to her billing: Small-

★ Lya Graf, a twenty-seven-inch little woman from Germany, gained fame in 1933, during Senate Banking and Currency Committee hearings in Washington, when she hopped onto the younger J. P. Morgan's lap for a publicity photo.

est Mother in the World. At thirty-one, she was due to have a child. In March she gave birth by cesarean section to a three-pound-twelve-ounce baby boy. The newborn, afflicted by respiratory trouble, did not survive.

MR. *and* MRS. FISCHER, THE WORLD'S TALLEST MARRIED COUPLE

Circa early 1900s–?

★ In the late 1930s, Gottlieb and Elfrieda Fischer were exhibited as the World's Tallest Married Couple. Billed as eight feet, one inch and only 240 pounds, the Austrian-born Gottlieb found his perfect mate when they were both booked in a London dance act. Elfrieda, also Austrian, stood seven feet, eleven inches and weighed a svelte 209 pounds.

Gottlieb and Elfrieda Fischer, the World's Tallest Married Couple, dressed in western garb for the Ringling Bros. and Barnum & Bailey show.
Collection of James G. Mundie

With two-inch heels, the giant bride could have looked her groom in the eye on their wedding day, November 30, 1933.

The Fischers arrived in the United States on April 1, 1937. They were known as Mr. and Mrs. Long when they toured with the Hagenbeck-Wallace and Cole Bros. circuses the following year. The Longs reverted to the name Fischer on a stint with Ringling Bros. and Barnum & Bailey, during which they otherwise completely ditched their heritage and dressed in cowboy regalia. The boots and hats most likely boosted them closer to their advertised height. Since their non-cowboy accents would've ruined the Wild West image, presumably the Fischers didn't speak much to onlookers.

Ringling Bros. did not renew the Fischers' contract after the 1948 season. Rather than join another circus, the giants hung up their hats, kicked off their boots, and retired to Sarasota, Florida, where they ran a motel.

FREDA-FRED
1908–?

The half man, half woman known as Freda-Fred was born in New York City on February 22, 1908, or so claimed the pitch card sold at shows. The card further explained that the child was initially believed to be male, and so was named Fred. The young lad enjoyed his boyhood until puberty thrust his body into limbo. At twelve years and three months, the changes began. The right side of his body grew larger and more muscular than the left. Fred's concerned mother had him examined by a doctor who determined he was "neither boy nor girl, but both combined in one body." A week later his mother did what his body could not—she chose a gender. Fred was dressed as a girl, sent to private school, and renamed Freda. But the inner Fred wasn't ready to be ignored. By age sixteen, he had hair sprouting on both sides of his face, but only on the right side of his body. Freda-Fred put nature's work to work by putting his dual sexuality on exhibit.

In actuality, Freda-Fred was a female impersonator named Fred Van. He toured the country for years as a half-and-half in various sideshows. Wearing a bikini top, Freda-

Fred appeared to be a woman, but obviously had a full set of male genitals.

After a lengthy career of playing dress-up, Van hung up his fake breasts and ran a carnival geek show. The wig Van wore as Freda was demoted to the less prestigious job of covering his geek's head. Van did make another appearance as Freda-Fred when he was well into his sixties. He was recruited for one last hurrah by Ward Hall, who found himself in need of a half-and-half act at the end of a season. Van accepted the invitation, reclaimed his feminine hairpiece, and reached into his old wardrobe. As Hall pitched the show, he realized it wouldn't be an easy sell, because of Freda-Fred's advanced age. Hall gave his bally and added a clincher: "I know what I have been telling you about this woman, you may find hard to believe, but I know it's true, because this is my mother." The plan worked.

Afterward, Freda-Fred retired for good to his home in Miami. The former sideshow star began a new career in the less glamorous business of furniture sales.

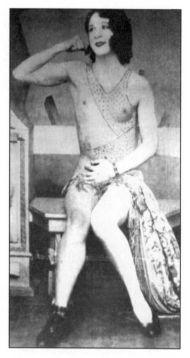

Freda-Fred, posing as both woman and man. Note the mismatched shoes and the unshaved leg on the male half. *Kobel collection*

LORETT FULKERSON
Born 1915

Lorett Fulkerson was born Loretta Love in Oklahoma on July 17, 1915. Young Love lived up to her name, marrying by the age of sixteen. The union was short-lived. Yet love, or at least the pursuit of it, would be a theme for Loretta, as she ultimately married

Lorett Fulkerson, circa 1980s.
Author's collection

five times. She eventually shortened her first name to Lorett and took her last husband's surname, Fulkerson.

At seventeen, already divorced, she planned to visit her ex, who was working on the railroad. But standing between home and her former husband was something much more enticing—a carnival. Fulkerson never made it past the show. She became a roustabout, finding work in girl shows and the cookhouse. Employment didn't come so easily when she returned home for the winter: "No one wanted to give me a job, so I said, 'Well, piss on them! I know where I can get me a job and work as long as I want to work.'" She did exactly that.

Fulkerson's path to becoming a Tattooed Lady started with a star on each foot, one red and one green. "Stop and go," she describes. After a few more "pieces of garbage here and there," she met the renowned tattoo artist Tats Thomas in Chicago. She fell in love with the design of an eagle battling a snake, and told Thomas, "Boy, if I ever had that money, that's what I want." He offered to ink her completely if she would advertise his name on her card as she traveled. Fulkerson agreed, and had ninety percent of her body finished before Thomas died. The work took five and a half months. Her beloved eagle and snake dominate her back, while 106 roses cover her arms. Four more roses, on the inside of her lower lip, blanket the tattoo of an ex-husband's name. Genghis Khan, snakes, and other designs decorate most of the rest of her body. She never let another artist mark her.

The Tattooed Lady started with her first show in Kansas in the 1930s, and traveled the country until her retirement in 1992. This living art gallery earned good money with the Ringling Bros. and Barnum & Bailey show for twenty years, then with the promoter Dick Best, and finally with Ward Hall for her last thirty-two years in the business. During the off-season she often worked at New York's Hubert's Museum in Times Square.

In her younger, thinner years, Fulkerson flaunted her scantily clad body as the talker introduced her. As she grew older and thicker, she revealed a bit less, by wearing a full one-piece swimsuit. Asked if she felt ashamed about her markings, she typically replied, "No, I got your two dollars up there at the ticket box."

Fulkerson was forced to retire in order to care for her fifth husband when he began suffering from Alzheimer's disease. Since his death, she has remained self-sufficient at home in Louisiana, taking care of herself, and as she says, "sittin' on my butt."

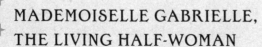

MADEMOISELLE GABRIELLE, THE LIVING HALF-WOMAN

1884–?

Mademoiselle Gabrielle, as she was known in show business, was a Legless Wonder of the early twentieth century. Born in Basel, Switzerland, she first exhibited her perfectly formed but abbreviated body at the Paris Universal Exposition of 1900. Shortly afterward, she arrived in America to continue her career.

Mademoiselle Gabrielle's body was described in a 1929 *London Life* magazine article

Mlle. GABRIEL
The living half woman
Dreamland Circus Side Show,
Coney Island, N. Y.

Mademoiselle Gabrielle, circa 1920. (Her name
is spelled differently here.) *Author's collection*

as "finishing neatly and smoothly a little below the waist, with nothing in the way of stumps being present." Though she had no legs, she was blessed with a striking face. She complemented her natural beauty with Victorian dresses fitted for her torso and opulent jewelry adorning her neck and wrists.

Self-esteem was not an issue for her, and Mademoiselle Gabrielle didn't bother feeling sorry for herself. "Women really do not need legs," she once said. "I have never had them and have never missed them. I can enjoy life and do everything I want to do without them. In any case they are not always particularly beautiful things, and I don't envy any woman in possession of them." Men apparently didn't believe she needed legs, either. She was married in the early 1900s (and used her married name, Hunter, outside show business), but for how long is not known. *London Life* reported that she wed twice more, the third time to a German nobleman.

In 1912, after Mademoiselle Gabrielle had gained fame at Coney Island as the Living Half-Woman, a booking agent signed her to a vaudeville contract, by which she was to appear under his management at New York's Hammerstein Theatre. She subsequently broke her agreement and left the show to work for other managers. Four years later the agent won $2,000 to cover his expenses after a court ruled that the legless woman had "jumped her contract."

Mademoiselle Gabrielle also worked with Ringling Bros. and Barnum & Bailey. She returned to Coney Island and appeared with the Dreamland Circus Side Show in the 1920s.

RONNIE *and* DONNIE GALYON

Born 1951

Born on October 28, 1951, in Dayton, Ohio, Ronnie and Donnie Galyon are currently the world's oldest living conjoined twins. The brothers weighed eleven pounds, eleven and a half ounces at birth. Their surprised father, Wes, told the Associated Press: "We were expecting twins and were hoping for them, but this came as a terrific blow to us." He and his wife already had two normal children and later added several more.

Ronnie and Donnie could not be separated as babies, nor do they want to be as adults. Joined at the abdomen, each has his own set of arms and legs and his own stomach, kidney, and small intestine. However, they have only one colon, one

Ronnie and Donnie Galyon outside their show, circa 1961. *Collection of Bob Blackmar*

set of sex organs, and one bladder. Both can feel the need to use the bathroom, but Donnie controls the equipment to do so. With careful coordination, the Galyons are able to walk freely, though a bit awkwardly. Like most men, they enjoy sports, particularly baseball, and are ardent Cincinnati Reds fans. Occasionally they take a swing of the bat themselves with their siblings pitching and catching. Bowling, hunting, and fishing are also favorite activities. In their youth, they often liked fighting as well, particularly with each other. Many a fist was thrown across their shared body.

The Galyons using a jacket to hide their connection in public. *Collection of Bob Blackmar*

From a societal standpoint, the twins are often counted as two. In the documentary *Sideshow: Alive on the Inside,* the Galyons explain that each may cast a vote during an election and each owns a Social Security card, but they need only one passport.

The Galyon's sideshow career began shortly after birth. Their parents didn't want to exhibit them, but as their father explains in the documentary *Being Different,* "Regardless of where they go, they're on exhibition. This way they get something from it. What else can Siamese twins do?" The twins have proved to be an extraordinary attraction for decades. They toured with their father, as well as a variety of showmen, including Ward Hall and Chris Christ, Sam Alexander in a Single-O show, and Papa Fuentes in the Mexican Circo Unión. During their exhibition years, they often sat in a trailer while spectators peered through a window to watch them play checkers or watch TV. When they were appearing as ten-year-olds under their father's management, their show was shut down in San Bernardino, California, after a woman complained of becoming ill after witnessing their act, or rather, witnessing them. Authorities invoked an obscure 1873 act prohibiting the exhibition of human deformities for money. The Galyons simply moved on to other towns, undeterred by the incident.

Now retired in Ohio, Ronnie and Donnie Galyon live self-sufficiently in a home they purchased. Their many years in the sideshow earned them a healthy living. They have no plans to exhibit themselves again; they did appear on *Jerry Springer* in 1997, however, and were filmed for the aforementioned documentaries.

MARY *and* MARGARET GIBB, AMERICA'S SIAMESE TWINS

1912–1967

America's Siamese twins were born on May 20, 1912, in Holyoke, Massachusetts. Their mother is thought to be the first woman in the United States to survive such a birth. The girls were pygopagus twins, joined at the base of the spine. Each had two arms, two legs, and her own rectum. Like all conjoined twins they were identical, although Margaret, at four-foot-ten, was two inches taller than Mary.

When the sisters turned three, their parents considered separating them, but then chose not to take the risk. They were given another opportunity in 1928 after a doctor's examination, but again the Gibbs decided against it.

Mary and Margaret were kept out of public as children, sheltered at home until they were fifteen. A private tutor came to the house to educate them. Apparently they learned to sing and dance at home, as they

Mary and Margaret Gibb. *Author's collection*

finally embarked on a public career in vaudeville. The twins worked with the Loew's theaters for two years and then spent four years on the Keith circuit.

In 1930, Mary and Margaret decided to see the world and let the world see them. They performed in Paris, Brussels, and Switzerland. They then moved on to an even bigger stage, joining the Ringling Bros. and Barnum & Bailey Circus in 1934. Four years later they switched to the Cole Bros. Circus. They jumped back and forth between shows until 1941, when they retired to their hometown.

Their circus life over, the Gibb sisters decided to sell something other than glances at themselves. They made and sold novelties, cards, and other items at the Mary-Margaret Gift Shoppe. The business closed in 1949.

The sisters spent their last years much like their first—in seclusion. In 1966, Margaret was diagnosed with bladder cancer. It spread through their shared circulatory system and to their lungs. The disease claimed Margaret as its first victim on January 8, 1967. Mary followed two minutes later. At age fifty-four, they had been the oldest living conjoined twins.

Mary and Margaret Gibb claimed to be happy as they were. They never wished for a separation.

Artoria Gibbons, circa 1970s.
Ward Hall collection

★ ARTORIA GIBBONS
★ *Born circa 1905–?*
★

★ Before adorning her body with tattoos, Artoria was Anna, the daughter of poor farmers in Wisconsin. By age fourteen, she had left home in search of a better life, which came in the form of a touring sideshow. Anna soon met the man who would become her husband—a tattoo artist, Charles "Red" Gibbons. He offered his services to help her land a job with the show as a Tattooed Lady. With more than eighty percent of her body inked, she adopted her stage name. From the neck down she was covered in reproductions of masterpieces by Raphael and Michelangelo; designs of vines, roses, and Americana; and an image of Leonardo's *Last Supper*.

Artoria toured the country with Ringling Bros. and Barnum & Bailey from 1921 to 1923, Hagenbeck-Wallace in 1924, and a variety of other shows over the next fifty years. When exhibiting, she wore a full-length robe and slowly revealed her illustrated arms and legs before removing the garment. A one-piece swimsuit, cut low in the back, left to the imagination whatever designs adorned her breasts, belly, and behind. In addition to displaying herself, the Tattooed Lady had to field ridiculous questions from spectators. "You wouldn't believe how many people come up an' ask me was I born this way," she once told a journalist. "I always say yes, an' the doctors figure it was on account of my mother must have gone to too many movies."

Gibbons stopped exhibiting after the death of her husband in the late 1940s, but the retirement was short-lived, and she was back onstage by the early 1950s. She enjoyed her job, and always maintained a strong work ethic. In her later years, she once broke her arm when leaving her circus trailer, but refused to go to the hospital until after the show.

By the mid-1970s, Gibbons was working with Ward Hall's sideshow. She began to suffer from senility and a loss of balance, and despite her pleas to let her continue working, Hall retired her at age eighty-six, when her condition grew too dangerous.

Other than at the sideshow, Gibbons could also be seen regularly in church. The religious Tattooed Lady was said to have never missed a Sunday.

LUCIO *and* SIMPLICIO GODINO
1908–1936

 Lucio and Simplicio Godino were born on March 2, 1908, on the Philippine island of Samar. The brothers were joined at the base of the spine, and were thus forced to face life back to back.

They had only a brief encounter with sideshows. In 1915 they were exhibited at Coney Island, but the Society for the Prevention of Cruelty to Children protested their appearance. Their career ended, the twins returned home to the Philippines.

Samar (Siamese) Twins.
Lucio and Simplicio
Two boys, 5 years old, joined
together for life.

Lucio and Simplicio Godino, circa 1913.
Author's collection

Lucio and Simplicio were determined to live a normal life. They exemplified teamwork by mastering the art of coordination. They learned to swim, golf, roller-skate, dance, play tennis, and drive, and even managed to be normal high school students. They had girlfriends—a pair of twin sisters, Natividad and Victorina Malos. In July 1929, the Godinos married the sisters, but not without a struggle. The marriage license clerk refused the union because he believed the Godinos were one individual, and he couldn't allow one person to have two wives. The Philippine Department of Justice overruled the clerk and permitted the marriage.

Marriage wasn't the Godinos' only legal problem. One of them (it's unclear which) once got drunk and injured a child while driving. Though the twin was found guilty, the judge could not imprison him without punishing the innocent brother. Instead, a hefty fine was inflicted and the Godinos were spared jail time.

By 1930, accompanied by their wives, the brothers had returned to America to perform in vaudeville. Their programs began with a talk, which was followed by dancing. This prosperous career was halted in 1936, when Lucio was stricken with rheumatic fever. On November 25, his death imminent, doctors tried to save his brother with an emergency separation. The operation was the first successful division of adult conjoined twins. Lucio died hours later, as expected, of rheumatic fever. Simplicio appeared to be on the road to recovery, but eleven days later cerebrospinal meningitis claimed his life.

Lucio and Simplicio lived full lives in their twenty-eight years and never expected a separation. "We accept the inevitable and make the best of it, convinced that united we stand, divided we fall," they once said. "And we have no desire to fall," they added.

THE GREAT OMI

1892–1969

THE
GREAT
OMI

Draped in thick black zebra stripes from head to toe, the Great Omi was the greatest tattooed attraction of the early twentieth century. Before becoming a sideshow star, Omi was a British war veteran named Horace Ridler. Born in Surrey, he joined the military in World War I. During his time in the service, the young soldier was promoted to major, and more important, he received his first tattoo.

After the war, Ridler inherited a handsome sum of money. He quickly squandered much of it, but by 1922 he decided to use what remained to break into show business as a Tattooed Man. A Chinese artist helped him achieve his goal, albeit with somewhat unrefined designs. They proved good enough for Ridler to make a living exhibiting himself. But the tattoo addict wasn't satisfied. And he had more money to burn.

The Great Omi, circa 1940s.
Ken Harck archives / Bros. Grim Side Shows

In 1927, Ridler employed the services of a well-known tattoo artist, George Burchett. He accepted Ridler's unprecedented challenge, and 150 hours and $3,000 later, Ridler had been transformed into the Great Omi (also called the Zebra Man). Not only was the pattern striking, it also covered many of his earlier tattoos.

The Great Omi's popularity spread quickly and earned him a spot with the Ringling

Bros. and Barnum & Bailey show and the Ripley's Believe It or Not! Odditorium in New York City. Rather than boast of Burchett's expensive and meticulous work, Omi regaled audiences with a tale of having been captured by savages in New Guinea and being marked against his will. Although his spectacular appearance and exotic story would have sufficed for most paying customers, he wasn't finished entertaining. Accessorizing with a nose ring, he continued to amaze the masses by hoisting an anvil from his nasal cartilage. The show made Omi one of the best-paid Tattooed Men in the business.

Omi wasn't alone in his permanent striped suit. His wife adorned her flesh with the zebra design and called herself Omette. Perhaps Omi was inspired by her look, too; he later grew more outlandish by applying lipstick and nail polish.

With the outbreak of World War II, Omi attempted to relive his days as a major and reenlist. The army rejected him on the basis of his appearance. If only he had chosen a camouflage tattoo theme instead.

In 1969, after more than forty years of his being on exhibit, death closed the curtain on the Great Omi's show.

The Great Waldo brings a mouse back to freedom. *From the collection of Milo Anthony and Cristina Boothe*

THE GREAT WALDO
Circa 1920–?

Before he became the Great, a young Waldo suffered growing anti-Semitism in his homeland. As a youth in pre–World War II Germany, he was frequently abused by other youngsters. Carnivals provided his only solace. Waldo loved the music, the costumes, the idea of traveling, and the freaks. He respected the human oddities for profiting from their differences. But it was the performers who swallowed and regurgitated objects that especially captivated him. He soon learned their secrets and developed his own stomach muscles to perform similar feats. Having this complete muscle control was handy not just for performing, but also for preventing indigestion—he could expel whatever wasn't agreeing with his stomach. Bellyaches would never again be a problem.

In the late 1930s, Waldo took his new talents on the road, performing as far as Vienna for an audience of doctors. When Hitler invaded Austria in 1938, Waldo fled to Switzerland. He did his act in nightclubs and was soon discovered by an American sideshow agent. The talent scout wasted no time in bringing him to the United States.

> ★ Agnes C. Schmidt suffered from an affliction that thickened the skin on her hips and caused it to droop to her knees. During performances in 1933 at the Ripley's Odditorium in Chicago, she would stretch her skin like rubber, then let it fall back against her leg.

The Great Waldo was also known as the Human Ostrich, because like an ostrich, he would eat anything. But unlike the big bird, he always dressed in formal wear. This allowed him to look very distinguished even as he swallowed white rats and brought them back up, alive and well. In addition, he swallowed rings, watches, lemons, goldfish, coins, frogs, and anything else the audience offered him. When swallowing frogs, he would first drink water so the frog would have a pool to swim in. After swallowing a watch, Waldo would invite an audience member onstage to listen to the ticking through his stomach. Perhaps even more astounding was his ability to swallow different-colored balls and then bring up whatever color was called for. The Human Ostrich worked in many shows, including Ringling Bros. and Barnum & Bailey, and Hubert's Museum in New York.

In his book *Step Right Up!*, Daniel Mannix recalls asking Waldo why he started swallowing rats. "One morning," he told Mannix, "I simply thought, 'I want to swallow a live rat.' So I did. Then it became a hobby with me. Other people go in for golf or bridge. I swallow rats."

Melvin Burkhart, who performed as the Anatomical Wonder and the Human Block-head for more than sixty years, recalled the Great Waldo as one of the most amazing acts he'd seen.

The Human Ostrich committed suicide by gassing himself in his home. Reportedly, a woman who left him had caused him great distress.

Tiny Hicks.
Ward Hall collection

★ **TINY HICKS**

★ *1919–?*

★ Clyde "Tiny" Hicks was born in 1919, and lived up to his nickname only through infancy. As he got older, Hicks was anything but tiny. Billed anywhere from 505 to 762 pounds, and standing six feet tall, he worked as a sideshow Fat Man for more than twenty years.

Hicks's illustrious career began in 1945 when he left his hometown of Warren, Illinois, to join Standard Shows in Wyoming. He then brought his massive frame east, where he performed with Ringling Bros. and Barnum & Bailey and with Ward Hall for eight years at Madison Square Garden. The Fat Man later traveled with Hall through the South and as far as Texas. Hicks didn't like the South. He had exhibited himself there earlier in his career and wasn't paid. His employer claimed this was because fat men weren't an attraction in the Confederate states. Hicks believed the crooked showman and never wanted to risk missing a meal again.

Although his weight may have been exaggerated, Hicks was still a force to be reckoned with. His breakfast was said to consist of six slices of toast, two eggs, two bowls of oatmeal, and six doughnuts. Such a meal easily helped him require pants measuring forty-five inches long and seventy-six inches at the waist, large enough for two adults to stand in comfortably.

DICK HILBURN

1918–1971

Dick Hilburn, circa 1958. *Kobel collection*

Handicapped with very limited appendages, Dick Hilburn was known as both the Quarter-Boy and the Half-Man. He was born in North Carolina on January 15, 1918, with one arm, no legs, and a foot with two toes jutting out from his left hip.

Yet Hilburn overcame his physical disability and lived self-sufficiently. With the aid of a skateboard he was able to move about with relative ease. He had a keen business sense, and with his one fully developed arm he ran a diner and operated a Single-O show, featuring himself and a younger attraction named Carl Norwood, whose parastremmatic dwarfism earned him the title Frog Boy. Hilburn also possessed great artistic talent. He could wield a tattoo needle with flair, and he earned extra income in the winters as a commercial painter of trucks and semitrailers. The Quarter-Boy experienced success also in his love life, marrying a woman with a full set of limbs.

Dick Hilburn ran his sideshow until he died, in June 1971.

THE HILTON SISTERS, DAISY *and* VIOLET

1908–1969

On February 5, 1908, in Brighton, England, an unwed barmaid named Kate Skinner gave birth to twin daughters, Daisy and Violet. They were pygopagus Siamese twins, joined at the hip and the buttocks. While the girls would be forever connected, their

Program cover for a Daisy and Violet Hilton vaudeville performance, 1929. *Author's collection*

mother severed herself from them and allowed her midwife, Mary Hilton, to "adopt" them. Hilton understood immediately that the girls would be a source of profit. Once Daisy and Violet could speak, she made them address her as "Auntie" and her husband as "Sir." Hilton and her husband knew that by training the girls properly, they could sell more than just peeps and stares at them. They could offer an entire show. The couple gave Daisy and Violet endless singing, dancing, and music lessons, turning them into versatile entertainers and, at the same time, virtual slaves.

By age three, Daisy and Violet were performing with circuses, carnivals, and fairs. Over the next few years they traveled the world, venturing as far as Australia. They arrived in the United States when they were eight and settled in San Antonio. Daisy and Violet were never upset that they were joined together or that they had to endure constant stares. "We're used to it," Daisy once said. "We've never known anything else." What made life difficult was the fact that Auntie was essentially joined to them as well. She never left them alone, never let them meet men or be young women on their own. Mary Hilton had been making a fortune and keeping every penny to herself, though Daisy had managed to hide away fifty cents, and Violet twenty-five. They held on to this money dearly, thinking that once they were eighteen they would have their freedom. It appeared that freedom would come even earlier when Auntie died, but the girls were willed to the midwife's daughter Edith and her husband, called "Sir." Their new managers were as wicked as the former, controlling the twins' every move. By age seventeen the sisters were vaudeville headliners earning thousands a week, but not for themselves.

Strangely enough, it took an absurd lawsuit for $250,000 filed against the twins to finally gain them their freedom. A fellow who worked as their advance man had asked for an autograph on their publicity photo. They signed it, "To our pal, Bill, with love and best wishes from your pals, Daisy and Violet Hilton." When their pal Bill's wife later filed for divorce, she blamed the twins in her suit, for apparently "loving" her husband. Naturally, the twins were shocked by this nonsense and sought legal advice. Accompanied by Edith's husband, they met with an attorney. The lawyer sensed something was wrong, and insisted to be left alone with the defendants. As soon as Sir left the room, Daisy and Violet told the attorney everything, and he took their case. Freedom was finally theirs.

Soon after, the twins played themselves in Tod Browning's 1932 movie *Freaks*, where they demonstrated their ability to have independent love lives. Even though they shared sensations, they learned to block each other out mentally. It was a trick inspired by the greatest magician of all. Harry Houdini had met the twins at a performance and told them that with the power of concentration they could achieve anything. Their love life was the focus of another film, *Chained for Life* (1950). Off screen, each sister married separately, but neither marriage lasted long.

At the height of their career, Daisy and Violet were earning $5,000 a week. But the public eventually lost interest. In 1960, when *Freaks* was re-released, to become a cult classic, the sisters capitalized by going on a publicity tour. They were left stranded in North Carolina at their last public appearance, after their tour manager failed to pick them up. At this point they were penniless. The once famous entertainers were forced to take jobs at a grocery store, one twin working the register and the other bagging. On January 6, 1969, Daisy and Violet failed to show up for work. They were later found dead at home, victims of the Hong Kong flu.

FAKED ACTS

One thing sideshows were not typically known for was honesty. Promoters frequently attracted paying customers with gaffed, or fake, acts. P. T. Barnum launched his career by fooling the public with the supposedly 161-year-old Joice Heth, who in reality was no older than eighty.

(*continued*)

Adolph and Rudolph,
the fake conjoined twins.
Author's collection

Siamese twins weren't the easiest attractions to find, but with a little creativity, "twins" could be conjoined for the stage. One such pair was Adolph and Rudolph, in the late 1800s. The Austrian "brothers" were rigged in such a way that one seemed to sprout upward from the other's waist. In 1930, the Milton Sisters capitalized off the Hilton Sisters' fame with performances at Coney Island. Their act came to an end after an argument at a show in Atlantic City: the sisters performed their own separation surgery onstage, cutting through their dress with a pair of scissors.

A two-headed man named Pasqual Pinon gained fame in 1917 when he appeared with the Sells-Floto sideshow. The second, smaller head—complete with facial features—appeared to grow from Pinon's forehead. Audiences were led to believe it could once see, hear, and speak. However, it had conveniently lost these abilities after a stroke years earlier. The superfluous head may have been a nicely decorated giant tumor, which still would have been freakish even without the makeover.

Bearded ladies were often bearded men in drag. In the early 1940s, one particular furry fellow donned a dress to evade the FBI after dodging the draft. He was eventually caught and promptly sent to the army. In 1911, a newspaper reported a fraudulent act revealed by an innocent young boy. The child indicated to the sideshow talker that he was related to the bearded lady, so the talker asked if the performer was his mother. "No," he told her, "she is my father."

Simple props helped create other shams. Dried, cracked glue smothered over children's bodies simulated reptile skin for alligator girls and boys. Hairy masks helped clean-shaven men imitate Jo-Jo the Dog-Faced Boy. Strategically placed dolls or children could create the impression of a parasitic twin or a four-legged woman (for reasons unknown, such attractions were generally named Margarite Clark). And birdseed filled the breasts of many hermaphrodites who were nothing more than female impersonators (see the sidebar "Half Men, Half Women," page 111).

ROBERT EARL HUGHES

1926–1958

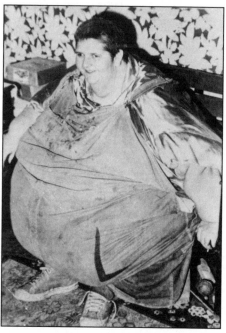

A mammoth of a man, Robert Earl Hughes was the heavyweight of heavyweights. Born in Fishhook, Illinois, the eleven-and-a-half-pound baby was off to a modest start in his claim to fame. According to Hughes, a case of whooping cough at three months made his glands go haywire, and thus his obesity. Whether the illness was to blame or not, Hughes grew into a very big boy. By age ten he weighed 375 pounds. At thirteen he had to quit school because he simply couldn't handle all the walking involved—to the classroom, to the lunchroom. He weighed 550 pounds.

Hughes lived on a farm with his parents. It

Robert Earl Hughes. *Becker Collection, Special Collections Research Center, Syracuse University Library* must have been handy for the family to grow their own food, although his father said his hefty son didn't have an excessive appetite. Updates on Hughes's weight came only a few times a year, when light farm work allowed them. His two brothers would help him onto a truck and drive him to Fishhook's general store to use the commercial scale.

Clothing was made to order. Five yards of material were required for a shirt that would fit his six-foot, 710-pound frame. The Associated Press described his shirts as looking like pup tents and his overalls like "deflated blimps." Hughes slept on a very sturdy double bed and used a strong bench for a chair.

Despite the hardships of being so massive, Hughes never complained. He was said to be good-humored, and he enjoyed reading, listening to the radio, and writing letters. Now and then he even took a walk around the farm. One thing he clearly didn't like was dieting. He tried once, to no avail, and gave up.

By age twenty-five, Hughes had passed the 800-pound mark. Traveling sideshows had made offers, but he refused them all. Five years earlier, in 1946, he had appeared in the Baylis, Illinois, Fall Festival, billed, naturally, as the Heaviest Man in the World. It was true, but only because the former heaviest man in the world (Martin E. Luotto, at 720 pounds) had died the previous July.

Hughes eventually toured with Gooding Amusement. The company listed his weight at a whopping 1,065 pounds. He measured ten feet, two inches around the waist. By February 1958 he had reached his maximum weight—1,069 pounds—earning his place in the *Guinness Book of World Records* with the heaviest documented weight for a human. The rotund Hughes could even be in two counties at once. This was not a cruel joke, but the truth: the dividing line between Pike and Brown counties actually ran through his living room.

Perhaps Hughes was right to avoid traveling shows in earlier years. While on tour in Indiana with the sideshow, he was stricken with the measles. He was taken to a community hospital in the town of Bremen but was too large to fit through the doorway. With the aid of a ladder, nurses attended to him in a specially built home on a truck bed parked at the rear of the hospital. Within days, on July 10, 1958, Hughes died from a case of uremia. The funeral service was held at the cemetery, as his converted piano-case casket was too large to get inside a church or mortuary. The 1,100-pound casket was lowered into the ground by a crane.

WILLIE "POPEYE" INGRAM
1932–?

Willie Ingram wasn't called Popeye because he had freakish forearms like his cartoon namesake. But his act was, in a sense, cartoonish. Popeye did exactly what his name indicates—he popped his eyes out. "The Man with Elastic Eyeballs" could push his eyes nearly an inch out of their sockets.

Ingram was born in Decatur, Alabama, and he learned at the tender age of four the skill that would be his livelihood. He once described his discovery: "I was playing hide-and-seek with some kids. I hid in a dark place, but they found me, and I was so startled my eyes popped out." His friends must have been even more startled.

The stunt was painless and effortless for Ingram, and enabled him to spend many years performing with the Walter Wanous shows. "Popeye was a very powerful act," promoter Ward Hall attests. Ingram would shock audiences by alternating his popping eyes, right, left, right, left. Then he would make them roll around as if they might fall out any second. One of his performances was at the Texas State Fair in Dallas in the early 1970s. After the Wanous show left, Hall played the fair for seventeen consecutive years. "And in the

> In 1927, Clarence H. Alexander, better known as Elastic Skin Joe in the Ringling Bros. and Barnum & Bailey Circus, committed suicide before a crowd gathered under the sideshow tent. He swallowed a bottle of strychnine after failing to win the affections of the show's Tattooed Woman.

seventeenth year we were there, people would still walk up to the office and say, 'Is this where you got the guy who pops his eyes out?'" Hall remembers. People who saw Popeye never forgot him.

Other than thrusting his peepers, Ingram enjoyed drinking. For this reason Hall never employed him. Drinking often led Popeye to pop his eyes a little too freely. Doing the stunt in public just for fun was a great way to spoil the act.

Popeye's elastic eyeballs can still disturb audiences, thanks to his role in the 1973 film *The Mutations.*

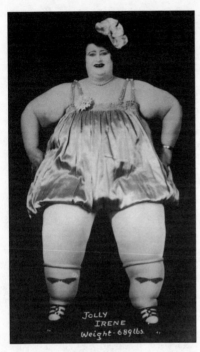

Jolly Irene, circa 1930s.
Author's collection

★ Amanda Siebert wasn't always the jiggly Jolly Irene. Born in Jersey City, New Jersey, she was quite normal for the first twenty-one years of her life. In 1901 she weighed a respectable 120 pounds and gave birth to a child. Not only was a baby born, but because of a few glands gone awry, so was Jolly Irene.

The pounds piled up and the flesh got fleshier. Diets were ineffective, leaving her helpless against her newly acquired mass. One reporter later described her as having "biceps three times as large as Jack Dempsey." But at 620 pounds, rather than box the heavyweight champion, she turned her tragedy into profit by joining Ringling Bros.

Jolly Irene had gotten so big, measuring seventy-nine inches around the waist, that simple things became exceedingly difficult. Traveling was degrading, as her obesity would require her to ride in a freight car. She refused, and thus performed with Ringling only when the circus was in New York. Of course, living in New York presented problems as well. Subway turnstiles were way too narrow, as were theater seats. Even a dentist's chair was a torture device, as it needed to be dismantled so she could get in and out of it.

In addition to Ringling, Jolly Irene posed her plump figure at the Harlem Museum. There she met another fleshy performer, Joe Cramer. He had the unique ability to stretch his skin several inches, and was known as the Rubberneck Man. He was thin, but his skin seemed to have the potential to expand like his hefty admirer. Jolly Irene was convinced that neither he nor any other man would ever seek her hand in marriage, so she decided to seek his. It was 1924—a leap year—and she planned to take advantage of the leap-year tradition permitting a woman to propose on February 29. Numerous newspaper reports suggest it was merely a publicity stunt; no answer from the Rubberneck Man was ever confirmed.

Jolly Irene's longest sideshow stint was at Coney Island, where she became one of its best-known Fat Ladies. Peaking at 689 pounds, she was well liked, always joking with onlookers and appearing, as her name promised, jolly. She may have been especially jolly when she eventually reeled in a husband, George Siebert. The 170-pounder was a hotel clerk who served as her talker during the summer season.

Her portliness started taking its toll. In 1937, while suffering from a cold, she fell off her bed. Neighbors heard the thump and called the police. It took five officers to hoist the Fat Lady back onto her mattress. Illnesses continued to plague her, and in a few years she lost 150 pounds.

On November 27, 1940, the sixty-year-old Jolly Irene passed away in her Coney Island home after a heart attack. Friends and family attended a requiem mass held at the curb outside a Brooklyn church. The casket was too large to fit through the doorway.

JOLLY FAT MEN AND WOMEN

The fat people who've exhibited themselves in sideshows could easily fill a book. They could fill a lot of things, for that matter.

There are those who have argued that these heavyweights were exploited—and perhaps some were. But others enjoyed their jobs and were proud to earn a living. At least the sideshow didn't discriminate, as many other employers would have when a 500-pounder turned in an application. Some fat people got their start in sideshows and moved on to other careers. Wisconsin's Clifford "Tiny" Krueger, for example, shifted his 485 pounds out from under the tent and into the United States Senate.

Of course, those who were happy in their position couldn't always keep a smile. The obese also suffered from health problems and often faced dangers the average person

(continued)

didn't—falling through a floor, for example. Not such a jolly situation. Regardless, many were given stage names beginning with "Jolly," whether they were or weren't.

Jolly Babe, 635 pounds	Jolly Lee, 600 pounds
Jolly Daisy, 700 pounds	Jolly Mary, 525 pounds
Jolly Ema, 620 pounds	Jolly Nellie, 642 pounds
Jolly Ethel, 580 pounds	Jolly Ollie, 640 pounds
Jolly Irene, 689 pounds	Jolly Pearl, 643 pounds
Jolly John Webb, 600 pounds	Jolly Ray, 457 pounds
Jolly Josephine, 550 pounds	Jolly Trixie, 687 pounds

Otis Jordan during his years at Coney Island. *Author's collection*

OTIS JORDAN, THE FROG BOY *and* THE HUMAN CIGARETTE FACTORY

1925–1990

Otis Jordan managed to do quite a lot for a man whose body remained in a fixed position since birth. His ossification began in Barnesville, Georgia, on his first day in the world, November 2, 1925. Otis had full movement from the shoulders up, and in two fingers. But that was it. Because of his twisted limbs, he grew no taller than twenty-seven inches.

Otis had six normal brothers and sisters. His brothers

carried him to school until the fifth grade, at which time a goat pulling a cart took over the duties. With the help of his family and the family pet, Otis got his education and graduated with honors. The goat also pulled him around town to sell pencils and powder. Undeterred by his handicap, Jordan eventually retired the cart and learned to drive a specially designed car. The ambitious man developed a mechanical sense and enjoyed repairing small appliances.

While sitting on his porch, Jordan learned to roll, light, and smoke a cigarette. This was a feat made famous by the Armless and Legless Wonder Prince Randian. Yet Jordan had never heard of Randian, or any other sideshow performer for that matter. That would soon change. Jordan realized that sitting on the porch rolling cigarettes wasn't earning him a living, but sitting on-stage and doing it would. When a carnival came to town in 1963, he demonstrated his talent to the sideshow manager. He was hired immediately and exhibited for

★ Earl Hall, known as Smokey, got into the sideshow after entertaining and winning bets in his hometown of New Ulm, Minnesota, by smoking cigarettes and making the smoke appear to come out through his skin, rather than out of his mouth or nose.

years as the Frog Boy. When he began working at Coney Island in 1987, his act was repackaged with a less demeaning, and much more specific, billing—the Human Cigarette Factory.

Jordan was proud to be independent, and he earned enough money to buy himself a winter home. His pitch card claimed he enjoyed traveling and meeting people. He was also a spiritual man. "I have a deep faith in God and this has seen me through many hard times," he wrote.

The Human Cigarette Factory rolled his last smoke in 1990. He left a wonderful memory with everyone who knew him.

KOO KOO
THE BIRD GIRL

1880–?

★ **K**oo Koo's name may have been the best way to describe her. Born Minnie Woolsey in 1880, she would grow up to be a short woman with sparse hair, skinny legs, large ears, and a beaked nose. In other words, she looked like a bird. She was said to have a brain to match. According to showman Bobby Reynolds, Woolsey made herself up for the act. "She had kind of a funny face and she was a very homely lady." In the documentary *Freaks Uncensored!*, Jeanie Tomaini spoke of Koo Koo as being "very funny, very entertaining . . . Of course, she was a little birdlike in the head. But she really was a good person." Others have claimed that she suffered from a form of dwarfism called Virchow-Seckel syndrome, or "bird-headed dwarfism."

Koo Koo the Bird Girl.
The Doghouse Collection/showhistory.com

Koo Koo the Bird Girl first performed as the Blind Girl from Mars. Perhaps Woolsey got a stronger prescription on her large, thick glasses and noticed that she looked more like a bird than a Martian. She was much more successful as the Bird Girl, even making an appearance in *Freaks* in 1932. Dressed in a furry outfit with tights, oversize bird feet, and a big feather protruding from her head, she shimmied about in a bizarre dance. Koo Koo's strange yet entertaining act was successful for many years at Coney Island and with the Sells-Floto and the Ringling Bros. and Barnum & Bailey shows.

MARTIN LAURELLO

1889–1955

★ Martin Laurello didn't look like a freak, unless both his face and his rear end were directed toward you at the same time. The so-called Human Owl could rotate his head a full 180 degrees.

Laurello came to the United States from Germany in the early 1920s. Decades before *The Exorcist* shocked audiences with Linda Blair's revolving head, the demon-free Laurello astonished crowds at the Coney Island Dreamland Circus Side Show, the Ringling Bros. and Barnum & Bailey show, and the Ripley's Believe It or Not! Odditorium in the 1930s. Ripley advertised him as "the only one in the world who can walk straight ahead and look straight behind." Laurello could also walk in reverse. His head later swiveled at the 1939–1940 New York World's Fair and at Hubert's Museum in Times Square. Laurello's oscillating antics earned him as much as $50 a week.

The rotating-head act was short, so he extended it by opening his performance with an unrelated routine—an animal show. The presentation usually featured cat fights, complete with little feline boxing gloves, or young dogs performing old tricks. After that came the grand finale—pushing his head around with his finger.

Laurello was married, but in 1931 he abandoned his wife in New York and left for Baltimore. His wife didn't accept the desertion. Police were dispatched and told to search for a man with a rotating head. Two detectives combed carnivals and dime museums, and sure enough, they found their culprit on a platform under a tent. Laurello's back was to the crowd as he stared directly at them—and the cops. He winked at the officers, and they winked back and arrested him. He was released on $500 bond, which he earned right back after a few head turns.

The Human Owl believed anyone could accomplish his special feat. He claimed to have spent three years practicing daily, slowly twisting his head farther and farther. After six months he could rest his chin past his shoulder. He kept going until he could have eyes in back of his head, or at least at his back. In reality, this is the ultimate "Do not try this at home" stunt. Any normal human being who attempted to imitate Laurello, doctors said, would suffer strangulation or dislocation of the neck vertebrae and most likely instant death. Yet Laurello felt no pain during his unusual routine.

It is likely, however, that he did feel pain when a sudden heart attack claimed his life in 1955.

FRANCESCO LENTINI, THE THREE-LEGGED WONDER

1889–1966

Francesco Lentini was born in Sicily in 1889. He was one of twelve children—there would have been thirteen if his undeveloped twin had been born complete. Instead, the unborn brother's leg protruded from the base of Francesco's spine. He also had a second set of genitals, sixteen toes, and a fourth foot growing off the third leg. The three legs were of different lengths, varying by several inches. As one might expect, Lentini didn't much care for his abnormalities. Doctors determined that removing the bonus leg, which was attached to the spine, could result in death or paralysis. So Lentini was stuck with his extra appendages. His parents, hoping to help him deal with his abnormality, took him to a home for disabled children. There he saw

FRANCESCO LENTINI
WORLDS FAMOUS DOUBLED BODIED THREE LEGGED WONDER

Francesco Lentini. Note the extra foot
on his third leg. *Author's collection*

children who couldn't even walk and were worse off than he, and he gained a new appreciation for life and a better attitude. After all, he could do all the things other people did.

He walked, ran, jumped, rode a bicycle, and ice-skated, and he eventually learned to drive a car.

Lentini came to America in 1898 at the age of eight. He finished school before embarking on a career in the sideshows that would span some fifty years and include appearances with Ringling Bros., Barnum & Bailey, the Buffalo

> ★ In 1944, Betty Eagley—a four-legged woman who briefly exhibited herself at Coney Island— was sought by police in the kidnapping of a three-year-old boy. Eagley, also known as Betty Embry and Darlene Egan, ultimately returned the child to his mother.

Bill's Wild West and Walter L. Maine shows, at Coney Island, and on his own. During shows, this Three-Legged Wonder and King of Freaks would demonstrate his extra limb's ability by kicking a football. He even developed a sense of humor about his superfluous leg: He could use it as a stool, thus claiming to be the only man who always carried around his own chair. When he swam, he said, the leg worked as a rudder. And he had a quick answer for the inevitable question of how he would buy three shoes: "I buy two

pairs and give the extra left shoe to a one-legged friend." Slim Price, who performed at Coney Island, later remembered how Lentini answered when asked how he coped with three legs: "If you lived in a land where everybody had one arm, how would you cope with two?"

> ★ Just as rare as a four-legged woman was a lady with three legs. One such attraction was the Norwegian Alma Von Lynd, who appeared in the Ripley's Believe It or Not! show in 1936.

The Three-Legged Wonder married and had four children, each born with the standard two legs and one set of genitalia. Lentini continued touring until he became ill. He died at the age of seventy-eight in 1966.

ALZORIA LEWIS *and* JOHANNA DICKENS, THE TURTLE GIRL *and* THE BEAR GIRL

Born circa 1920s

Through the late 1940s and 1950s, Coney Island's Alzoria Lewis and Johanna Dickens were paired as the Turtle Girl and the Bear Girl, respectively. They were often billed as the Most Unusual Sisters in the World, and sometimes referred to as cousins. Of course, as with any turtle and bear, there was no relation.

Johanna Dickens and Alzoria Lewis.
Author's collection

Alzoria the Turtle Girl was born in Kentucky. All of her limbs were stunted; she had small stubs where her legs and arms should have been. However, nature compensated by giving her extra digits—six fingers on each hand, six toes on each foot. As the Turtle Girl, Lewis crawled around on all fours and told audiences that her mother had been frightened by a turtle while fishing. When erect, Lewis stood two feet tall. Despite her appearance, she married twice. At least one of her husbands was known to have been after her money.

Johanna the Bear Girl had a normal torso, normal hands, and normal breasts. Contrarily, her legs were very short and thick, and her gait like that of a little bear. Slim Price, a sword swallower and fire eater who worked with her, recalled her looking more like R2-D2. She also walked on her hands and feet.

The Turtle Girl and the Bear Girl worked primarily at Coney Island, but also traveled with showmen Bobby Reynolds and Milt Levine.

JEAN-JACQUES LIBBERA, THE DOUBLE-BODIED MAN

1884–1936

The brothers Jean and Jacques Libbera were born in Rome, the fourth (and fourth-and-a-half) of thirteen children. Jean would have the burden of carrying his brother around for his entire life. The helpless Jacques was a parasitic twin leeching off Jean's body, sharing his circulatory and nervous systems. One of their siblings also had a parasitic twin, but the baby died shortly after birth. Jean's partial brother had two each of arms, legs, hands, and feet.

While Jean provided nourishment for Jacques, Jacques earned good money for Jean. Libbera toured with various circuses as the Double-Bodied Man. A pamphlet sold at shows claimed that a "very thorough and complete" X-ray had found a head embedded in Jean's body, with a circumference of about six inches.

JEAN LIBBERA. THE DOUBLE BODIED MAN

Jean Libbera with his parasitic twin, circa 1920s. *Author's collection*

Being more man than most, Libbera found himself a wife. She bore him four perfectly normal children. After retiring from show business, he moved back to Italy, where he died in 1936.

Stella MacGregor.
Ward Hall collection

★ To friends and family, Stella the Bearded Lady was better known as Betty MacGregor, from Battle Creek, Michigan. As a young woman, she fought her furious facial hair growth, but it wasn't easy. Shaving couldn't keep up with its growth. MacGregor's razor visited her face as many as six times a day to keep it clean.

The high-maintenance hair caused problems as she pursued careers in teaching and nursing. When MacGregor sought her master's degree from the University of Michigan to work with gifted children, classmates were often unable to suppress their giggles. While working at the hospital, she was forced to slip away for a shave to avoid funny looks from patients and doctors. Specialists surrounding her at work offered shots and pills, but nothing helped.

Her greatest embarrassment came in dating. She described her dilemma in an interview for Arthur Lewis's *Carnival*: "If I didn't have a chance to sneak off during the evening for a quick shave or two, by the time the guy was ready to kiss me good night, either I'd have to slam the door in his face or else let him think he'd been planning to make love to another man."

In her early twenties, the redheaded MacGregor did what other bearded lasses had done before her—she exhibited her whiskers in various sideshows. Having accepted her facial hair, she found she still exuded enough femininity to attract men. The bearded lady landed two husbands (one died in World War II, the other after a car accident).

MacGregor didn't earn the big bucks that some of her predecessors had. During the mid-1960s, when she worked for showman Nate Eagles at Madison Square Garden, she made only $50 a week. She attempted to supplement her income by offering souvenir pitch cards to circusgoers, but few sold. According to Ward Hall, for whom MacGregor also worked, she didn't know how to present herself properly: "She spent her money on gowns, but they were kind of plain and not show-type gowns, she wouldn't wear makeup, and so on."

Stella the Bearded Lady eventually dropped her stage name and left the sideshow business. In fact, she didn't just quit being a Bearded Lady, she quit being a lady. Hall claimed that MacGregor underwent a sex change and spent his remaining years working as an accountant.

EDDIE MASHER, THE SKELETON DUDE

1892–1962

Edward C. Hagner was born in 1892. By the time he reached adulthood and a height of five feet, seven inches, he weighed little more than he did as a toddler.

Hagner changed his name to Eddie Masher and put his thin frame to work in the sideshow. The human skeleton dressed in a twig-size tuxedo and called himself the Skeleton Dude, just like his distinguished predecessor James W. Coffey.

During a 1917 appearance of Masher's with the Barnum & Bailey Circus, one journalist sarcastically wrote

Eddie Masher. *Kobel collection*

that he "may have to go into training before being permitted to appear here. His careless trainer allowed him to take on a full meal last week and the dude gained two ounces."

Even if he had gained two pounds, Masher would still have been a remarkable attraction. The *Guinness Book of World Records* lists him as one of the lightest adults in history, at an alleged forty-eight pounds. A newspaper article in 1924 reported he weighed ten pounds less than that. Either way, the Skeleton Dude lived up to his billing.

Masher exhibited himself for twenty-five years before retiring. He passed away at age seventy.

★ YVONNE *and* YVETTE McCARTHER
★ *1949–1993*

★ Twins attached at the head (craniopagus) occur in about two percent of conjoined births. On May 14, 1949, in Los Angeles, Yvonne and Yvette Jones beat the odds and made it into that unlucky two percent. The girls had separate brains and hearts, but shared a circulatory system. Surgery was deemed too risky. The sisters were not expected to live more than a few months. But they bested the expectations—as would recur throughout their lives. Their biological father was out of the picture by the time they were born, and their mother, Willa, remarried about four years afterward. They eventually rose to fame under the name of their stepfather, Charles McCarther.

Yvonne and Yvette spent their first two years of life in the hospital. Their mother had a deep faith in God and was determined He would help her raise them. Whether it was God's work or just an attentive showman's ear, help with medical bills (at least $13,000) came in the form of the Clyde Beatty Circus. The circus offered the twins a private trailer, complete with traveling nurses. Though resistant, Willa had little choice. She had five other children to support. Yvonne and Yvette were side-show stars before they took their first steps, which finally happened when they were three. Willa taught her daughters to walk with their heads bowed to form an arch. She also nurtured them with her strong religious faith, and raised them to accept their condition and to live as two, not one. Yvonne, born first, was the more dominant sister, bossy and more talka-

Yvonne and Yvette McCarther, circa 1950s.
Collection of Bob Blackmar

tive. As with other conjoined twins, one could be sick and the other healthy. And despite their being joined at the cranium, one twin could have a headache while the other felt fine.

The sisters remained with the circus for only a few years. During that time they toured throughout North America. While audiences may have been impressed simply watching them walk, Yvonne and Yvette were developing other talents. At age six they began singing gospel, and when they quit the show, it was to pursue a vocal career. They found success with gospel music and traveled the United States through the 1970s.

Yvonne and Yvette were living remarkable lives largely because of their confidence, perseverance, and sense of humor. They never saw each other eye to eye, but they did see eye to eye with each other. They got along and even acted like typical twins. Yvonne and Yvette dressed alike and carried the same purses. They often joked about whose hair was whose. When asked how they slept, they gave the obvious answer: In a bed.

In 1987, the ambitious sisters, now living in California, decided to further their education. Tutors had provided them with the rudiments when they were young, but now they had hopes of becoming children's nurses. They enrolled at Compton Community College, and a year later took another big step—moving into their own Long Beach apartment. At thirty-nine, Yvonne and Yvette were true college girls. By late 1992, they were almost through with school and set to receive their degrees the following June. But on January 2, 1993, Yvonne's enlarged heart stopped beating while she was lying in bed. Yvette's heart failed her shortly after. The sisters were forty-three years old.

Yvonne and Yvette McCarther were awarded degrees posthumously at their funeral.

Grace McDaniels.
Collection of Bob Blackmar

GRACE McDANIELS, THE MULE-FACED WOMAN
1888–1958

★ Billed as the Ugliest Woman in the World, Grace McDaniels probably could have added the word "Ever" to her title. She was afflicted with progressive tumors on her lips and mouth. Her face looked like a slab of raw meat. Her grotesque appearance earned her the title of Mule-Faced Woman. McDaniels has often been described as a beautiful woman inside, however. She was very generous with her wealth and frequently gave money or gifts to single mothers with babies in her audiences.

Born in Valeska, Iowa, McDaniels got her start in the business in the 1920s. Ward Hall recalls a time when his former partner Harry Leonard was lecturing on McDaniels at a store show (a show held in an empty store building after the carnival season). "All of a sudden," Leonard said, "Grace decided she wanted to be pretty, and pretty she was not. She started putting lipstick and rouge on, which only made her more grotesque." As Leonard went on about the Ugliest Woman in the World, McDaniels got upset and demanded he stop describing her in such a way. The owner of the show dismissed her complaint, as she was earning a lot of money to be called ugly—much more than a beautiful woman could earn. McDaniels initially resisted, holding her fingers in her ears while onstage. But eventually she got over it, and realized that she had turned her misfortune into a fortune.

In 1933, McDaniels exhibited her mule face at the Chicago World's Fair. One reporter, offensively, wrote: "This was no fake because the lady did look exactly like a mule and she could flap her lower lip in a way to make a boy from Mexico break down and cry of homesickness."

It has been falsely reported that McDaniels married a "Prince Charming" and had a son. She did have a son, Elmer, but there was no Prince Charming. A worker at the show, apparently intoxicated, had a one-night stand with the unattractive attraction. The son evidently took after his ill-mannered father. Though he looked after his mother, Elmer was a drunk who treated her poorly and spent nearly all her money. The illegitimate son lived up to the pejorative meaning of bastard. His mule-faced mother died in 1958, and forty-year-old Elmer died just six months later. It seems he couldn't live without her love, or more likely, her money.

ROBERT MELVIN, THE MAN WITH TWO FACES
1920–1995

 Others have been advertised as the Man with Two Faces, but none fit the bill better than Robert Melvin. Born on May 9, 1920, in Lancaster, Missouri, he was stricken with neurofibromatosis on the right half of his face. This caused benign but bulging tumors to grow under his skin. The left half of his face was normal. Children like Robert were often hidden away. But this wasn't the case for Robert. His small town accepted and loved him, and he attended public school in Lancaster.

Melvin was a phenomenal attraction and, according to many who knew him, a wonderful human being. Johnny Meah worked with him for a season with Royal American Shows, and the two became inseparable. Meah said that Melvin "always looked like Popeye—he looked like a cartoon." Like those around him, he accepted his condition. He believed it was God's will, and never considered himself handicapped in any way.

When not exhibiting himself onstage, Melvin kept busy handling the bookkeeping and accounting for the show. After the sideshow season finished, he spent the winter working at a hardware store.

Even his personal life was normal. Melvin married his childhood sweetheart, Virginia, and the couple had a daughter. Later they became grandparents.

This Man with Two Faces appeared in the 1977 horror film *The Sentinel* and the 1981 documentary *Being Different*. He died on November 16, 1995.

Mignon, showing off her figure.
Kobel collection

MIGNON THE PENGUIN LADY

Circa 1910s–?

Suffering from a condition called phocomelia, Ruth Davis (née LaArgo) was born with stunted arms and legs. Her abbreviated lower limbs likened her gait to that of a penguin, thus earning her her stage name. She was also known as Mignon and Mickey Mignon. *Mignon* is French for "tiny" or "dainty," which certainly described the diminutive Davis.

The Penguin Lady exhibited her birdlike physique and played the marimba at the 1933 Century of Progress Exposition in Chicago, at the 1939–1940 World's Fair in New York, and at many sideshows, before retiring in the 1960s. She often wore a two-piece bathing suit to display fully her unusual shape.

With her marriage to Earl Davis in the 1950s, Mignon added a partner to her act. Earl had once been an aerial acrobat, but he became crippled after falling from the air and missing the net. He was billed as Hoppy the Frog Boy. However, Hoppy wasn't the first suitor Mignon's waddle attracted—a previous relationship resulted in a normal son.

MAJOR MITE
1913–1975

MAJOR MITE
AGE 20 YEARS
WEIGHT 20 POUNDS
HEIGHT 26 INCHES

Major Mite, 1933. *Author's collection*

Born on February 9, 1913, in McCleary, Washington, Clarence Chesterfield Howerton was the third of five children. He was also the shortest, peaking at a Lilliputian twenty-eight inches. As a child, Clarence was protected by his family and never attended school, perhaps because of his physical and emotional fragility.

Little Clarence wouldn't be tucked away forever. He put his compact size to better use than hiding, by joining Ringling Bros. and Barnum & Bailey in 1923. He was only ten, but in typical circus fashion he was advertised as eighteen and given the name Major Mite. He soon bonded with the giant Jack Earle over games of penny-ante poker. The star midget's stint with Ringling would last nearly twenty years. During that time he also worked briefly with the Cole Bros. Circus and the Coney Island Dreamland Circus Side Show.

Major Mite may have been tiny, but he had a big mouth. He filled it with cigars and beer and often yelled obscenities. When feeling especially mean, it was said, he would run down the length of a bar, kicking anything in his way. At silent movies he would yell at others to read the captions; either he couldn't see over the seat in front of him or his lack of education had left him illiterate.

In 1938, Major Mite took a small break from the circus and headed off to Munchkinland. He was featured in *The Wizard of Oz* as Herald #3, announcing the arrival of the mayor.

By 1948, the Major was starring in his last circus. He retired at age thirty-five. Little is known about how he spent his remaining years, which were many. Major Mite lived until November 18, 1975, when he died of pneumonia in McMinnville, Oregon.

Born on October 18, 1932, in Wetumpka, Alabama, Pete Moore was more fragile than the average baby. He was afflicted with osteogenesis imperfecta, better known as brittle bone disease. The condition caused him to break sixty to seventy bones during childhood and left his legs curled beneath him, preventing him from walking. Pete attained a height of sixteen inches and a weight of thirty-two pounds. He had four brothers and four sisters, all normal.

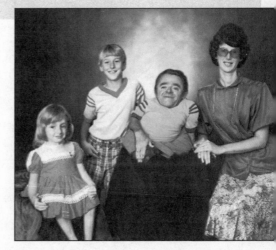

Pete Moore with his wife Adena, daughter Carol, and son John. *Courtesy Adena Baker*

Despite all this, young Pete was an accomplished child. When he might have been going through the terrible twos, Pete was inventing the skateboard instead. The innovative toddler asked his father to attach some metal skates to a board so he could scoot around on it. His genius would continue to flourish at home, since he was not allowed to attend school until the age of eleven. A pregnant teacher at the local school believed her baby would be cursed if she gazed on someone "different." Pete's father helped him study at home, and by the time he was allowed at school he was well advanced in his learning. He completed twelve grades in just nine years—with an A average. He learned to drive a car by using specially designed hand controls to work the pedals. He was involved in only one accident—a minor one, and caused by the other driver.

Once out of school, and after his mother's death, Moore worked to help support his family. He sold magazines, newspapers, and cigarettes on a corner in downtown

Wetumpka, and later was an inspector at a bottling plant. Then the sideshow came to town. The show had a sign advertising the "World's Smallest Man." Moore went inside and found himself dwarfed by the man supposedly shorter than he. The owner of the show saw the tiny twosome and asked Moore, "What are we doing? Multiplying?" He offered Moore a two-year contract.

After the contract expired, Moore realized he could work on his own. He ended up running his own tent show for twenty-eight years. In 1967, at a fair in Hamilton, Ohio, a tall, beautiful woman came to see the World's Smallest Man. Not only did Adena Snyder see an attraction, she felt one. As did he. "When I saw him, I saw a smile," she later recounted. "When I walked out, I couldn't get him out of my mind." So she went back, they spoke, and subsequently they corresponded. After about a year, and much grief from her family, Moore and Snyder were married. The couple had two children. The first, a son named John, was normal. The second, a daughter named Carol, was also born with osteogenesis imperfecta. Moore was able to provide treatment for her with the money he earned from the show. His success in the business enabled him to buy a home on fifty-six acres of land and provide quite well for his family.

In his early fifties, Moore fell victim to hereditary heart disease; he died in 1984, while on his way to a fair. His wife, now Adena Baker, described their interesting life together: "I think our fifteen years was packed more full than some people who were married fifty years."

RASMUS NIELSEN

Circa 1870–?

Born normal in the early 1870s, Rasmus Nielsen slowly transformed himself into a freak. In his youth, he worked as a blacksmith in a mining camp in Angels Camp, California. Rather than relax at the saloon each evening, Nielsen entertained himself by acquiring tattoos on nearly every inch of his body. Eventually he was shrouded from the

Rasmus Nielsen lifting an anvil, circa 1930s.
Collection of Bob Blackmar

neck down. Nielsen's flashy flesh featured a large Statue of Liberty on his back, sequoia trees adorning his legs, and numerous other designs.

With his skin serving as a personal art gallery, Nielsen left blacksmithing for show business. But he found he wasn't unique within the circus scene. Undeterred, he upped the ante to set himself apart. He had his nipples pierced and developed enough strength and elasticity to hoist heavy objects attached from those piercings.

Like other tattooed performers, Nielsen altered his history for the benefit of his audiences. His intense inking was blamed on savages in the South Seas. The depraved wild men hung him from trees by piercings through his chest. Nielsen escaped their evil clutches, but not before he had developed his magnificent nipple power. He could now stand before crowds and lift anvils said to be as heavy as 200 pounds. This was likely an exaggeration, and the larger anvils may have been made of aluminum. Nielsen also reportedly lifted a 115-pound rock attached to one nipple, ten-pound hammers from rings through his ears, and a twenty-five-pound mallet from his nose. Banners occasionally proclaimed him as the Scandinavian Strong Man, but among some in the industry, he was called "Tough Titty."

★ The *Chicago Tribune* called Captain Ringman Mack "the man who does not know the feeling of pain." The early-twentieth-century performer lifted weights from his pierced nipples and as a grand finale stuck a needle through his eye. No reports on whether he crossed his heart and hoped to die.

Nielsen was an attraction with Ringling Bros. and Barnum & Bailey for much of the 1930s and 1940s, working at an advanced age. The tattooed wonderman also revealed his nipple potency in Ripley's Believe It or Not! Odditorium at the 1939–1940 Golden Gate Exposition in San Francisco.

FRANCES O'CONNOR, THE LIVING VENUS DE MILO

1914–1982

Frances O'Connor. *Author's collection*

Frances O'Connor was born on September 8, 1914, on her grandmother's farm in Renville County, Minnesota. The young armless girl quickly learned to use her feet as substitutes and became adept at everyday tasks.

O'Connor was a natural sideshow attraction and soon joined the Al G. Barnes Circus in Wyoming. She later worked with Cole Bros., Sells-Floto, and Ringling Bros. and Barnum & Bailey in the 1920s through the 1940s. O'Connor was very close to her fully limbed mother, and made sure she always traveled with her.

In 1932, O'Connor's handy feet were featured in the movie *Freaks*. As in the film, her live performances demonstrated her astounding dexterity. She ate, drank, and sewed with ease. She could pull a cigarette from its pack, light it with a match, then puff away. O'Connor could even aim a rifle and pull the trigger. Such displays often required her to show a little more leg than was decent at the time, which may have drawn men to see Venus de Milo in action. The beautiful young woman with a sweet disposition reportedly turned down many marriage proposals.

When O'Connor's mother died, the era's most famous Armless Wonder felt too old to marry and retired to a life of relative obscurity. Frances O'Connor moved to California, where she died at the age of sixty-seven.

BARON PAUCCI
The smallest perfect man on earth, height 27 in.

Baron Paucci. *Author's collection*

BARON PAUCCI
1894–?

✴ **I**n the early 1900s, one of several fellows billed as the Smallest Man in the World was the twenty-seven-inch-tall, thirty-six-pound Baron Paucci. He hailed from Sicily, born as Peppino Magro. At the age of fifteen he was left buried under a pile of bricks and plaster after an earthquake, but he was dug out from the rubble—evidently saved by his small size. It would prove advantageous again in America, where it earned him a healthy living with the Ringling Bros. and Barnum & Bailey Circus and at Coney Island Dreamland.

Paucci spent much of the 1920s at Coney Island, where he was known to be a ladies man, with a big, multilingual mouth (obnoxious in four languages). The little man had little fear, once telling the press he would fight Jack Dempsey if the boxing champ would train down to his size. Unfortunately, Paucci's big talk was often foul and eventually led promoter Samuel Gumpertz to fire him.

The Baron rejoined the Ringling show, despite his having shot up to thirty-six inches. In 1931 the pint-size Casanova married five-foot-three-inch Mavis Lane, under the big top. Jealousy caused the romance to fade. "So many women would pick him up and exclaim he was cute," Lane once said. But there was enough love early on to produce a baby girl in April 1932. The marriage lasted at least another two years, for he could proudly inform the press: "I am one of the little people, but I got a big wife and a nice two-year-old daughter who will grow up like anybody, and a big house, and I can eat as you can. Maybe more."

JOHANN PETURSSON, THE VIKING GIANT
1913–1984

Born in Dalvík, Iceland, on February 9, 1913, Johann Petursson grew up to be one of the most gigantic giants. He reportedly stood eight feet, eight inches.

Petursson's career began in Europe. He performed in music halls, in an act with two midgets. His companions played miniature accordions while Petursson played a large one between them. This continued until World War II, when the music halls closed. During the conflict, Petursson found himself working in shipyards in Copenhagen.

After the war, John Ringling North discovered him and debuted him in the 1948 Ringling Bros. and Barnum & Bailey season. Petursson dressed formally, with a top hat and a Prince Edward–style coat. He earned $200 a week for allowing people to look up to him. A shrewd businessman, he started selling giant rings as souvenirs, something many giants did. Petursson's were so large you could pass a silver dollar through them.

Johann Petursson with an unidentified man, circa 1950. *Ward Hall collection*

He stayed with Ringling only briefly before joining a sideshow belonging to another promoter, Glen Porter. Porter and his wife developed the character that would ultimately become Petursson's trademark, the Viking Giant. Mrs. Porter created the costume, consisting of Viking regalia and a giant helmet. Petursson spent several seasons with the sideshow, until Porter went into the monkey speedway business.

Petursson branched out on his own in a Single-O show, which he ran out of a trailer. It earned him a sizable fortune—he saved up $50,000 after just five years in the country.

Petursson also exhibited his size on the big screen. In 1950 he played a nine-foot grunting prehistoric giant, Guadi, in the B movie *Prehistoric Women.* Thirty years later he appeared in *Carny,* starring Jodie Foster.

Petursson eventually retired to Gibsonton, Florida, where he was taller than the Giant's Camp's own giant, eight-foot-four-and-a-half-inch Al Tomaini. Like many retirees, Petursson found a passion for bingo. One cool night in January, while returning home from bingo, Petursson slipped outside his specially built van. The giant fell hard and couldn't get up. It wasn't until morning that a neighbor found him and helped him to a hospital. Petursson recovered partially, and returned to Iceland to live out the rest of his days. He died on November 26, 1984.

GIBSONTON, FLORIDA— FREAK CAPITAL OF THE WORLD

Movie stars have beautiful, sunny Beverly Hills. On the other side of the country, sideshow stars have sunny, swampy Gibsonton, Florida. In its heyday, you couldn't pass through the small town just south of Tampa along U.S. Highway 41 without noticing a few resident human oddities. Gibsonton, or Gibtown as it's affectionately called by its inhabitants, has been home to more freaks than perhaps any other place in the world. Sadly, only a few remain today.

It all started in the early 1920s. Carnival concessionaires Eddie and Grace LeMay happened to stop for a rest near the Alafia River. There wasn't much more than a dirt road at the time, but the LeMays soon met a handful of welcoming locals and decided to stay. Word traveled and soon other show folks were wintering in the hospitable town. Land was cheap and zoning laws allowing for "residential show business" made it convenient for trailers and carnival equipment.

In the late 1940s, Al and Jeanie Tomaini made their home in Gibtown. The giant Al decided to take advantage of the spectacular fishing in the Alafia and opened Giant's Camp right next to it, complete with a restaurant and cabins built by his own

Giant's Camp restaurant,
Gibsonton, Florida, 2003. © *Liz Steger*

enormous hands. The entrepreneur also founded the town's fire department and became its chief. In keeping with the character of the community, the police department was headed by a dwarf. Before long, carnies and freaks not only wintered in Gibtown, but retired there as well. Giants, little people, bearded ladies, fat men, fat ladies, and the Lobster Boy's family could stroll about free from other people's stares.

Many of the town's unusual residents have passed on. Yet colorful vending booths and trinket-filled carnival game concessions still appear in lots and yards. The Showtown Bar & Grill, with its ever-changing murals and painted illusions, is still popular among the locals. The International Independent Showmen's Association is headquartered just off the highway. Every February it hosts the International Independent Showmen's Foundation Trade Show & Extravaganza, which brings in about 6,000 circus and carnival operators and nearly doubles the town's population. The club houses a small museum, which is currently being expanded to a larger facility to showcase its many treasures properly.

Giant's Camp still stands, but the restaurant has changed ownership. The wonderful sideshow memorabilia has been removed, in favor of NASCAR decorations. The owners feared the reaction the former adornments might bring. Apparently, they don't know what town they're in.

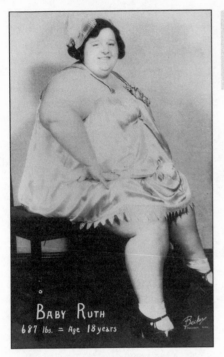

Baby Ruth Pontico, 1922. She appears to be seated on two chairs. *Johnny Fox's Freakatorium*

★ When Ruth Smith was born in Kempton, Indiana, she was well on her way to Fat Lady fame. Her mother, a circus Fat Lady, weighed 600 pounds on that February 8, 1904. Actually, she probably weighed a little less, after delivering the sixteen-pound baby. Ruth followed in her mother's heavy footsteps, weighing fifty pounds in her first year. By age ten, she had reached 300 pounds. She clearly hogged all the obesity genes for herself, as Ruth's one and only sister grew up to be a fashion model.

Young Ruth was content to be a fat lady, but not professionally. She had aspirations of being a businesswoman. Unfortunately, the first business she got into was a candy factory. Perhaps fate was giving her a message. The factory helped her earn enough money to go to secretarial school, but finding an office where she wouldn't be stared at or a chair that would hold her became a challenge for the new 400-pound Ruth.

She continued to gain weight, and the circus beckoned. Her first stage name was Ima Waddler. A lesser woman may not have endured the heckling provoked by such a name, but Ruth learned to handle it. It became even easier to handle with all the money she was earning, and she could afford all the food she wanted. Ruth even began to flaunt her sexuality, attracting many suitors.

Ima Waddler soon became known as Lady Beautiful, then finally settled on Baby Ruth, perhaps inspired by the many candy bars she must have eaten. In 1931 she joined the Ringling Bros. and Barnum & Bailey show. While exhibiting her girth in New York City, she met her husband, Joe Pontico. He was also fat, but not as fat as Ruth. Pontico saw her from across the room, as many could, and fell in love instantly. Ruth was equally attracted. Joe's passion for cooking made him quite alluring. The two married and had one daughter and many meals. Their home had reinforced floors.

Promotional photographs of Baby Ruth claimed that she weighed more than 700 pounds. For a time, that was an exaggeration, and Ruth didn't like it. So she determined to make honest men out of the promoters, by eating more. In 1934 typhoid fever set her back, causing her to lose 200 pounds. By the next year she had regained the lost weight, and was back in top exhibition form, over the 700-pound mark. While working with Royal American Shows she averaged 725. At her peak, Baby Ruth weighed 815 pounds. A New York journalist said that when she smiled, she "dimpled in fourteen places."

After the 1941 circus season, Baby Ruth discovered a tumor inside her left thigh. It was as large as a football, but benign. A first attempt at surgery failed because the operating table collapsed. Armed with a stronger table, doctors tried again. The procedure was successful, but the mammoth patient died in recovery, officially as a result of cardiac failure. A casket weighing 200 pounds was built to hold her body.

Baby Ruth was one of the fattest of the Fat Ladies, and proud of every pound. In the middle of the Depression, she was earning an astonishing $300 a day.

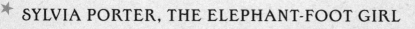

SYLVIA PORTER, THE ELEPHANT-FOOT GIRL
Born circa 1920s

Sylvia Porter was born in a shack in Mobile, Alabama, and her feet quickly outgrew the humble dwelling. The Elephant-Foot Girl, also known as the Woman with the Biggest Feet in the World, suffered from a form of elephantiasis that resulted in extremities estimated at about twenty-four inches long and twenty-four inches around the instep. The warm southern climate frequently saved her from the necessity of shoes, but when they were needed, Porter wore a size 60.

The Elephant-Foot Girl's career spanned from roughly the 1940s to the 1970s. Ward Hall remembers an instance in the winter of 1960 when the operator of Hubert's Museum wooed the Elephant-Foot Girl to New York City. Porter was hesitant because of the cold weather, but the operator convinced her she would be fine and booked her a hotel room a block from the museum. A week into the gig, as luck would have it, a heavy snowfall blanketed the city. Porter left immediately.

Aside from her feet, Porter was an attractive woman. A circus train porter named George Jackson appreciated her beauty from the ankles up and asked her to be his wife. She said yes.

The sideshow gave Porter the opportunity to travel and find her mate, and for this she was thankful. In Arthur Lewis's *Carnival,* she responded to those who opposed the exhibition of freaks by saying, "Where are they gonna send me? Back to the farm? No, thanks, I'd rather be dead."

Sylvia Porter under a sideshow tent, 1971.
Photo by Mac Bradley. Johnny Fox's Freakatorium

FRIEDA PUSHNIK,
THE ARMLESS, LEGLESS GIRL WONDER
1923–2000

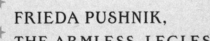

Frieda Pushnik was born without arms or legs, on February 10, 1923, in Conemaugh, Pennsylvania. Her condition was said to be the result of a botched appendectomy on her pregnant mother. Pushnik's family had little money and couldn't afford a wheelchair for her. Instead, they attached wobbly wheels to a high chair. She was carried to public school by her mother and carried home by her brother or sister. Young Frieda didn't concern herself with her lack of limbs. At an early age she learned to adapt and do as much with her stumps as possible. She was able to feed herself, sew, crochet, write, and type. She even earned an award for her penmanship.

In 1933, at age nine, Frieda appeared at Ripley's Believe It or Not! Odditorium at the Chicago World's Fair as the Armless, Legless Girl Wonder. She would sit on a plush pillow and introduce herself to the audience, then give a short demonstration of her abilities. Pushnik also was exhibited at the 1939 New York World's Fair. She performed with Ringling Bros. and Barnum & Bailey's sideshow from 1943 to 1955 (with a two-year break in the 1950s). Pushnik reached a weight of thirty-eight pounds as a full-grown adult.

After her exhibition years she moved to California. There she enjoyed her savings from the sideshow, cruising about in her

Autographed pitch card of Frieda Pushnik.
Author's collection

"Jaguar," a wheelchair she'd had upholstered with fake jaguar skin. She also appeared in the movies *House of the Damned* (1963) and *Side Show* (1981).

Pushnik died of bladder cancer on December 24, 2000, at age seventy-seven, in Costa Mesa, California.

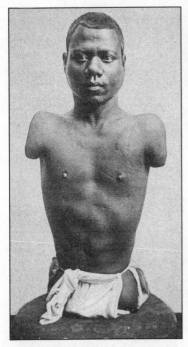

Prince Randian. *Author's collection*

PRINCE RANDIAN,
THE LIVING TORSO

1871–1934

Randian was born in 1871 in Demerara, British Guiana, completely limbless. He was brought to the United States by P. T. Barnum in 1889 and became known as the Living Torso. Randian's typical wardrobe consisted of a one-piece wool garment that looked somewhat like a potato sack. He appeared at Huber's 14th Street Museum and in carnivals, circuses, and dime museums—including a stint at Coney Island—for forty-five years.

The aggrandizing title of Prince and the Living Torso were only a few of the names used to advertise Randian through the years. He was known also as the Snake Man, the Human Worm, the Sausage Man, the Pillow Man, the Human Torso, and the Caterpillar Man—the last because of how he wiggled his hips and shoulders to move.

In addition to his live acts, Randian enjoyed a brief moment of stardom with his role in Tod Browning's 1932 movie *Freaks.* Though his one spoken line in the movie is practically indecipherable, he was said to speak Hindi, English, German, and French. *Freaks* did showcase his mouth's other impressive abilities: in one scene, he rolls a cigarette with his lips, then lights a match to smoke it. Randian even built the box he kept his smoking materials in. Among his other skills were painting, shaving, shooting marbles, and writing with his lips. He was also said to have quite a sense of humor, which may have been one of the qualities that helped him attract a wife. As a married man, Randian was able to make use of his one working appendage; he and his wife had five children.

Prince Randian and his family lived in Paterson, New Jersey, during the off-season. The Living Torso died in 1934 at the age of sixty-three, shortly after a performance.

LADY SANDRA REED *and* HAROLD SPOHN

Reed: Born 1945–

Spohn: 1936–1980

Best known as the Queen of Swords, Lady Sandra Reed originally joined the sideshow to lecture on her albinism, along with her equally pink sister, Doreen.

Born in 1945 near the Adirondacks in New York state, Reed didn't exhibit herself until 1969. In an interview for *James Taylor's Shocked and Amazed*, she described how she got her sideshow start by talking to showman Whitey Sutton at the New York State Fair. Sutton offered her a job, and Sandra became Lady Sandra. Her family proved very supportive. Doreen later joined the show, and their father sold tickets; their mother had worked in vaudeville and girl shows.

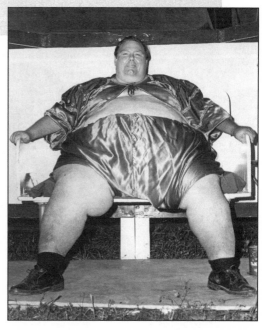

Harold Spohn. *Ward Hall collection*

Not only was Reed a performer in the show, but she became a fan as well. Like the thousands who attended the fairs, she was fascinated by the sword-swallowing routine. At the end of her inaugural season, she decided to learn the stunt herself. While wintering in Gibsonton, Florida, she diligently mastered the art under the guidance of a local swallower, Ricky Richiardi. The next season, she was set to continue her albino routine, until the show's resident sword swallower suffered a fall and was hospitalized. Reed stepped into the role and suddenly became a double attraction.

Lady Sandra's sword-swallowing prowess allowed her to travel across the country with Ringling Bros. and Barnum & Bailey, the Clyde Beatty–Cole Bros. Circus, Ward Hall and Chris Christ's sideshow, and other shows. In the late 1970s, she claimed a Guinness world record by swallowing five Japanese ceremonial dress swords at once.

While working with the Hall and Christ sideshow, Reed fell in love with its Fat Man, Harold "Big Jim" Spohn. Born in 1936 in Lancaster, Ohio, Spohn ran away from home at an early age to pursue a life in show business. He spent several years as a big clown before turning to professional wrestling under the alter ego of Happy Humphrey. His increasing weight eventually prompted his career change to the sideshow.

The albino sword swallower and the Fat Man married and lived happily together for several years. In April 1980, Spohn suffered a fatal heart attack, and afterward Lady Sandra left the sideshow and retired to Tampa. She didn't drive and claimed it was economically unfeasible to continue performing. It's likely that heartbreak was also a reason for her retirement. She received many offers to return to the stage, but she refused them all.

Lady Sandra was immortalized as a performer in a photograph by Diane Arbus, *Albino sword swallower at a carnival, Md. 1970.*

DOLLY REGAN, THE OSSIFIED GIRL
1919–1994

Dolly Regan was born in Saskatoon, Canada, in 1919 to a socially prominent family. Muscular dystrophy and ankylosis paralyzed her joints. At fourteen, she was four feet, one inch tall. As her body grew more stonelike, she shrank to three feet, nine inches.

Regan could neither stand nor walk. The few fingers she had command of allowed her to control an electric wheelchair. She was also able to hold a specially designed, multifunctional stick that helped her reach things, smoke, and poke people as needed.

In 1942, Regan was selling raffle tickets near a visiting sideshow. It was the first time she'd seen a sideshow, so she and a friend went to explore. A manager soon discovered her and offered her $50 to be his "stone lady." Though initially nervous about her new career, she adapted quickly. She was even asked out on her first date. It would be the first of many, and Regan eventually married three times (a juggler, a ride foreman, and a magician/sideshow manager). In the documentary *Being Different*, Regan claimed to have a good sex life.

Her career lasted for decades, and enjoyed a rejuvenation when showman Bobby Reynolds renamed her the Half Lady, Half Baby. "From the waistline up," he described her, "a perfectly normal, beautiful well-developed girl. But from the waistline down, she has the body of an infant!" Regan's new billing proved itself successful in her own Single-O show.

The Half Lady, Half Baby was still traveling with Ward Hall's sideshow in the 1970s. She wintered in Gibsonton, Florida, enjoyed being active in town, and was always happy to support herself. Her mind was sharp, and she never wanted to be confined because of her body's condition.

Dolly Regan died in 1994 at age seventy-five.

BOBBY REYNOLDS

Bobby Reynolds is the self-proclaimed Greatest Showman in the World. Along with fellow showman Ward Hall, he has been making an impact in the business for more than fifty years. "I wasn't waiting for the world to change, I changed it," he observes.

Reynolds was born in Jersey City, New Jersey, on October 5, 1932. He got his start in show business performing magic across the Hudson River at Hubert's Museum in New York City thirteen years later. The teenager used someone else's birth certificate to show he was sixteen years old and obtain a work permit. It proved to be the first trick in his reign as the World's Youngest Magician.

While at Hubert's, he learned to swallow swords from a master of the art, Alec Linton. Hidden away in the boiler room, where the smoke wouldn't bother anybody, Reynolds picked up fire eating from another master, Chief Woo-Foo. But his greatest skill was honed by pitching Professor Roy Heckler's flea circus. Reynolds recalls his first opening

(continued)

Bobby Reynolds at home with his dog and a two-headed baby, 2004. © *Liz Steger*

word for word: "Once every hour, ladies and gentlemen, Hubert's Museum proudly presents none other than Professor Heckler's trained flea circus. In this enclosure you're going to see dozens of real, live trained performing fleas. Fleas that juggle, jump through hoops, play football, tiny little fleas hitched to a chariot, they actually run a race. But the predominating feature of the entire show is little fleas dressed in costume dancing to the strains of music. It is without a doubt the most fascinating sight you'll ever see. Now, the Professor is on the inside, ready and waiting to give the performance. There will be no show out here on these stages until it is over. If you would like to go, there is a small admission. We do not apologize, it is only nine cents. Fleas that juggle, jump through hoops . . ."

In addition to the many human curiosities Reynolds met at Hubert's, he met a Hawaiian dancer who became his first wife. Just as he did in show business, he got an early start as a husband. Reynolds was only sixteen when he married the dancer—the first of ten wives.

After Hubert's, Reynolds headed to Coney Island, where as a child he had shined shoes and spent many nights sleeping under the boardwalk in a cardboard box. Although he had added the human blockhead, bed of nails, anatomical wonder, human pincushion, and knife-throwing routines to his repertoire, he preferred talking. "The people who got the most money were the talkers," Reynolds explains. "And when I became a talker I was afraid to swallow swords because I'd lose my voice." His mastery of the bally earned him as much as $600 a week in the 1950s. In 1964 and 1965, he worked on the Wonderland show at the New York World's Fair, raking in $150 a day.

The multitalented Reynolds also performed in nightclubs and theaters. He was often booked for his ventriloquism act when he was in his twenties. Later he traded his dummy in for a slightly more intelligent partner—a chicken. By attaching Scotch tape to the fowl's feet, Reynolds was able to have it tap-dance with him on the Palace Theatre stage. Over the decades, he worked with most of the great sideshow performers and owned several shows himself. Not all of his attractions were human oddities. He once exhibited Henry the Tattooed Dog, and he still has a Giant Killer Rat: "More feared than a sniper's bullet. Capable of shredding a man's arm off in thirty seconds." The fearsome rodent is actually a South American capybara. Dwarfing this "rat" was his Giant Bat, which weighed 500 pounds. Reynolds professed it was big enough to kill a horse. What he didn't tell the marks was that the deadly bat was of the baseball variety. "People laughed. It was so damn silly it was pitiful."

Bobby Reynolds with Henry the Tattooed Dog.
Collection of Bobby Reynolds

Until recently, the showman was traveling with his museum of curiosities, including, among the more amazing pieces, a two-headed baby preserved in a jar. Now "retired" at his ranch in California, Reynolds has hopes of opening a museum in Texas and would like to remake Tod Browning's *Freaks*. "I know where there's enough mutations to be able to do that," he claims.

GILBERT A. REICHERT

1912–?

★ Gilbert A. Reichert's career as a giant began as a thirteen-pound baby on November 9, 1912, in Cleveland. By adulthood he had skyrocketed to seven-foot-six, though like any giant, he was always billed as an eight-footer.

In 1936, the young Goliath put his height and 365 pounds to athletic use, playing center for an obscure basketball league (he was on the House of David team). Unfortunately for him, he was too early for the NBA.

Reichert's stature earned him a role as an eight-foot-four-inch giant for the Ringling Bros. and Barnum & Bailey show in the 1950s. His stint with the circus ended after the 1956 season—Ringling's last outdoor show under the big top.

Unemployed, Reichert returned home to Cleveland to find a new way to earn money. Too old for hoops and without a circus, the giant took a job suitable for a man of any height: shoe salesman. "Shoe selling is a little better than [circus] life," he once said. "You're home every night that way. Course it doesn't pay as well." Perhaps he also felt that if he could find size 29 shoes for himself, he could find a pair for anyone.

At his height, Reichert had little choice but to marry a woman he looked down on. His significant other was significantly shorter, at five-foot-two. In his biographical pamphlet sold at shows, a list of personal facts concluded with: "Sex life is normal." His four children were proof of that. The pamphlet also mentioned his fourteen-year-old son as already being six feet, three inches, apparently en route to following in his father's giant footsteps.

Schlitzie performs a magic trick.
Collection of Bob Blackmar

✶ SCHLITZIE
✶ *1892–1972*

✶ Schlitzie was born Simon Metz in 1892. It's been said that he and a sister, Athelia, were children of a wealthy family in Santa Fe, New Mexico, and that the two microcephalics had been hidden in the attic for several years. A sideshow operator adopted them, but then turned Schlitzie over to another promoter, George Surtees. Schlitzie would go on to be one of the most famous performers of the era, billed as Schlitzie the Monkey Girl, the Missing Link, and the Last of the Incas.

Except for the tip, Schlitzie's pinhead was shaved to emphasize his small skull. He was also exhibited as a she. This wasn't solely for showmanship. Rather, it was because he had to be diapered, and the muumuus he wore made it easier for his caretaker to change him. It was also because female attractions tended to do better at the box office. Schlitzie certainly wasn't one to complain. He didn't have the intelligence to carry on conversations. "He would gibber and didn't make much sense," Ward Hall observes. But he did parrot people. He would overhear a conversation and repeat it to someone else later. On-stage, Schlitzie charmed crowds with a magic act involving card tricks, a wand, and plenty of giggling.

Surtees died in the 1960s, and his daughter took Schlitzie to an institution in Los Angeles. Fortunately for him, a sword swallower by the name of Bill Unks was working in the hospital as an orderly and discovered Schlitzie in the waiting room. He summoned a promoter, Sam Alexander (also known as the Man with Two Faces), who came immediately. A psychiatric evaluation by the hospital concluded that Schlitzie wouldn't live six months under institutionalization. He needed the affection and adoration of the sideshow people and the audience. The State of California named Alexander to be Schlitzie's guardian.

They toured together for several years, until Schlitzie grew too old. He retired with a nurse to an apartment in Los Angeles, near a park, where he would often sit and enjoy the attention of neighborhood visitors. Schlitzie died at age eighty.

Schlitzie also entertained on the big screen. He was one of the stars of *Freaks* (1932); he appeared in *Meet Boston Blackie* (1941); and in *Tomorrow's Children* (1934), Schlitzie wore a full head of hair, moustache, and beard.

SEALO THE SEAL BOY
1903–1980

Before becoming Sealo the Seal Boy, Stanley Berent was a devout Catholic growing up in Pittsburgh. He was born in 1903 with phocomelia, which may have been a genetic

Sealo, circa 1940.
Collection of Bob Blackmar

condition or the result of a thalidomide drug his mother used during pregnancy. The affliction left him with no arms, only hands, like a seal's flippers. A showman is said to have discovered Stanley selling papers on a street corner. He ended the boy's days of hawking the news and put him in the sideshow.

Sealo loved performing. Onstage he demonstrated his abilities with his armless hands, which, according to the promotional cards he sold, often involved shaving. Sealo appeared with every major sideshow, including Ringling Bros. and Barnum & Bailey, Clyde Beatty, Cole Bros., Coney Island Dreamland, and Hubert's Museum in New York.

Those who worked with him found him a pleasure to be around—he always had a smile on his face. Even a chimpanzee enjoyed his company. One season, while working with Ward Hall and Chris Christ, Sealo befriended a great ape in the show. During one of the chimp's performances, three inebriated men began annoying the Seal Boy. The chimp saw this and threw his chair at the aggressors. No one was going to mess with his friend. Sealo also loved to play cards; he spent many years with the promoter Pete Kortes, whose show was known to have a backstage card game going all day.

While Sealo loved what he was doing, some people felt he was being exploited and wanted to save him. Don Driver, a magician and escape artist who worked with him, remembered Sealo's reaction: "Save me from what? If I wanted to, I could have lit cigars from five-dollar bills." It was a luxury he couldn't have afforded in an institution.

Sealo knew he had a right to perform and even fought for freaks' rights in the state of Florida. A 1921 law prohibited the exhibition of any malformed, deformed, or disfigured human, but no one had enforced it or even seemed to know about it. In 1972, Ward Hall saw an article about the law in a Florida newspaper. Along with Sealo and Pete Terhurne, a dwarf, he set out to have it overturned. After all, Florida was where many of the freaks lived and paid their taxes. They sued the state, and the law was rescinded. "One who is handicapped or in an unfortunate position because of physical handicaps or deformities, in no wise of his own choosing, must be allowed a reasonable chance within his capacities to earn a livelihood," the court ruled.

Sealo retired in 1976 and lived in Gibsonton. When he became ill, he checked into a Catholic hospital back in his hometown of Pittsburgh. He died there in 1980, at the age of seventy-seven.

SERPENTINA

1908–?

Serpentina, circa 1920s. *Author's collection*

While many sideshow attractions were subject to exaggeration, Serpentina's billing as "Nature's Strangest Living Enigma" was hardly an embellishment. The Serpent Lady from Oakland, California, was born with no bones in her body, except for her skull and a few in her arms. As such, she depended completely on the help of others for the simplest of tasks. A baby carriage was used to move her about, and her exercise was limited to having someone reposition her limbs. Had she been able to stand up, she may have measured somewhere between three and four feet. Surprisingly, Serpentina maintained good health and a positive outlook.

Hailed as the Eighth Wonder of the World, Serpentina's boneless body was exhibited at Coney Island and with various traveling shows. At Coney Island, she often worked the blow-off. For an extra fee, spectators stared at her sitting onstage with her legs tucked into a scaly stocking and her head propped up by a hand. Serpentina's snakelike flexibility was demonstrated by tying her limbs in knots.

Advertisements for the Traveling Mammoth Marine Hippodrome Show in the late 1930s called Serpentina the "sensational siren of the Seven Seas" and "nature's closest approach to a living mermaid." Illustrations portrayed her as the mythical creature, with scales over her legs and a tail instead of feet. A journalist added to the mystery: "Serpentina is one of life's tragedies and it will be up to the public to decide whether she is a fish or a human being."

According to her souvenir pamphlet, her bizarre condition had been diagnosed by a physician as "arrested ossification." Essentially, her cartilage never turned to bone, and she was left largely with that cartilage, like a shark. Or more exotically, like a mermaid. The doctor blamed the predicament on "a lack of developing power of the mother, probably due to over work before the child was born." The reasoning seems to lack the plausibility of the diagnosis. Of course, the pamphlet also described Serpentina as the "despair of doctors and the puzzle of scientists."

Though literally spineless, figuratively she was not. Serpentina triumphed over her physical plight and earned a fortune from it. She put her money into diamonds and filled her fingers with rings by the end of her career.

KITTY SMITH
Circa 1883–?

Unlike most Armless Wonders, Kitty Smith was not born as one. She was born healthy in Chicago. Her mother died when Kitty was still young, leaving her alone with her father. According to a booklet sold by Smith, "Story of My Life," she lost her arms at the age of nine after an unfortunate domestic accident. The girl stumbled across a bottle of whiskey at home and intoxicated herself. Her father, unaware, shouted from another room for her to put more wood in the kitchen fire. In her drunken stupor, Kitty fell upon the hot stove. By the time her father found her, her arms had burned off. Or so the story went.

Smith spent time recuperating in the hospital and at the Home for Destitute Crippled Children in Chicago. She quickly learned to use her feet as freely as she would have used her hands. She could write, draw, embroider, brush her teeth, and comb her hair.

Whatever the booklet's explanation, an 1892 newspaper article presents a more grue-some account of how she lost her arms. The report claimed that it wasn't little Kitty who was drunk, it was her father. In the winter of 1891, he demanded a meal from his eight-year-old daughter. When she failed to cook, he punished her by holding her hands on the red-hot stove. Kitty's burns were so bad that her arms had to be amputated. During a sub-sequent court hearing, the young amputee apparently forgave her cruel father. Perhaps it was this forgiveness that prompted Smith to alter the story for her pamphlet. Or maybe the sheer cruelty of the act made it too difficult to share with the public.

As early as 1905, Smith was capitalizing on her tragedy with the Kitty Smith Company in South Whitley, Indiana. Backed by an investor/manager, Frank Miner, and with the help of a small staff, she mailed out 22,000 pamphlets a month, across the country. Each booklet had a return card with a slot for a quarter. By 1906, the company was earn-ing $1,625 a week—on pace to reach more than $80,000 within a year. Americans were paying the armless girl considerably more than they paid Theodore Roosevelt to lead the nation. A year later, Smith enrolled at Taylor University in Indiana in search of a higher education. She hoped to be a financial secretary at the National Children's Home, an in-stitution that helped crippled youngsters.

Although Smith made a fortune with her booklet business, she later exhibited herself as an Armless Wonder with Ringling Bros. and Barnum & Bailey, the John Robinson Cir-cus, and other shows during the 1930s.

ELVIRA *and* JENNY LEE SNOW

Elvira: 1900–?

Jenny Lee: 1912–?

In 1929, Coney Island's sideshow impresario Sam Wagner presented two pinheads billed as Pipo and Zipo. The microcephalics were sisters, Jenny Lee and Elvira Snow, from Georgia. Elvira (Zipo) was born in 1900, and at forty had the mental equivalency of a five-year-old. Jenny Lee (Pipo), twelve years younger, wasn't nearly as intelligent. She achieved the brainpower of an eighteen-month-old.

Also called Pip and Flip, the sisters filled the pinhead void left by the death of Zip, the What Is It? Perhaps their names were meant as a tribute to their famous predecessor, or as an attempt to capitalize on his name's popularity. Like Zip, they had shaved heads, except for a patch at the tip, to accentuate the small size. The Snow sisters became one of Coney Island's greatest attractions during the Depression and after. They were paid $75 a week. "Life is pretty nice for them," Wagner once told a newspaper. "They spend their winters in Georgia at home and have all the money they need. They have nothing to worry about and, I suppose you could say, nothing to worry with."

Jenny Lee and Elvira Snow were featured in the 1932 movie *Freaks*, alongside fellow microcephalic Schlitzie.

GRADY STILES, JR.
1937–1992

Ectrodactyly, hereditary in the Stiles family, was passed along to a new generation with the birth of Grady Jr. in 1937 in Pittsburgh. The gene, which had run in the family since at least 1840, caused the baby's fingers as well as his toes to merge together, creating the appearance of claws at his hands and feet. His legs were stunted below his knees. Grady's family had been in the carnival for years, and he would make his sideshow debut as the Lobster Boy at the tender age of seven. He eventually operated his own 10-in-1 show, accompanied by an oddity museum and a Single-O show in which he starred. The Lobster Boy enjoyed his sideshow life, once saying, "If I'm not doing this, I'm appearing at universities and hospitals and they're giving lectures on me. At least out here they're not poking me."

In 1959, Stiles met and fell in love with (Mary) Teresa Herzog. They settled in a Gibsonton, Florida, trailer park. While his career was in the sideshows, his life at home would also prove to be a circus.

The Lobster Boy grew quite strong, having to use his upper body to compensate for his nearly useless legs. He was able to crawl about on his arms and do most anything with his claws. Too often, unfortunately, Stiles used them to drink alcohol and physically abuse his wife. Despite these problems, the couple had three children together. Only one daughter, Cathy, was born with electrodactyly. She was affected in the same manner as her father.

Grady Stiles, Jr., circa 1940s.
Kobel collection

Eventually Teresa moved away from her crustaceanlike husband. She took her children to live with a friend in Ohio, Harry Glenn Newman, also known as the Midget Man. Tall, dark, and handsome was evidently not a big priority for her. Teresa and Newman soon had a son, Harry Glenn Jr., called Glenn. Meanwhile, Stiles had filed for divorce without Teresa's knowledge, and he gained custody of the children. He found another woman to marry, Barbara Browning Lucille, who bore him a son, Little Grady, who also had the lobster syndrome.

Stiles's rage wasn't reserved for his wife and kids. When his daughter Donna attempted to elope, Stiles disapproved. Aiming with his lobster claw, he shot and killed her fiancé. The Lobster Boy went to trial, but astonishingly didn't serve a day in prison. The court claimed there was no handicapped access in the prison, and that a jail sentence might constitute cruel and unusual punishment for him. He was freed on probation.

In spite of all the Lobster Boy's faults, Teresa was still in love with him. She left Newman and rekindled her relationship with Stiles. The two continued to live in Gibsonton.

But Stiles hadn't changed; the abuse and the drinking went on. So much so that Teresa finally snapped. She wanted her husband dead before he wound up killing her. She enlisted Glenn, her son, to help, and he hired a friend and neighbor, Chris Wyant, to do the job. On the night of November 29, 1992, Wyant earned his $1,500, shooting Stiles in his trailer. Teresa, Glenn, and Wyant were prosecuted and convicted for the murder.

Teresa served only a few years of her sentence and is now happily retired, though on probation. Cathy has been married for fifteen years and has a fourteen-year-old daughter representing yet another generation with ectrodactyly. Cathy, who as a girl sat onstage with her father, now works at a pet store and has appeared in HBO's *Carnivàle*, and in Tim Burton's *Big Fish* and a few other small films. As for the past, the family tries to leave it behind. "The only positive thing I could ever say about him [Stiles] was that he had a good mind for business," Cathy has commented.

Grady Stiles's tragic life is the subject of a biography by Fred Rosen, *Lobster Boy*.

SUSI THE ELEPHANT-SKIN GIRL
1904–?

Although ichthyosis derives its name from the Greek term for "fish," those afflicted with the disease are usually referred to as Alligator Men or Women in the sideshow. In Susi's case, the skin disorder earned her the title of the Elephant-Skin Girl.

Susi was born Charlotte Vogel in Germany. In childhood an extreme case of ichthyosis caused her skin to grow thick, rough, and discolored like that of an elephant. Generous applications of oil helped prevent it from excessive cracking. Unable to perspire or even tear, she rubbed ice on her body during the summer to avoid overheating. Even blinking posed a problem, as she could rest her eyes only by closing her lids with her fingers. Vogel peeled the dry skin off her face nightly, allowing at least that part of her to appear normal, temporarily.

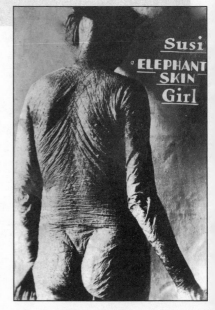

Susi the Elephant-Skin Girl, from the back. *Author's collection*

As Susi the Elephant-Skin Girl, she exhibited her pachyderm hide at Coney Island and Hubert's Museum in New York City, and in a variety of sideshows from the 1930s through the 1960s. She lived in a New York apartment with her manager, who as a side-line sold church pews. Perhaps it was his small way of getting more people to pray for his attraction's well-being.

After her manager died, Vogel retired the Susi name. Through her career, the Elephant-Skin Girl often kept to herself. While she did not complain about her coarse skin, her feelings were expressed in the pitch card her manager wrote and sold: "She is happy and contented but advised not to marry. She hopes by showing her strange body to you to prove that life is still worth living." Indeed, many spectators left her shows comforted by the fact that no matter what problems they faced, at least they did not have skin like an elephant's.

JIM TARVER, THE TEXAS GIANT

1885–1958

James Grover Tarver was born in September 1885 in Franklin, Texas. An abnormal growth spurt shot him up to a reported eight feet, four inches and 435 pounds (some accounts claim eight-six and 460). He was so big that when he occasionally rode into town on a mule, his feet dragged against the ground. Once cars were invented (much to the relief of his mules), Tarver would lean over the roof of a vehicle to open the door on the other side. Though these stunts were impressive, they didn't lead to a normal job, so he used them in the circus.

Tarver's career as a circus giant lasted

Jim Tarver, circa 1920. *Author's collection*

from 1909 to 1935. During that run he worked with the Forepaugh-Sells, Ringling Bros. and Barnum & Bailey, Sells-Floto, and Hagenbeck-Wallace shows. He was billed as the Texas Giant and, of course, the Tallest Man in the World. Tarver often told audiences, "I was a cowboy until I got bigger than the pony."

During his stint with Ringling, he learned that he wasn't actually the world's tallest man. An even taller man, Jack Earle, attended a show in Texas and proved to be the new Texas Giant. He took over the title of World's Tallest Man and subsequently traveled with Ringling. Tarver and Earle were also both giants in separate film productions of *Jack and the Beanstalk*, with Tarver playing the role of Blunderbore in the 1917 version.

Like children and grown men, but perhaps for their own reasons, women flocked to Tarver. He married several times. One wife died; another marriage ended in divorce. Perhaps the latter wife found it difficult living with his custom-made oversize furniture.

Tarver retired from the circus—and from Texas—to take up farming in Turrell, Arkansas. This career lasted nearly as long as his days as a performer. Tarver spent twenty-three years on the farm before dying in his home on January 21, 1958. He was seventy-two.

The former Texas Giant hasn't been forgotten by locals. A store in Gilmore, just north of Turrell, placed a marking eight feet, six inches up on a post to commemorate his height.

PETE TERHURNE
Born 1930

Norbert Terhurne was born in Breckenridge, Minnesota. Twenty-four years later, the four-foot-one dwarf joined the sideshow, dropped the Norbert, and became Little Pete, or Poobah (taken from Gilbert and Sullivan's *The Mikado*). His names haven't changed since.

Terhurne's career began when Ward Hall's sideshow was playing his hometown fair in 1954. A woman in the show noticed the little man, and Hall arranged for him to become part of the production. Terhurne was put in clown makeup so the locals wouldn't recognize him, but the plan failed. He stayed with the show regardless. Although Little Pete was happy, his mother was not. She didn't want her son traveling with the sideshow, and repeatedly instructed him to return home. He didn't want to, and he never did. Terhurne finally retired in 2003.

In his many years in the business, Little Pete became quite the versatile dwarf. Having no particular skills in the beginning, he ultimately became an accomplished clown, juggler, snake handler, and fire eater. He also entertained audiences with his "iron tongue," from which a hook helped him lift dangling weights. The daring dwarf even served as a knife thrower's target, weathering just a few minor cuts. In 1963 the multitalented Terhurne put his entire arsenal to work in the Pygmy Village. Ward Hall and his partner at the time, Harry Leonard, developed the venue, which promised six acts inside. The leopardskin-clad Terhurne turned out to be the only "Pygmy" and performed all six acts.

In addition to working with Hall, Little Pete spent six years clowning for Ringling Bros. and Barnum & Bailey at Madison Square Garden shows. Out from under the tent, Terhurne enjoyed success on bigger stages. In the early 1960s he played Puss in Boots in three Santa Claus films and in 1980 he found himself looking up to Jodie Foster and Gary Busey in the movie *Carny*.

Having settled in Gibsonton, Florida, Little Pete now prefers eating grilled cheese sandwiches rather than fire. According to Hall, even though he's enjoying retirement, Terhurne still asks every day, "Have I got a booking yet?"

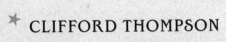

CLIFFORD THOMPSON
1904–1955

Known as the Scandinavian Giant, Clifford Thompson was indeed from Scandinavia. Scandinavia, Wisconsin, that is. He weighed in at twelve pounds when he was born in Waupaca County, on October 18, 1904. In time he became the tallest man in town—and perhaps the world. It wasn't until he graduated from college with a bachelor's in

Weight 460 Lbs.
Height 8 ft. 6 in.
—
Born
October 18, 1904
Oslo, Norway

CLIFF THOMPSON

Clifford Thompson demonstrating his height.
Author's collection

education that Thompson decided to profit from his unusual height.

He spent twelve years as the Tallest Man on Earth, showing off his size 22 shoes, size 10 hats, and oversize everything else. Besides the Scandinavian Giant, he appeared as Count Olaf. Under this name, Thompson was said to have come from Norway, a direct descendant of a Viking, Olaf Sigurdsson.

Thompson kept growing taller until the age of twenty-seven, with some reports claiming he reached eight feet, seven inches. Once he stopped getting taller, he got thicker. In three years he gained 100 pounds and tipped the scales at 460. A typical meal for him consisted of three pounds of steak, three large baked potatoes, three dishes of vegetables, a quart of milk, and one apple pie.

The giant didn't limit his audience to circus gawkers. In 1937 he expanded his fan base to include the pro wrestling crowd. He was billed not as an exotic Norwegian, but as the more American "Wisconsin Paul Bunyan."

In 1939, Thompson married a former circus dancer, Mary Mars, whom he'd met while they performed in the same show. Mars stood only five feet, five inches.

The newlyweds did not return to the circus. Rather than represent Earth as its tallest citizen, Thompson worked as a salesman at Blatz Brewing Company in Wisconsin for four years. Having peddled enough beer, he aspired to help people in a different way. He enrolled in Marquette University's law program and earned his degree in 1944, then worked as a practicing attorney in Iola, Wisconsin, and in Los Angeles and Portland, Oregon. While there is no official record for the world's tallest lawyer, Thompson most likely holds the title.

Clifford Thompson died on October 12, 1955. His widow said that gallstones and a liver ailment were to blame, and that his height did not contribute to his illness.

AL *and* JEANIE TOMAINI

Al: 1912–1962

Jeanie: 1916–1999

Al and Jeanie Tomaini, with Baby Ruth Pontico seated in the back. *The Tomaini Collection*

Although they weren't the only pair touted as the World's Strangest Married Couple, the title fit them especially well. Jeanie was born without legs, and measured two feet, six inches as an adult, while Al had legs long enough for the both of them, standing eight feet, four and a half inches.

Jeanie was born Bernice Smith on August 23, 1916, in Bluffton, Indiana. One of seven children, she began to perform locally at age three, walking on her hands, climbing ladders, and doing other ordinary things extraordinarily without legs. When she was thirteen, her mother died. Her father had left the family years earlier, but returned with his girlfriend after the funeral. They cared for Bernice and her siblings, until one day her father left again. The girlfriend continued caring for the children, but soon they were placed in an orphanage. A woman named Lizzie Weeks discovered Bernice there and adopted her, perhaps sensing the fortune to be made exhibiting her on the road. When not performing, Weeks would keep her hidden, so as not to "ruin people's appetites," as Bernice once said. Weeks decided to call her star Genie, and had a banner painted with her new name. The sign artist misspelled it, and Genie became Jeanie.

Aurelio "Al" Tomaini was born in Long Branch, New Jersey, on February 25, 1912. He weighed fifteen pounds. Al too was one of seven children. By age twelve he was more than six feet tall. Doctors attributed the rapid growth to an overactive pituitary gland, and his concerned parents eventually had the doctors remove the gland. The surgery was suc-

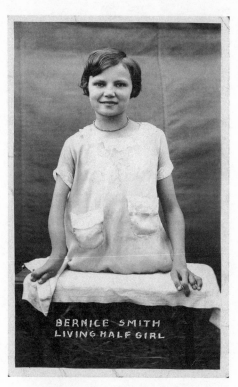

Postcard of Jeanie Tomaini as a child,
circa 1920s. *Author's collection*

cessful, but Al had already reached an enormous height.

Al and Jeanie met when their separate shows chanced upon each other in the same town. They quickly fell in love. An opportunistic Lizzie Weeks thought she had two meal tickets, but big Al wouldn't stand for it. Six months later, on September 28, 1936, the couple eloped, believe it or not, in Ripley, New York. Lizzie Weeks was left behind. The Tomainis went on to work with Ringling Bros. and later ran their own sideshow.

After wintering in New Jersey with Al's family, Jeanie put her proverbial foot down and asked whether Al wanted to be married to his brothers or to her. Their next winter was in Florida—their first of many.

In 1946 the couple adopted a daughter, Judy. They retired in 1950 from performing and settled down to raise their daughters; in 1954 they adopted a second child, who would later go to live with her biological family. Now living in Gibsonton, Florida, Al and Jeanie opened a restaurant and fishing camp alongside the Alafia River. They weren't sure what to call the place, but Al's friend Francesco Lentini (the Three-Legged Wonder) suggested an obvious name: Giant's Camp. The name stuck, and the place is still there today. Al organized Gibsonton's first fire department and served as its chief. Following the Tomainis' lead, many sideshow performers began wintering and settling in Gibsonton.

Jeanie never worried much about people staring at her. And people did stare. She went about life normally. She would often dine out with her armless friend, Frances O'Connor. "[Everybody would be] staring at Mother when they walked in, because Frances would be wearing a cape," daughter Judy Rock recalls. "They would sit at the table and everybody would be checking Mother out and Frances [would be] sitting there eating with her feet and they didn't even notice."

Al died on August 30, 1962. Jeanie operated Giant's Camp for decades more. She lived there until her death, on August 10, 1999, just weeks before her eighty-third birthday.

Judy Rock never thought anything unusual about her unique parents. "Our home life was wonderful," she remembers. "It was what everybody wishes theirs was: no talk of divorce, no big fights, no drinking, no smoking. Just a family."

VIOLETTA, THE TRUNK WOMAN

1907–?

Violetta, the Trunk Woman, seated elegantly on a pedestal at the World Museum, Los Angeles, circa 1926. *Johnny Fox's Freakatorium*

Having not a single arm, leg, or stump, Violetta was known as the Trunk Woman and the Human Torso. She was born Aloisia Wagner in Germany in 1907, and came to America in April 1924 to exhibit herself at Coney Island Dreamland. The Limbless Wonder also performed with Ringling Bros. and Barnum & Bailey.

Violetta was exhibited on a velvet-topped stand. She had a beautiful face, styled hair, and a chic wardrobe covering her svelte three-foot body. Aside from beauty, she had talent. Violetta performed simple tasks with her mouth, using her tongue and lips in place of her missing limbs in remarkable fashion. In

1940, *London Life* magazine printed an account of a performance in which she lit a cigarette and smoked it, drew cartoons with a pencil in her mouth, washed herself with a sponge, and even threaded a needle and sewed. Of course, she also used her mouth to speak and sing. Violetta hopped about on her torso and bowed to the audience at the end of the show. The lecturer joked about how economical a wife she would be, as any husband would save a bundle by not having to buy shoes, gloves, pants, or anything with sleeves for her. What the lecturer did not reveal was that Violetta was indeed married, and had such a lucky husband. The limbless beauty, who was accompanied by a nurse during her act, was said to be happy and content with her condition.

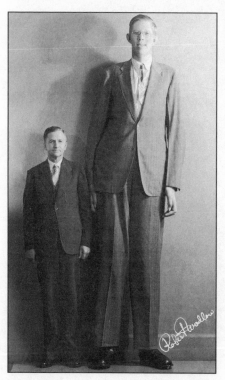

Robert Wadlow with an unidentified man, possibly his father, circa 1930s. *Author's collection*

ROBERT WADLOW
1918–1940

★ **O**f all the circus giants, Robert Pershing Wadlow was the only one who had absolutely no need to exaggerate his height. Wadlow topped them all. During his one brief stint with the Ringling Bros. and Barnum & Bailey show in 1937, he stood eight feet, seven inches tall. And he wasn't done growing. Classified as an acromegalic case, the "Gentleman Giant" continued to shoot skyward until his premature death, reaching an astonishing eight feet, eleven and a half inches and 491 pounds.

Weighing nine pounds at birth, on February 22, 1918, in Alton, Illinois, Robert appeared normal enough. An overactive pituitary gland would change that. He quickly grew into a big baby, weighing 62 pounds by his sixth month. At five years old he was already five feet, four inches tall and weighed 105 pounds. Within four years he could carry his 150-pound father around like a puppy. By age thirteen he was easily the world's tallest teenager, at seven feet, four inches.

The giant youngster kept busy with more than just growing. Wadlow became the Boy Scouts' tallest member in 1931, requiring fourteen yards of material to make his uniform. A year later, at seven-

⭐ Francisco Sandoval Ríos left Central America to exhibit his colossal feet at state fairs. Of his 180 pounds, thirty of them were attributed to one of his feet.

foot-five, he started playing high school basketball. He enjoyed photography and was an above-average student. In 1936 he graduated from high school and began attending Shurtleff College on a scholarship. He hoped to enter the legal profession.

At first, Wadlow's father refused to let his son be exhibited. But by 1937 he had changed his mind, and Wadlow signed a short-term contract with Ringling. He was never with the sideshow, however. He insisted his appearance be dignified, and therefore wore a suit and appeared only in the center ring.

His short circus career was followed by public appearances for the International Shoe Company. The colossal spokesman promoted the business in forty-one states and received custom-made size 37AA shoes for free. Other stores hired him for publicity stunts. An advertisement for a midwestern shop called Gately's promised a $7.98 electric clock lamp to every customer Wadlow greeted: "Let the World's Biggest Boy give you the biggest free gift we've ever offered!" the ad proclaimed.

In July 1940, Wadlow was making an appearance at the National Forest Festival in Manistee, Michigan, sponsored by his shoe company. Although the shoemakers were thrilled with his large feet, Wadlow was not; they had often been a source of trouble. A blister formed under a leg brace during the festival, and infection set in. Local hospitals were unable to accommodate him properly, and the infection lingered and worsened. Wadlow developed a fever of 106 degrees. Doctors performed minor surgery and gave him a blood transfusion, but it was to no avail. Robert Wadlow died on July 15. A coffin ten feet, nine inches long was needed to bury him.

Today, Wadlow still holds his spot in the *Guinness Book of World Records* as the tallest man recorded in history. His hometown of Alton erected a life-size bronze statue in 1985 to memorialize its beloved giant.

Fred Walters, the Blue Man.
Johnny Fox's Freakatorium

★ **L**ong before the Smurfs were animated and the Blue Man Group started painting their faces, blue men populated the sideshows. These colorful characters suffered from a disease called argyria, which results from prolonged contact to or ingestion of silver salts. This stains the skin a gray or bluish color.

The English-born Fred Walters was one of these blue men. Walters was in the British army, serving as captain of the Seventeenth Lancers. He came to the United States in 1891 and exhibited himself in various dime museums and sideshows, including Barnum & Bailey, Huber's 14th Street Museum, and Coney Island in the 1920s.

Walters used silver nitrate to treat his locomotor ataxia, a progressive degeneration of the nervous system that affects muscular coordination. The treatment resulted in his argyria. Walters realized that the more silver he ingested, the deeper blue his pigment became. And the bluer the blue man became, the more profitable his act would be.

In August 20, 1923, Walters reached his final shade of blue, succumbing to heart trouble in Brooklyn. Doctors who performed an autopsy were shocked to discover the amount of silver poisoning in his body, declaring it "the most remarkable case of its kind" ever brought to their attention. Walters left behind a wife and a six-year-old daughter. Neither was blue, except perhaps emotionally.

Another theory on Walters's blue condition was reported in 1922, in an article in *Illustrated World*. During his military days in India, Captain Walters had been injured when a horse fell on him. He spent four months in a hospital and began to turn blue after his recovery. It's possible that the accident caused the ataxia. The article's author claimed that the injury disrupted an opening in his heart, resulting in cyanosis, a condition in which oxygen flow through the blood is impaired. It often affects newborns and is the reason for the term "blue baby," used for infants with congenital heart disease. But these babies generally don't grow into Blue Men or Women.

JOAN WHISNANT

1924–?

Joan Whisnant attends to her baby with her foot. *Collection of Bob Blackmar*

Despite Joan Whisnant's apparent handicap, her parents refused to believe their daughter would be a helpless girl. Joan was born without arms in Oklahoma in 1924. Instead, her parents taught her to use her feet as hands. By age four she was holding a pencil between her toes and making marks. At six, she could write, eat from her plate with a knife and fork, drink from a glass, cut paper dolls, embroider, and do just about anything else a child her age needed to do.

The armless girl went to a normal school and sat at a special desk where she could raise her foot with ease. She had no trouble keeping pace with her schoolmates. In addition to regular classes, Whisnant took up guitar lessons and with years of practice developed into a talented musician. She continued her academic education through a correspondence course at the University of Oklahoma, studying music, history, and English. Her extraordinary musical ability soon led to a job, though it was her very lack of arms that landed her the position. After all, her employer was Ripley's Believe It or Not! Odditorium.

By the late 1940s, Whisnant was busy not only strumming tunes with Ripley's or at state fairs; she was starting a family. She married, and had a baby in 1947. Fortunately for both, her dexterous feet had no difficulties changing diapers.

Betty Lou Williams at a Ripley's Believe It or Not! Odditorium, 1934. *Author's collection*

★ Born on January 10, 1932, in Albany, Georgia, Williams was the fourth of thirteen children. She was a beautiful girl, normal except for the miniature twin growing out of the left side of her body. The twin's body was formed from the waist down and had two legs and an arm.

At the age of three, Williams was performing with Ripley's Believe It or Not! Odditorium. According to a Ripley's pamphlet, X-rays revealed a perfectly developed head inside her chest. Despite the extra body, Williams moved about with ease like a single-bodied person. When she was in public she wore maternity dresses to walk about with her twin unnoticed.

Williams's parasitic sister helped her earn a handsome living—nearly $1,000 a week during her heyday. She worked with Royal American Shows and was said to be the highest-paid human oddity ever. Showman Dick Best, who employed her, once said: "Betty Lou Williams was not only one of the greatest freaks ever born, she was one of the finest, most generous persons I ever knew." Williams put her eleven siblings through college and purchased a 260-acre farm for her parents. Such generosity came to a premature end when she died at her Trenton, New Jersey, home from an asthma attack. She was only twenty-two.

THE KNOTTY MEN

Throughout its history, the sideshow business has been peppered with several Knotty Men. They earned the descriptive name courtesy of a disease, neurofibromatosis, that covered their bodies with lumpy, benign tumors under the skin. The condition either is inherited or results from a spontaneous mutation. The first signs may not appear until puberty.

The most famous Knotty Man worked for Dick Best on Royal American Shows in the 1940s and the Kraft shows in 1947, and made appearances at Hubert's Museum in New York City. He was better known as Knotty Knot. Hundreds of lumps—gumball to golf ball size—punctuated his body from head to toe.

Sideshow performer and banner artist Johnny Meah remembers a Knotty Man whose mental condition rivaled his physical state. Although he was an undeniable attraction, Meah believes this was one case where the sideshow may have been exploitative. "It was the only time in my life I was appalled at something in the sideshow. Your heart had to go out to this poor soul."

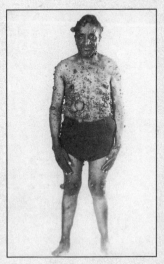

A Knotty Man.
Author's collection

PART THREE

It took ten months to get them to size. I did an operation every two months, popping out the old, popping in the new. People are all stunned, but women have been getting breast implants for years now.

THE ENIGMA, *on getting horn implants, 2003*

The

MODERN AGE

From the LAST *of the* OLD SIDESHOWS
to the EMERGENCE *of the* NEW

(circa 1970s *to* 2005)

The Coney Island Sideshows by the Seashore cast, 2003. Standing, left to right: Serpentina, Tyler Fyre, Scott Baker, Madame Electra / Madame Twisto, Dick Zigun. Seated: Insectavora. Not pictured: Eak. © *Liz Steger*

What did you want to be when you grew up? A fireman? Baseball player? Doctor? How about a professional freak? In the past fifty years that career has been an enthusiastic choice for those truly inspired by the magic and wonder of the circus. This section features performers who worked in the last of the old sideshows and who've carried on the tradition, along with the younger generation of fire eaters, sword swallowers, human blockheads, and others pushing the body to its limits.

THE AMAZING BLAZING TYLER FYRE

Born 1976

The day newborn Tyler Fleet came home from the hospital, a tornado struck his family's backyard. Perhaps it was a harbinger of his future career in danger.

Born March 29, 1976, in Atlanta, Fleet was first drawn to the circus arts six years later while attending a Ringling Bros. and Barnum & Bailey show. After witnessing the array of amazing acts, he knew he had found his destiny. But it wasn't until years later, when Fleet was studying playwriting at New York University, that he pursued his dream with a few extracurricular circus classes. He had never seen a hu-

Tyler Fyre eats fire at Coney Island, 2003. © *Liz Steger*

man blockhead until Todd Robbins guest-lectured. "I realized I had a predisposition for human blockhead," Fleet says. "Normal kids will laugh and shoot milk out their nose. I would laugh and shoot spaghetti and meatballs out my nose."

Classes and training soon gave birth to the Amazing Blazing Tyler Fyre. He performed his newly acquired fire-eating, machete-juggling, and human blockhead acts in amusement parks around the country before stumbling upon Sideshows by the Seashore at Coney Island in the spring of 1998. He met with Dick Zigun and rattled off his many talents, but to his dismay, all the positions for the inside acts were filled. Zigun needed an outside talker, however, and asked him if he could do the job. Fyre wondered what a talker did, exactly, but told Zigun, "Yes, of course I can do that." He was invited to return on the weekend, which happened to be the season-opening Memorial Day weekend. When he arrived, a performer gave him a crash course and sent him atop the bally platform. Ten hours later Fyre stepped down. After a month of training, he got the job. When a position opened on the inside, Fyre brought his talking skills to the stage as master of ceremonies, introducing the various performers, himself included. His repertoire has expanded to include sword swallowing, escapism, and magic, as well as razor blade eating and glass eating.

Fyre flirts with danger, and danger has flirted back. A glass sword filled with neon cracked in his throat during the summer of 2003. The sword was designed with fishing line so that broken shards might be extracted from his throat if necessary, but the toxic neon left him without a voice for a few days and without an appetite for even longer. A week later he was back onstage performing.

When not at Coney Island, Fyre travels with his own Lucky Devil Circus Sideshow and works occasionally with the Bros. Grim Side Shows.

THE AMAZING MR. LIFTO
Born circa 1970

Joe Hermann, better known as the Amazing Mr. Lifto, gained notoriety in the early 1990s by dangling heavy objects from pierced body parts with the Jim Rose Circus sideshow. He was one of the earliest members of the troupe and has stayed with the show throughout the years.

According to Jan T. Gregor's *Circus of the Scars*, a teenage Hermann discovered that his circumcision had been botched, leaving him with "a private hiding place—a hole in his penis into which he inserts pens, pencils, forks, what have you." He made use of the unfortunate error to win bets with school friends. They called him Spermin' Hermann. In the late 1980s, Hermann moved to Seattle from his small town near Puget Sound and found work as an insurance salesman. At night, he ditched his shirt and tie and became active in the grunge/club scene. Tattoos and piercings soon followed.

By age twenty, Hermann added to the modification of his penis with his first extreme piercing, a Prince Albert. He performed the genital prick himself with a sterilized safety pin. Heading north on his body, he had a needle poked through each nipple. Mr. Lifto now has piercings in eleven places, including his ears, nose, and tongue. His body has also been altered with facial implants aligning his temples, and tattoos down the center of his forehead.

His many body modifications were inspired by the self-proclaimed Modern Primitive, Fakir Musafar, who has studied and practiced self-mutilation and ancient rituals since the 1950s. Pierced weightlifting acts of the late 1800s and early 1900s influenced Mr. Lifto to help revive the art and push the limits to new boundaries. Cinder blocks and irons swing from his stretched nipples and penis, stools sway from his ears as he spins in circles, and suitcases and kegs of beer are hoisted by his mighty bands of cartilage.

Jan Gregor, who worked as the Jim Rose Circus sideshow's tour manager, described Lifto as "beautiful, photogenic, androgynous, and charismatic. Rose's introduction of his act would practically cause a stampede of people trying to witness the spectacle." Gregor's first question at the end of each performance was, "How many faints tonight—did anyone get a faint count?" Inevitably, Lifto's act was responsible for two or three per show.

Mr. Lifto's unusual weightlifting has caused the occasional stretching or tearing of flesh, but he heals quickly and fearlessly gets back to work.

SCOTT BAKER

Born 1948

While Scott Baker has made himself unique by perfecting sideshow working acts, he's also distinguished for being the only person who's starred in both a Broadway show (*Oh! Calcutta!*) and a Coney Island sideshow.

Born in 1948 in Tulsa, Oklahoma, Baker went to his first 10-in-1 sideshow at the state fair when he was six years old. "I was completely blown away," he recalls. Baker already considered himself a magician at the age of five.

Eventually he became a master conjurer, as well as a human blockhead, an anatomical wonder, a two-faced man, a glass eater, a fire eater, an outside talker, and much more. Baker proudly claims to be the only performer who still reenacts Melvin Burkhart's classic two-faced man (smiling and frowning at the same time) and anatomical wonder routines (particularly expanding and contracting his stomach so that he looked either nine months pregnant or on the brink of starvation, respectively). Of course, Baker adds his own shtick to the legend's pitch: "Don't try this at home—wait till you get to church," he said once as he pounded a large nail into his nose, "And then they'll know you're a god."

Baker's numerous talents are on display in his own show—Geek Circus: The Twisted Shockfest—and at Coney Island, where he also uses his gift of gab from atop the bally platform to draw crowds.

Scott Baker sucks his stomach in as part of the anatomical wonder routine at Coney Island, 2003. © *Liz Steger*

THE BINDLESTIFF FAMILY CIRKUS, KEITH NELSON *and* STEPHANIE MONSEU

Nelson: Born 1970
Monseu: Born 1968

The Bindlestiff Family Cirkus is a traveling troupe dedicated to preserving the arts of sideshow, vaudeville, and burlesque. More than 200 entertainers, including aerialists, jugglers, clowns, magicians, contortionists, and glass musicians have joined them for performances throughout the United States, Canada, and Europe. Based in New York City,

Stephanie Monseu and Keith Nelson at the
Bindlestiff Family Cirkus Palace
of Variety, 2002. © *Liz Steger*

the Cirkus took a break from the road in 2002 to open the Bindlestiff Family Cirkus Palace of Variety in the heart of Times Square. For nearly a year, the Palace brought the circus arts back to Forty-second Street for the first time in nearly a generation.

The nucleus of the Bindlestiff Family Cirkus was formed when Stephanie Monseu persuaded Keith Nelson to teach her fire eating. At the time, the two were working the graveyard shift at an all-night diner in Manhattan's East Village. By 1995 the Cirkus was born, reviving the spirit of traveling entertainment.

The name Bindlestiff "leapt off the page of my thesaurus!" explains Monseu. The word was used for the migrant jobless of the Depression era. Bindlestiffs had a strong network and united to demand wages and fair social treatment. "DIY was our motto," Monseu says. "In the years of traveling we have done, Bindlestiff has been instrumental in creating a network of venues and performers who want to keep variety arts flourishing."

Nelson, born in 1970 in Massachusetts, became interested in sideshows and clowning when he was given an Emmett Kelly ventriloquist doll as a child. In college he learned to juggle from David Hunt, founder of the New Orleans School of Circus Arts. "A few months later I traded a bottle of whiskey with a group of jugglers who taught me to eat fire," Nelson recalls. Before forming the Bindlestiffs he performed on the street and in community theater—"though I think being a camp counselor and leading songs gave me most of my chops," he adds. Nelson also worked with Ward Hall and Chris Christ's World of Wonders, swallowing thirty to fifty swords a day (which gave him the occasional sore throat). With the Bindlestiffs he performs a variety of acts as both Kinko the Clown and Mr. Pennygaff. As the latter, Nelson throws knots in ropes, fashioning three in one swing like an über–Boy Scout. To add a touch of the grotesque, he attaches the rope to his pierced tongue and keeps the loop spinning by shaking his head. Pennygaff's many other acts include the human blockhead with a hand drill, an array of juggling routines, gun twirling, and of course, his top act—a lectured demonstration on the history and manipulation of one of the oldest toys on Earth, the top.

Monseu, born in 1968 in Queens, New York, was a competitive ski racer and runner as well as a visual artist before becoming a Bindlestiff. Sideshow acts gave her the opportunity to combine theater with extremely physical stunts using the body as the primary instrument. "Whether eating fire or performing in a comedy character, the stage gives me the same adrenaline rush that running a super giant slalom course at forty-five miles an hour in icy conditions used to!" she says. And as a former singer in a top-forty cover band, Monseu was no stranger to the microphone. Besides serving as ringmistress under the name Philomena, Monseu shreds roses in the mouths of audience members with a bullwhip, walks on broken glass, and shares balloons with Pennygaff by stuffing them up a nostril and locking lips to exchange them via the mouth.

BROS. GRIM SIDE SHOWS

Circus historian Ken Harck has set up this authentic 1920s-era sideshow in select locations since the year 2000. He and his late partner, John Hartley, conceived of the idea after seeing the Clyde Beatty–Cole Bros. Circus. They felt that young, hip crowds were unaware of what a great thing the circus has been for the last hundred years and more. "We were trying to think of a way to bring a version of it to a younger audience," Harck says. "The sideshow made a lot of sense."

Having collected circus and sideshow memorabilia for most of his life, Harck sought to share his passion in a show that would replicate the experience of the early twentieth century. Achieving this required meticulous attention to detail and plenty of hard work.

(continued)

Harck's shows sport a hundred-foot banner line, a vintage fairground organ, sawdust on the ground, and a museum of oddities sharing space with the stage under the canvas. His mission, he believes, "is to give this to the world and say, 'Look at how cool this is! Isn't this better than sitting at home watching *American Idol?*'"

Many of the rotating cast of performers are not exclusive to the Bros. Grim show. These include: The Enigma and Katzen, Zamora the Torture King, Tyler Fyre, Keith Nelson and Stephanie Monseu, fire manipulator and juggler extraordinaire William Darkë, bearded lady Vivian Wheeler, Danielle Stampe (aka Slymenstra Hymen, formerly of GWAR), belly-dancing sword swallower Natasha Veruschka, the Rubber Boy, and Tahar the Mighty Moroccan Alligator Wrestler. Harck has also discovered new talent, such as fat lady Fannie Bryson and two human oddities—legless wonder Jesse Stitcher and a fellow called the Cyclops Boy. The latter is missing an eye, and has a hole in his head the size of a cue ball. This hole has opened the door to many creative—but disturbing—forms of entertainment. With the lights turned down, he'll shine a light in his mouth to create a glow in the vacancy. Beer can be guzzled through the opening and spit out of his mouth. And as a grand finale, Cyclops Boy will actually stick his tongue out of the empty socket. "You see that and you'll never forget it," Harck promises. "It'll burn into your psyche."

The costly production has been a labor of love. It certainly hasn't made Harck rich. Rather, the reward has been the roar of the crowd and the return of the sense of awe that the sideshow once offered.

SES CARNY

Born 1980

Ses Carny is here today courtesy of the band KISS. Of course, his parents are also responsible, having brought him into the world in December 1980. As a kid growing up in Raynham, Massachusetts, the future performer attended a KISS concert and was blown away watching front man Gene Simmons blow fire onstage. He was determined to do the same one day.

Carny spent several years learning to manipulate flames, and then progressed to other stunts. He's mastered the gamut of sideshow arts: sword swallowing, the human block-head, the bed of nails, the human dartboard, walking on and eating broken glass, the human pincushion, and more. He has performed them all since he was twenty years old, with his own Ses Carny Sideshow. His wife, Boo Boo, assists and performs with him. Carny's show has entertained audiences of all kinds, from gamblers at Las Vegas's Circus Circus to heavy metal fans as an opening act for Warrant.

Of all the stunts, his favorite is the eye hook. He learned to dangle and swing heavy chains from his eyelids under the tutelage of Harley Newman. "It is definitely an act you don't forget," Carny says.

Although he treats his body like a torture chamber, Carny feels little pain. During the human pincushion act—where he puts skewers through his forearm or pectoral muscles—he places himself in a state of self-hypnosis. "I actually feel the pain as something other than pain," he explains. He has suffered various minor injuries, including severed nerves in his face and lip and the occasional punctured vein. A pulled tooth led to the retirement of his glass-eating routine. All the teeth are needed for the stunt, and the risk of eating glass minus one tooth was too great. "It was a real bummer for me, because I loved eating lightbulbs," Carny says. "People think it's just a trick. Well, no, it's not a trick. You just don't know you can eat a lightbulb."

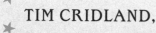

TIM CRIDLAND, ZAMORA THE TORTURE KING

Born 1963

Tim Cridland was born in December 1963 in Pullman, Washington. His studies of the torturous arts began in childhood. "I read this book in my elementary school library which had descriptions of people in India and other countries doing various things with

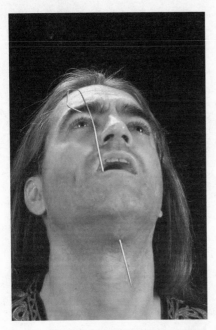

Zamora the Torture King tortures his mouth and chin. *Photo by Richard Faverty*

skewers, and people in sideshows swallowing swords," Cridland explains. "I said, Wow, I want to see people doing that." But since there weren't many people doing that anymore, he decided to learn it himself.

By the age of seventeen, Cridland had performed his first daring act. After reading about fire eating, he coaxed members of a small traveling circus to give him personal instruction until he accomplished the feat. The budding torture artist relocated to Seattle, where he ate fire in street performances and then added glass walking to his repertoire. He took his act off the street and onto the stage at punk-rock concerts. But Cridland's act was just beginning. His studies of fakir stunts soon turned him into an extreme human pincushion.

Meditative techniques, self-hypnosis, and a full knowledge of his anatomy allow him to pierce his flesh with skewers all over his body without experiencing the pain any normal person would feel. Cridland pushes needles through the bottom of his mouth and out his chin, straight through the middle of the biceps, and into other places whose piercing is guaranteed to disturb the squeamish. "I have managed to change my internal reactions to the trauma," he says. "Because I change how I react to external stimuli, this changes external reaction."

Cridland's sideshow career took off in 1991, after he hooked up with the Jim Rose Circus sideshow. His extraordinary stunts earned him his apt title, the Torture King. He added the name Zamora (a northern California town) because "Tim the Torture King" just didn't emanate excitement or mystique.

Besides poking long, sharp things through himself, the Torture King enjoys standing on two dozen raw eggs without breaking them; swallowing several feet of string and cutting himself right under the chest to pull it out from beneath his skin (the "Bizarre Yogi Internal Floss"); and swallowing swords. Of course, he has felt some pain: "I've hurt myself, but never enough to stop the show or go to the emergency room."

Cridland currently stars in his own Las Vegas show called *Shock*. His most shocking stunt has yet to come: the Torture King would like to have a sword pushed through the center of his body. The stunt was performed by Mirn Dajo in Switzerland in the late 1940s with a fencing sword that went through various points of his torso.

When not torturing himself in the sideshow, the Torture King conducts lectures and demonstrations on the history of fakir acts at conferences and universities.

MATT "THE TUBE" CROWLEY
Born 1962

In addition to being one of the original members of the Jim Rose Circus sideshow, Matt the Tube was simply original. While others in the troupe were reinventing old sideshow stunts, Crowley was inventing his own. His stomach-pumping "gavage" stunt and various other acts have been adopted by many performers working today.

Crowley was born in Helena, Montana, on August 20, 1962. Chemistry, Houdini, and Ripley's Believe It or Not! were among his childhood interests. Aside from these early fascinations, Crowley's eventual foray into the sideshow can be linked to a gift from a nurse he befriended in the mid-1980s. The nurse helped himself to certain items from the hospital that would have been deemed garbage by many. One such item was a gastric lavage unit (a stomach pump), which consisted of a large syringe connected to a long, thin plastic tube that would be pushed up the nose and threaded down into the belly. Plunging the syringe would retrieve the contents of the stomach. The nurse gave a unit to Crowley, and his wheels started spinning with ideas.

At the time, Crowley was a vocalist in a band. Rather than sing, he "lectured" on scientific subjects with jazz musicians in the background. Inspired by a Sid Vicious vomiting stunt, Crowley wondered whether he could regurgitate in a more "scientific" way. He pulled the tubing out of the unit and pushed it up his nostril and down behind the soft palate, but he couldn't resist the gag reflex. Frustrated, he put the tube away. But the urge to regurgitate returned several years later, after he had moved to Seattle; his curiosity was revived when he swallowed large nutritional supplements and the pills occasionally came up on their own. He recalled reading that Houdini would conceal keys or picks in the back of his throat, then bring them up when necessary. Crowley thought that "maybe it would not be too tough to become a regurgitator simply as a show-off stunt," and practiced with a piece of potato on a string, but had no luck. Still eager to perform a stunt, he remembered his friend's gift. By then he was able to push the tubing into his stomach. He also discovered a softer, more stomach-friendly brand of tubing. Finally, he developed a stunt primed for winning bar bets: "I can put the beer from this bottle into my stomach without a drop touching my lips," he would say. The syringe pump would push the beer into his stomach, then suck it out.

Shortly after developing the stomach-pumping routine, Crowley met Tim Cridland, the future Torture King. Cridland booked Crowley to perform during an intermission of a show and taped the performance. Jim Rose saw the video just before Labor Day 1991, and Crowley then joined Rose's group as Matt the Tube. His anatomical creativity continued. By feeding rubber tubing from his nose to his mouth, then pulling each end back and forth, he developed "mental flossing." Thanks to a suggestion from Cridland, the act evolved from using a tube to using a condom. Another oft-imitated Tube stunt is his grinder act, in which an angle grinder meets a piece of steel to create a shower of flying sparks. This act is frequently seen in sideshows and before mainstream audiences during segments of *Late Show with David Letterman*. The Tube welcomes others to perform his acts. "I see others doing my stunts as a testament that I created something good," he says.

Crowley left the Jim Rose Circus sideshow in 1994. He returned to his pre-sideshow work as a pharmacist for several years. Today he spends his time with his girlfriend, his truck, books, and Internet porn. "I think this is called 'bumming around,'" he admits. He has no plans of performing again. Instead, he's focused his creativity toward building custom furniture. But his years with the sideshow made an impact. "The experience 'reprogrammed' me. I began to perceive fundamental human issues like social status, human sexuality, attractiveness, money, fame, journalism, TV, hype, in totally new ways. Ten years later, I find myself still changed."

EAK

Born 1962

Eak at home in New York's
East Village, 2004. © *Liz Steger*

Coney Island's Eak earned his name not because his burly physique and heavily tattooed flesh scared people, but rather as an acronym for "Eddie, Are you Kidding?" Friends used the Frank Zappa phrase as a reaction to his various outrageous antics. But before being christened Eak, the tattooed wonder, pain-proof man, bouncer, and poet was simply Eduardo Arrocha from Mexico City.

Arrocha is the son of one of Mexico's most prominent corporate lawyers and an American mother. Born on January 12, 1962, he left Mexico in 1981 to experience a bigger world, beginning in New Mexico.

Arrocha's adventures began at a state fair in Albuquerque, where he sold balloons on the midway. The hustle quickly became a habit. After traveling the country working swap meets and fairs, playing in hardcore bands, and writing poetry, he landed in New York as a street vendor. The job was short-lived, but it opened the door to a new opportunity at Coney Island after a friend put him in contact with Dick Zigun, who was in need of a ticket seller. Arrocha was his man. Not only was he hooked on the fast-paced selling, but he fell in love with the Coney Island atmosphere. "It's addictive even in the smells—grease and cotton candy—and it's really beautiful," he says. "The way the sands would shift in colors and tones. It was just this little perfect piece of the universe."

Eak also cleaned up and acted as general security: "Back then I was a lot more willing to pull people out by their ears." He enjoyed his role as an outside observer and captured his experiences in endless journals. More than 3,000 pages filled with his observations line the shelves of his apartment in Manhattan's East Village.

Eak had no ambition to become part of the show as a working act. But after he had his face tattooed, he was thrust onto the stage by Zigun. After all, he was now a sideshow freak. Becoming a freak wasn't his intention; the facial tattoos were something he had contemplated for nearly ten years. The final push came one summer, after he fell for a girl who lost interest once the sideshow season was finished. "That created this incredible awakening. I thought, What am I holding back at? I'm never really going to get accepted back into that world. I told myself, Just go for it." Yet he waited another two years before going for it. He still feared turning himself into a permanent walking sideshow.

The summer after Sideshows by the Seashore moved from the Coney Island boardwalk to Surf Avenue, Eak tattooed his forehead. He took the next year off and had the rest of his face inked with images of the universe. "We're part of something so much bigger than we are. So I kind of consider the universe my higher power in some strange way." Eak ultimately returned to Coney Island, but he refused to adopt a stage persona. With a hood covering his illustrated face, he helps gather crowds (and size them up) from atop the bally platform. Inside he performs on a bed of nails and helps with other acts, plugging holes where needed.

Eak has no regrets as a self-made freak: "It completely changed my life. I actually became a lot happier after I did it. I was a mean bastard [before]." Forced to accept who he is, he no longer tries to escape his character. Outside Coney Island and his neighborhood, Eak spends time in the classroom. He recently returned to college, and hopes to teach performing arts to children one day. He also intends to keep writing poetry and someday publish his work. One of his goals is to break the stereotypes attached to the heavily tattooed. "I might have tattoos on my face, but get over it. I still have to eat and sleep, fall in love, get heartbroken, I still like watching my corny TV shows. I read *The New York Times* every day." Just like everybody else, with the possible exception of that every day part.

THE ENIGMA *and* KATZEN

The Enigma: Born 1968
Katzen: Born 1974

The Enigma and Katzen are the reigning World's Strangest Couple. The Enigma is completely tattooed with puzzle pieces filled with an enormous amount of blue ink.

Katzen is tattooed with tiger stripes across her entire body. Their onstage performance is as breathtaking as their appearance.

The Enigma was born on December 20, 1968, in Long Beach, California, and grew up near Seattle. The seed was planted for a career in entertainment when he began piano lessons at age six. His musical training continued with ballet, tap, flute, and singing lessons. The young talent hit a turning point when he joined a magic club in grade school, and soon stumbled onto some old sideshow material. Sword swallowing piqued his interest. By the age of sixteen, he gulped down his first blade. "I felt it was the impossible possible, and how beautiful it was," he remembers. "It was all a gamble, and one I wanted to take." Combining music and sideshow stunts, he began performing at small events. The show

The Enigma and Katzen with the Bros. Grim Side Shows at Seaside Heights, New Jersey, 2003. © *Liz Steger*

took off and he joined a small group of performers who would become the Jim Rose Circus. Their breakthrough came with an appearance at the first Lollapalooza music festival in 1991. The Enigma was known as Slug the Sword Swallower at the time.

Katzen was born in Atlanta on December 10, 1974. While The Enigma's upbringing centered around music, Katzen's was around art. In grade school she created a dream-inspired self-portrait in which half of her face was tattooed with tiger stripes. Katzen later became involved in Atlanta's avant-garde art scene, and by age seventeen in tattooing.

In 1991, The Enigma was contemplating how to change his act. A day job pressing shirts at a dry cleaner's freed his mind to brainstorm. The idea of becoming blue intrigued him the most. "I had other ideas—what if I was all paisley? All plaid? I also thought I could do puzzle pieces all over my body, then just fill it in." To accomplish the transformation, he would need a lot of tattooing. And someone to help.

At the 1992 Lollapalooza show, he found his partner in Katzen. His devotion to becoming blue inspired her to turn her dreams into reality and become a tiger. During a month off in January 1993, Katzen tattooed The Enigma from head to toe with designs of puzzle pieces. Since then, he's had more than 200 tattoo artists from around the world fill them in—amateurs and experts alike. Whatever they want, as long as it's a shade of blue.

The next phase of his transformation involved implanting horns on his head. That required a series of operations lasting ten months.

Katzen's tattoos are entirely her own design. She carried the tiger theme further by adding Teflon whiskers, which are actually attached from piercings. She had her earlobes removed, and the cartilage atop her ears reshaped into points.

"We're ambassadors for the tattoo community," Katzen explains. "When people see us, they're going to gauge our personalities and our reactions against what they think a tattooed person should act like." Their personalities give tattooed people everywhere a good name. Yet wherever they go, they still endure mobs of kids asking whether they're real.

The colorful couple has a ten-year-old daughter, Caitlin, who was adopted by Katzen's mother. She lives in Tennessee and sees her biological parents two or three times a year. Should she wish to follow in their footsteps, Katzen will be happy to tattoo her (but not until she's eighteen).

Performing as one of the Human Marvels, The Enigma swallows swords, pumps his stomach, and does other incredible stunts with dynamic flair. He's equipped with an electric guitar shaped like a puzzle piece, while Katzen plays a customized bass with an angle grinder, igniting giant sparks from which she lights a cigarette. When not playing the guitar, The Enigma connects wires to it, shoves them up his nose and out of his mouth, then connects a shining lightbulb to create the Human Spotlight.

"We show people things they didn't know they could do," he says. "Instead of thinking about the car payments they can't pay, or the wife and kids screaming at them, they think, 'Oh my goodness, I didn't know you could be a different color.' We take them out of their little shell and we open their minds." The two have toured the world and have been featured on a variety of TV shows. The Enigma has also gained fame from an appearance on an episode of *The X-Files*.

The Enigma hopes his music career will reach the level of success he's had with the sideshow. The Human Marvels have released a CD and contributed to two movie soundtracks. Yet many people still assume that he is only a tattoo artist, and have a hard time imagining that he can do other things. These are the thoughts that drive The Enigma. "This isn't about what I can't do. This is about what I can do. I can do anything, and this is proof of it. This is about self-empowerment."

JOHNNY FOX

Born 1953

Born on Friday the 13th in November 1953, Johnny Fox has never considered himself unlucky. Instead, he's had the good fortune to simply do the things he loves.

Growing up in Connecticut, Fox developed an interest in magic and theater. As a ten-year-old, he read about how Houdini practiced swallowing and regurgitating with a piece of potato attached to a string. "I thought, Wow, that was brilliant, if it got dislodged he could digest it," Fox remembers. Inspired, he swallowed a strand of spaghetti and brought it back up.

Johnny Fox at the Freakatorium, 2001, swallowing a sword with a live scorpion on his face. © *Liz Steger*

By age twenty, Fox began performing comedy and sleight-of-hand magic in Florida restaurants. He added other stunts, such as fire eating, which also helped him gather crowds for street performances. In 1978, he began training to swallow swords. Fox spent six to eight months slowly perfecting the art. "I didn't want to look like I was struggling. I wanted it to look really natural in front of a crowd," he says. Having achieved a level of effortlessness, Fox has swallowed swords for the past twenty-five years at the Maryland Renaissance Festival, as well as fairs in Colorado, Florida, and Illinois. His mastery of the blades has led to several television appearances, including a performance on *The Jonathan Winters Show* in which he swallowed sixteen swords. By the early 1990s, even doctors took notice when the Johns Hopkins University School of Medicine documented Fox's skills with an X-ray of his throat holding a sword, in a film produced to help people with swallowing disorders.

> ✳ Ukraine's Leonid Stadnik currently stands eight feet, four inches. His remarkable growth began at age fourteen, after a brain operation disturbed his pituitary gland. Stadnik is still growing and may ultimately soar past history's tallest man, Robert Wadlow. He has yet to exhibit his great height for profit.

Fox's inventory of stunts also includes contortion, glass eating, coin tricks, and the human blockhead. The last was inspired by old photos of Leo Konges, a blockhead from the 1930s. "I was using a spike, which was really like a nail," Fox recounts. "I noticed people in the audience were grossed out and disgusted. So I stopped doing it." But then he discovered photos of Melvin Burkhart using a giant, twenty-penny spike. "That's the way to sell that trick. That way people from the back row can see it." Today, Fox combines his talents with storytelling in a one-man show.

Fox founded a museum dedicated to sideshow memorabilia, the Freakatorium, El Museo Loco, which was located on Manhattan's Lower East Side from 1998 to January 2005. The collection featured an array of old photographs, posters, artifacts, and creatures (stuffed, gaffed, and living). Several pieces from his museum are reproduced in this book. "New York needs a place where people can come see the history of freakdom," Fox said when the museum was still open. "I want it to bring happiness, or wonder, or awe, or disgust, to people. Whatever it stirs up. Something like that should always be in Manhattan." His museum is missed.

GEORGE THE GIANT
Born 1969

George McArthur was a not-so-giant seven pounds, eight ounces, when he was born on September 19, 1969, in Bakersfield, California. He ultimately rose to seven feet, three inches, and while he is not the tallest of giants, unlike giants of the past, George the Giant has sideshow skills that stretch far beyond just standing there.

Among this Goliath's talents are sword swallowing, snorting balloons through one nostril and blowing them out the other, and fire manip-

George the Giant, 2004. © *Liz Steger*

ulation. Some stunts required years of research and practice, while others were mastered in just two hours. He learned to eat fire to overcome a fear that developed when someone broke into his brother's home, tied him up, lit him on fire, and left him to die. (He survived.) Oddly enough, McArthur also had a fear of heights, so he bungee-jumped in order to overcome it. He had no fear of swords, although he may have feared his teacher, Bobby Reynolds. On one of his first gigs, Reynolds used a coat hanger to teach McArthur the ancient art just in time for the show: "Go on! Shove it down your throat!" Reynolds told him. Sure enough, he got the hanger down his throat, and today he holds the record for the longest sword swallowed, a thirty-three-inch blade. Until a taller sword swallower comes along, the record should remain safe.

George the Giant is currently working with a dwarf on a show combining stunts, escapism, and comedy. "I want something I can bring any family member to and not have them feel ashamed," McArthur says. In addition to his live performances, he's played a giant on the big and small screens, most notably in the HBO series *Carnivàle* and in Tim Burton's movie *Big Fish*.

McArthur still lives in his hometown, with his loving wife—all four feet, ten inches of her.

THE GREAT FREDINI

Born 1965

✶ Fred Kahl was born on May 18, 1965, in Boston, but the Great Fredini wasn't conceived until seventeen years later. In 1982, Kahl went to New York City for art school, and there he developed an interest in magic and illusions. The famed magic shops Tannen's and Flosso-Hornmann became his hangouts.

The Great Fredini swallowing a curved sword. *Laure A. Le*

As Kahl's interest in magic grew, so did his curiosity about Coney Island's history. At the time, Dick Zigun had just started up Coney Island USA with Sideshows by the Sea-shore. Kahl, who had begun performing magic in Central Park, made frequent visits to Coney Island to watch Melvin Burkhart, Otis Jordan, and showman John Bradshaw. A couple of years passed, Burkhart didn't return, and Jordan died. This left an opening for younger performers, and Kahl stepped in and took the lead as the Great Fredini. "I knew enough, but not enough. I was really green," Kahl admits. He performed his magic, worked the electric chair and blade-box stunts, and pitched whoopee cushions to the audience.

With the sideshow reborn and flourishing in the early 1990s, veteran showman Bobby Reynolds decided to set up at Coney Island. Under his guidance the Great Fredini mastered the art of the bally. Kahl soon added the human blockhead routine to his newly polished talking skills. The next winter, it was time to expand his arsenal and learn sword swallowing. Yoga classes gave him the necessary relaxation capability. After failed attempts with wire hangers, success came at the start of the new Coney Island season. Kahl brought a coat hanger with him and announced to the crew that he was going to learn to swallow it. It went down on his first try. "It was just being in the space and knowing yoga well enough to be at that point of final relaxation," the Great Fredini said later. He began performing the stunt in shows that day. Kahl took the act a step further by swallowing a sword with a curved blade. "Sometimes it makes me a little sore," he allows.

The Great Fredini's next grand stunt was his marriage to another Coney Island performer, the Combustible Kiva. The wedding sparked a bit of media frenzy, as it was billed a Barnumesque "marriage of the freaks." It did not last long.

Kahl quit the show after a number of years and became great at another art: computers. He returned to school and earned a master's of professional studies from New York University's Interactive Telecommunications Program. "Whatever that means," he says. He uses these skills to develop websites and games.

The Great Fredini has moved beyond the sideshow, but he hasn't stopped performing. He launched a Friday-night burlesque series at Coney Island and incorporated it into a live show, *America's Favorite Burlesque Gameshow: This or That TV,* which he hopes will eventually be where its name suggests—on TV.

DICK ZIGUN AND SIDESHOWS BY THE SEASHORE

In the early 1900s, Coney Island was filled with the wonder and curiosity of sideshows. More human oddities were congregated at the shore in Brooklyn than in any other place in the world. But by the 1960s, the area once known as Sodom by the Sea had suffered fires, park closings, and changing attitudes toward freaks. The sideshow had all but disappeared until the 1980s, when a man from P. T. Barnum's hometown of Bridgeport, Connecticut, named Dick Zigun became Coney Island's latest impresario.

In 1979, the young Yale School of Drama graduate brought his two theater degrees to New York, intending to write plays based on vaudeville and burlesque. Rather than

Coney Island USA's
Funny Face logo, 2003.
© Liz Steger

(continued)

Broadway, he headed toward the Atlantic and began Coney Island USA as a not-for-profit arts organization. What started as a restored wax museum evolved into a dime museum with art installations and performances. But Zigun had bigger aspirations. He wanted to make a splash over the entire neighborhood. His ambition spawned the first Mermaid Parade—which continues as an annual Coney Island event today. The parade brought in funding, and in 1985, Zigun launched Sideshows by the Seashore.

The space initially booked performance art, poetry, and other forms of creative expression. Toward the end of the first season, veteran showman John Bradshaw ran a one-man sideshow. The show saved Zigun from bankruptcy. Sideshows by the Seashore dedicated itself to keeping the 10-in-1 tradition alive. Melvin Burkhart and Otis Jordan joined up in the late 1980s, along with the Illustrated Man, Michael Wilson. "That began the new generation, meeting the old," Zigun says.

Burkhart and Jordan retired after a few seasons, and Zigun brought in younger talent. Over the years, many performers have amazed Coney Island crowds: sword swallowers Frank Hartman and Diane Falk, fire eater Christine Hell, fat lady and singer Helen Melon, snake enchantresses Ruby Rodriguez and Stephanie Torres, Koko the Killer Clown (a dwarf), and others, some profiled in this book. Though most of the performers are self-made freaks, Zigun has made sure that natural-born oddities have a place. "We're performance-oriented, not gawker-oriented. It's a fine line." Yet even with a performance, the gawk factor certainly helps sell tickets.

THE GREAT NIPPULINI

Born 1974

Like the appendix, men's nipples have often been considered useless. It may be true, unless you're the Great Nippulini—possessor of the world's strongest nipples. "The abilities that I have with my nipples are really wide," he claims.

The Great Nippulini was born in 1974, unaware that he would grow up to become the
Schwarzenegger of nipples. A professional body
piercer, he had his own nipples pierced for five years
before he realized their potential. The inspiration
to tap into their power came from watching videos
of performers lifting objects with their chests. He
noticed his nipples were bigger than those of these
lifters, as were his piercings. So he could lift things
too. With that, the Great Nippulini was born.

As he began studying, he discovered an old circus performer who would become a major influ-
ence: Rasmus Nielsen. Nippulini's first lifting
challenge came from his father—a key chain,
weighted with numerous keys and clips. He worked
his way from this to a thirty-pound anvil.

The Great Nippulini, 2004. © *Liz Steger*

Nippulini's chest has towed heavy men on carts
and a one-ton 1922 Ford T Bucket Roadster. Despite his moniker, he doesn't discriminate with his piercings. His earrings of choice are three-and-a-half-pound regulation
bowling pins. The sixteen-pound bowling ball is lifted by his mighty nipples and swung
around toward the pins.

The Great Nippulini lifted forty-eight and a half pounds in May 2003, setting the
Guinness world record for the Heaviest Amount of Weight Lifted by a Nipple. This
weight included two anvils and the harness and chains that held them. By January 2004,
he shattered the record with a fifty-five-pound anvil.

The Great Nippulini had never been injured, until, in September 2004, a fan assist-
ing onstage failed to pay attention to instructions. As a result, an entire rigging of bowling balls jolted down onto one nipple and tore out Nippulini's nipple ring. "There wasn't
much pain at all," he later claimed. But the damage was extensive and he feared for the end
of his sideshow career. Depression, then acceptance, followed. The Great Nippulini realized he still had one healthy nipple—enough to continue performing with. His wounded
nipple will heal, and he'll be back at full strength. "I'll be swinging my grandchildren
from my nipples someday," he promises.

THE GREAT THROWDINI

Born 1946

Born in Brooklyn, New York, on December 5, 1946, the Great Throwdini didn't come to life until almost fifty years later. His résumé for the first half-century of his life is best summed up in the introduction to his performance: "Good evening, ladies and gentlemen, my real name is the Reverend Dr. David Adamovich,

The Great Throwdini with Ula at Coney Island. *Laure A*

retired professor, doctorate in exercise physiology, paramedic, pool hall owner, unabashed student of the culinary arts. And in my spare time, I throw knives."

Adamovich is a man of many talents. He has performed between 3,000 and 4,000 weddings as a minister and spent eighteen years as a professor. In his spare time he wrote a 414-page textbook on electrocardiography. After leaving his university job, Adamovich worked for an emergency medicine management company. The company was sold four years later, and he was out of work. Despite a wall full of diplomas, he wasn't finding a new position. So at age forty-eight, Adamovich pursued another interest—pool.

A few years after he bought a pool hall, a friend stopped by and interested him in knife throwing. The two walked outside and Adamovich threw his first knife at a tree. It stuck beautifully. "It was a natural skill for me," Adamovich says. He went out and bought an assortment of throwing knives. Months of practice—with both hands— sharpened his precision. Within a year he entered the world championship competition held by the International Knife Throwers Alliance. A virtual no-name in the contest, he placed second, only a point behind the winner. Over the next five years Adamovich won both national and world titles. His wife also took up the sport and won the women's national championship. After winning her title she hung up her knives. The Great Throwdini had other plans.

Holding numerous records and credentials, Throwdini moved from competition throwing into the impalement arts, or the art of throwing around a target. He had to put together a show and get onstage. That's when he met Chris McDaniel, another world champion. McDaniel, world champion in the Texas skip, is a master of the western arts, which include gun spinning, trick roping, and tomahawk throwing. He served as a mentor to Adamovich in producing a show.

The next thing the Great Throwdini needed was an assistant, but finding one is no easy task for a knife thrower. He currently works with Ula the Pain-Proof Rubber Girl, who would not have assisted for anyone less than the absolute best in the world. She may call herself "Pain-Proof" and "Rubber," but she needn't prove it by taking a knife in the gut. Fortunately, Throwdini has been Great, never stabbing Ula or any other assistant. "I scraped a girl once," he confesses. No harm was done.

Inspired by a line from the 1999 French movie, *The Girl on the Bridge*, the Great Throwdini calls his show *Maximum Risk*. And it is just that. Knives, axes, and machetes are flung—but with stunning accuracy. To add to the danger, Adamovich throws with a steel mask and a hood covering his eyes. Ula taps the board where the knife should hit, leaving him with only a sense of sound to throw by. But that's not maximum risk. Maximum risk goes a step further, removing both sight and sound clues. Ula holds a large sheet of paper in front of her entire body, and his knives are hurled through it.

"I take this very seriously, I think about it twenty-four/seven." Day and night, Adamovich says, he thinks about what he does and "how dangerous it is, and about that girl's safety." So far so good.

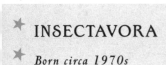

INSECTAVORA

Born circa 1970s

The exotic-looking Insectavora claims to have been stranded on the Fiji Islands: "No McDonald's, no Burger King, no four-star restaurants, no greasy spoons. No deli, no diners, no street vendors of any kind." The poor girl had only a plethora of insects to eat.

Insectavora at Coney Island, 2003. © *Liz Steger*

Insectavora's birth name is Angelica. The Brooklyn-born bug eater began developing her look with her first tattoo in 1987; she had her face inked in 1999.

Angelica's first Insectavora experience came at age five, when a neighborhood boy challenged her to eat an insect. "It grossed him out, it was such an awesome response!" she says. It continues to gross out adults and children of all ages at Coney Island.

Her Coney Island career began in 2002 after she was spotted by Sideshows by the Seashore performers at the New York City Tattoo Convention at Roseland Ballroom. "That's where these guys kidnapped me," she explains. She enjoys a "Fear Factor feast" of live crickets, grasshoppers, mealworms, maggots, and nightcrawlers. She has no particular favorite.

Insectavora walks up a razor-sharp ladder of swords and is currently working on a whip-cracking act. During the off-season she works in a tattoo and body-piercing shop, and probably eats a more balanced diet.

✷ THE LIZARDMAN
✷ *Born 1972*

✷ **E**rik Sprague is a self-made freak. He has tattooed nearly his entire body with reptilian scales, filed his teeth into fangs, implanted horned ridges over his eyes, forked his tongue, and pierced his ears and septum. These procedures have cost Sprague more than $10,000, not to mention plenty of discomfort, but it's all been worth it to him. "The implant procedure was incredibly painful, but I love the results," he says.

He hatched his plan as performance art in 1990, but didn't begin any tattoo work until 1994. Ten years later, Sprague isn't quite finished. "There is very little of me left to tattoo in terms of outlining. I am now like a big coloring book just waiting to be completely filled in." Friends and family have accepted Sprague's new look. "They can see how this is the most natural path for me and how it's just the ordinary course for my artistic development and expression."

Sprague didn't always plan on being a lizard man. During high school he considered being a marine biologist or a stockbroker. And during his lizard-free high school years, he worked at a Methodist church.

While Sprague looks like a lizard, he is much more talented than any reptile. His skills include sword swallowing, fire eating, insect eating, hammering nails into his head, walking on glass, lifting weights from piercings, and other stunts one shouldn't try at home. The Lizardman has performed with the Jim Rose Circus and independently, and has appeared on scores of television shows. He recently married his longtime girlfriend and is said to enjoy pizza and wax worms.

The Lizardman. *Photo by Allen Falkner, www.obscurephoto.com*

JENNIFER MILLER
Born 1960

Unlike Bearded Ladies of the sideshow before her, Jennifer Miller isn't just a hirsute wonder to be stared at. She's an entertainer who just happens to be a woman with a beard. Her circus career began before she ever sported her curious whiskers.

Jennifer Miller, 2004. © *Liz Steger*

Miller was born in California in 1960, but grew up on the opposite coast, in Hartford. She juggled in high school and expanded her skills in a clowning class. After graduating as a literal class clown, she worked with a local entertainment organization and a small one-ring circus in California.

In her early twenties, Miller moved to New York City and became involved in experimental dance and performance art. She also taught theater to children, including a third-grade Claire Danes. It was during this period that Miller's beard began to sprout. It wasn't an easy decision to keep the growth, and initially it caused her much private fear. "I was very alone in my experiences. And I was afraid. I had nightmares of groups of eleven-year-old boys surrounding me and chanting and beating the shit out of me. But that never happened." She believed her facial hair was nothing to be ashamed of, and nothing to be concerned about from a medical point of view. Plenty of women have the potential to grow a beard, they simply choose not to. Culture, rather than biology, dictates that they shouldn't. "Look at all the electrologists out there, the hair removal products," she says. Yet Miller did shave on a few occasions. Once it was for a bike messenger job, and another time, ironically, it was to work in a small circus. But when it came to teaching in an after-school program, the beard stayed.

In the late 1980s, as Coney Island's Sideshows by the Seashore was taking off, Miller joined and adopted the stage name Zenobia. Veteran talker John Bradshaw chose the moniker, which happened to be the name of his favorite pistachio company, in the Bronx. Zenobia's act consisted of a feminist/comic monologue, knife juggling, and straitjacket escapes. As she told *The New York Times,* "Ten times a day, I address in the strongest, most forthright terms feminist issues of appearance and dress. I use the platform of the sideshow to defreakify."

While at Coney Island, Miller met legendary talker Bobby Reynolds, who had his own show nearby. Eventually she had the honor of working for him as well. Though normally limited to New York, her act found a national audience with appearances on *The Joan Rivers Show* and *Jerry Springer.*

At the same time, Miller was developing her own show. Combining political commentary, postmodern dance, circus arts, and collaboration with a talented group of New York performers, she put together Circus Amok. It debuted as a single show, but was so successful and enjoyable that she decided to continue the production. By the mid-1990s, Circus Amok performed outdoors throughout New York's five boroughs. The one-ring, animal-free, politically based, queerly situated show attracted audiences of all colors, classes, and ages. Miller has little trouble helping the crowd get past her unusual appearance. "We have a big opening stilt dance, where I come down off the stilts and go through a transformation. I ask, 'How is everybody?' It just takes a fucking hello to get over the beard." Once she raises social topics the people in the audience can relate to, such as government budget cuts or police brutality, she simply becomes one of them—just another person dealing with the same problems they are facing. Of course, her beard does raise curiosity, particularly with children. Are you a boy or a girl, they'll ask. "At my age, you've got to say woman. It's a beard that just grows there. A lot of women have facial hair," she'll begin to explain. And by the time she's in the middle of that sentence, the kids are asking, "Can we play on the jungle gym now?"

Anyone who would doubt Miller's gender can simply inspect her nude photograph in Annie Leibovitz's book *Women*.

Circus Amok continues to perform in the summers. Miller also does solo shows and has been an adjunct professor at UCLA. She described her course, appropriately, as theory and practice of "outdoor political spectacle-making."

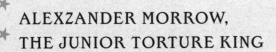

ALEXZANDER MORROW, THE JUNIOR TORTURE KING

Born 1989

If Al and Jeanie Tomaini were still alive today, they would be quite proud of their great-grandson, Alexzander Morrow, also known as the Junior Torture King. Alex was born in Tampa, Florida, on March 30, 1989. It wasn't long before his grandmother, Judy

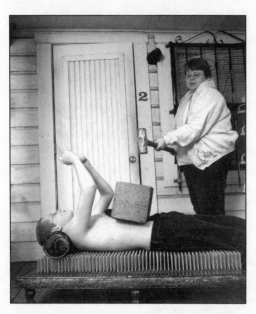

Alexzander Morrow lying on a bed of nails as his mother prepares to smash a sledgehammer over a cinder block on his stomach. At Giant's Camp, Gibsonton, Florida, 2003. © *Liz Steger*

Rock, started his training during visits to nearby Gibsonton. Rock is not your average grandma. She made him his first bed of nails (4,782 nice sharp ones) when he was eight. Rock scooped him up and laid him right down on it. "It's not easy. But it's not hard. And it does hurt like heck, I'll tell you that," Alex says. He's made the stunt even more challenging by having cinder blocks broken over his chest while he's lying there.

Grandma wasn't finished with the young torture king. She found her father's old swords in the attic and fashioned them into a ladder. Alex learned to climb it without slicing his feet, though he did suffer minor injuries simply from walking near the blades.

The Junior Torture King's greatest accomplishment to date is becoming the youngest person to lie on a bed of only two nails. Inspired by an eighteen-year-old woman who lay on four nails, Alex intended to match her, but before he could lie back on the last two nails, he found himself balanced on just two. "I can't believe I can do that," Alex says. "I'm working on one, I can do it, but it just hurts to put all my weight in one spot the size of your pinky."

As for any good torture king, beds of nails and ladders of swords are only a beginning for Alex. He walks and jumps barefoot on broken glass. At the 2003 Sideshow Gathering in Wilkes-Barre, Pennsylvania, he swallowed his first sword (twelve inches)—the youngest person ever to achieve the stunt. His flabbergasted friends think he's insane.

Alex's mother, Tina, fully supports his dangerous hobby. "I've been raised around it. If he likes it, let him do it," she says. Tina does a few stunts herself. She taught herself the human blockhead routine in the 1990s. "All the show people were around, so you just kind of pick up things. It's normal for us."

HARLEY NEWMAN, PROFESSIONAL LUNATIC

Born 1951

Born in Montclair, New Jersey, Harley Newman grew up to be a Professional Lunatic. It's a far cry from his original plan of becoming a doctor, although his performances do require an extensive knowledge of anatomy and physiology. He knows his own body as well as any doctor might.

Harley Newman lying on a bed of four nails, 2004. © *Liz Steger*

Newman's first professional gig was in 1972 as a clown, while he was in college. Afterward he became a mascot for an Indianapolis minor-league baseball team. These antics led him to the Hoxie Brothers Circus, where he helped run the sideshow. Spending time with performers such as sword swallower and fire eater Bill Unks (aka The Baron) later helped him train for his various stunts.

In 1978, Newman left the circus to put his master's degree in counseling to use. But after a few frustrating years in mental health, he returned to performing. "One of the most amazing puzzles is how the body works. And what got me going on that was the bed of nails," Newman explains. Solving the puzzle took no time. He got so good at the stunt that he was able to lie on the bed with 1,700 pounds resting on top of him. He worked his way down to a bed with just four nails, but he wasn't done yet. He took two nails out and, leaving no room for error, balanced his entire body on the remaining two. Editors considered the stunt too dangerous to include in the *Guinness Book of World Records*.

The bed of nails was only one puzzle Newman set out to solve. He heard of a stunt involving objects swung from fishhooks pushed through the eyelids, and set out to learn it. Newman hangs a stainless-steel cup from hooks in his eyelids, has it filled with water

Harley Newman performing his eye hook routine, 2004. © *Liz Steger*

to add weight, then rolls his eyes back to complete the gruesome feat. Though it sounds gross, gross-outs aren't his intention. Newman wants people to be amazed. The difference is all in the attitude. He claims he can put fishhooks in his eyelids at a children's show and get away with it.

Newman has also developed mind-boggling escapes that liken him to a modern-day Houdini. One such stunt features his body wrapped in a cocoon of a quarter-mile of Saran wrap, with a snorkel in his mouth to breathe. Then he has a cork put in the snorkel. He'll squirm around for a few minutes, then fall over limp to get the audience's hearts racing. People rush the stage to help in about eighty percent of his performances. "I'm probably evil for scaring people so badly," Newman confesses. He also picks locks in his mouth and escapes from a straitjacket, while riding a unicycle or hanging upside down from a burning rope (no net below). For Newman, it's all about the theatrics of the performance and involving the audience emotionally.

Newman has performed internationally for the last twenty years and is developing his show. "If all I want to do is go around disturbing people, I may as well go back into doing therapy," he says.

Over the years he has suffered many minor injuries, the worst being cracked ribs. He also injured his eye while having a cinder block smashed over his face. It healed.

When not performing, Newman can be found at home with his wife and daughter. "They used to cringe a lot more," he comments. A good cringe always meant he was on the right track. Aside from practicing stunts, Newman spends time sculpting shapes from various raw materials. "If I could make a decent living sitting in my workshop with a mallet and chisels and chunks of logs, I'd probably do that all the time," he says. "But I like to perform, too. I like having my mind go a lot of different directions." Like any lunatic, professional or otherwise.

THE PAIN-PROOF RUBBER GIRLS, ULA *and* SÄRKA

Born circa 1970s

Särka as a contortionist on a bed of nails.
Photo by Colby Katz

According to their "mythos," Ula and Särka were twins connected at the butt, born to nomadic Gypsies in the desert of Mauritania in 1974. They were sold to German scientists for "one hundred American dollars" at age four, then put up for adoption separately in the United States. The sisters remained separated until one magical evening at a fire eater's potluck dinner. "We recognized each other instantly and formed our act immediately," Ula recounts.

Mythos aside, the "sisters" were both attending college in New York City when they put a contortionist act together. In the winter of 1994 they performed in Austria with a show called Wild Style, in which their unnamed act was listed as the Schlangen Menschen (German for "snake people"). As the Schlangen Menschen girls, they adopted foreign-looking names, hence Ula and Särka. Joining them on the tour were a variety of established sideshow performers, such as Todd Robbins, the Bindlestiff Family Cirkus, Harley Newman, and the fire eater Indio. Ula and Särka were influenced by the various acts surrounding them.

Upon returning to the States, Särka built a bed of nails in her school workshop. Rather than simply lie on it, she used it as a platform for her contortionism. "I honestly think I'm the only performer who's ever done that," she says. "Because not a lot of circus performers acknowledge sideshow tricks and integrate them into their act." Ula joined her fearless sister and subjected her body to the pointy bed as well. "We started adding these sideshow tricks in our act basically to entertain each other," she explains. By then she and Särka were extinguishing cigars on their tongues, breaking (rigged) bottles of beer over each other's heads, and contorting on broken glass. Although they had liked being Schlangen Menschen, they changed their name to the more descriptive, and intelligible, Pain-Proof Rubber Girls.

The Pain-Proof Rubber Girls exhibited their limberness and gleeful self-torture around New York, including a short stint at Coney Island in 1995 and at Lollapalooza's 1996 New York City stop. It was at Coney Island's Sideshows by the Seashore that Särka met the Illustrated Man, Michael Wilson. He turned her on to a new passion—tattoos—and introduced her to area inkers. On a trip to San Francisco she met another tattoo artist, fell in love, and moved there to pursue what would become a "hopeless relationship." Särka retired in 2000 from her sideshow career, leaving Ula behind for her new love and a tattooing job out west. Today, Särka is a respected tattoo artist and is almost covered in designs. Only her hands, neck, and face remain unmarked.

Ula continues to perform as a Pain-Proof Rubber Girl. She developed her contortion act, replacing the bed of nails with a more menacing bed of merciless machetes. She demonstrates her rubbery abilities on the trapeze as well—skills she mastered working with a small circus before teaming with Särka. And she's taken on a separate act with an impalement artist, the Great Throwdini. Who better to work as a knife thrower's assistant than a Pain-Proof Rubber Girl?

★ TODD ROBBINS
★ *Born 1958*

★ Billed as a Purveyor of Amazement, Todd Robbins first began dabbling in the amazing as a boy in Long Beach, California. Born on August 15, 1958, Robbins grew up in a middle-upper-class family, or "three hots and a cot" as he describes it in carny terms.

As a child he grew interested in magic, but quickly realized it was all trickery. When the carnival came to town, he went to see a magic act and discovered a man swallowing swords and another eating fire. "They had extraordinary capabilities beyond the average person and, to me, were the closest thing to real magic I'd ever experienced," Robbins re-members. Not only was he enthralled, he wanted to learn their secrets.

The twelve-year-old Robbins met an older magician at a local shop who was willing to teach him "all the dangerous stuff," provided he was serious and didn't tell his parents. Robbins convinced the magician of his sincerity and soon learned to manipulate flames and hammer nails into his nose. Later, another magician taught him the delicate arts of glass eating and sticking a hand in an animal trap without losing a digit.

Although Robbins had built an impressive sideshow repertoire, he put his skills aside and pursued comedy and magic theater. After earning a theater arts degree, he went to San Francisco's American Conservatory Theater. But the pretentious characters sur-rounding him soon grew intolerable. In 1981, Robbins left for New York to explore the East Coast theater scene. He saw that traditional theater wasn't for him. "I found myself auditioning for roles in shows I didn't like for people I had no respect for. It was com-munity theater with pretensions of high art."

To gain control over his career, he revived his old magic act and added the animal trap stunt. The trap was the one thing that was real, but nobody believed it. Audiences were astonished. "I thought, Well, this is interesting. What else could I add?" He answered his question by inserting the human blockhead routine.

Armed with his new act, Robbins worked colleges and clubs, as well as the Big Ap-ple Circus, but by the early 1990s decided that if he was going to do sideshow stunts, he should do them in a sideshow. Coney Island's Sideshows by the Seashore had recently lost its veteran performers Melvin Burkhart and Otis Jordan and showman John Bradshaw. By the spring of 1992, owner and operator Dick Zigun was looking for help. Robbins au-ditioned and got a gig as an outside talker. Fortunately, legendary talker Bobby Reynolds was working his show right around the corner, and he helped Robbins perfect the art. Once Robbins moved inside the show, he ate fire, munched on lightbulbs, and walked barefoot on broken glass.

In the following seasons Robbins filled in for others as needed. "I became the relief pitcher of the show, [and that] continues to this day," he says. Over the years his stunts have expanded to include sword swallowing and—a remarkable feat of the lungs—blowing up a hot-water bottle until it explodes. Robbins serves as chairman of the board of Coney Island USA and is the professor to eager students ready to poke their nostrils with nails and flirt with fire at Coney Island's Sideshow School, which he founded.

Outside Coney Island, Robbins continues to work with New York's Monday Night Magic show. It was there that he pulled off an entirely new trick—turning the stage manager into his wife. Their wedding in 2001 featured the last performance of the original human blockhead, Robbins's good friend Melvin Burkhart.

Robbins recently starred in his own off-Broadway show, *Carnival Knowledge* (2002–2004). The performance re-created the experience of an old-time sideshow, from bally to blow-off, with Robbins's stunts in between.

Through his career, the Purveyor of Amazement has performed around the world and appeared on numerous talk shows. Although there is no official record for "Most Lightbulbs Eaten," Robbins surely holds it, having ingested approximately 2,000 sixty-watt bulbs (not to mention a few wineglasses). As amazing as his appetite is, it's more incredible that it has never caused his stomach any trouble. Nor have his teeth been affected, though his dentist doesn't approve. "He has two words," Robbins says: 'Tsk, tsk.'"

Todd Robbins eating a lightbulb, 2004. © *Liz Steger*

★ JIM ROSE
★ *Born 1956*

★ **M**uch of the rejuvenation of the side-show can be attributed to the success of the Jim Rose Circus sideshow, which hit it big in the early 1990s. It helped establish a new breed of performers and continues to inspire young artists today.

Its leader, Jim Rose, was born on December 21, 1956, in Oregon but grew up in Arizona. As a teenager he worked at the state fairgrounds, where he picked up the human blockhead and a few other stunts. This experience did not immediately lead to a career choice. Instead, Rose found work as an exterminator and a car salesman.

Jim Rose with his wife, Bébé.
Photo by Michael Sweet

Years later, he met his wife, Bébé, who came from a French circus family. On a trip to France in which they toured with her family, some of Rose's sideshow skills were rekindled. When he returned to the United States in the late 1980s, he developed a troupe in Seattle and sharpened his pitching skills at Venice Beach in California. "I looked around and saw no one was doing what I was doing," Rose says. "And there were sure a lot of kids showing up."

The stage show in Seattle began to take off, with Rose as talker. His former assistant Joe Hermann transformed himself into the Amazing Mr. Lifto with a cringe-inducing pierced weightlifting act. Zamora the Torture King, who had seen the show, brought his flesh-skewering talents, and introduced Rose to Matt "The Tube" Crowley. "He had some phenomenal stuff that no one had ever seen," Rose says about Crowley's stomach-pumping routine. The Enigma, then known as Slug, brought his sword-swallowing skills to the troupe. Bébé participated as well, climbing a ladder of swords and resting on a bed of nails. Word spread, others added their talents to keep the show fresh and different, and ripples went out across the country. And the continent. A promoter in Vancouver soon booked the circus, and the Canadian shows were sold out.

In 1992, the Lollapalooza tour booked the Jim Rose Circus and gave it a national audience and instant fame. Over the years, the show has featured such extreme stunts as pierced-penis weightlifting and a performer balancing on his chin a lawnmower slicing heads of lettuce. Rose found his value was greater as a talker; sharing the stage with others made for a better show. Yet he can perform many stunts himself. He'll often shove his face in broken glass or eat razor blades. His biggest show didn't feature the aforementioned insanity. Instead, it offered women's sumo wrestling and Mexican transvestite wrestling. The event reportedly sold 17,000 tickets per city. Overall, Rose claimed, his circus grossed more than any other sideshow in the twentieth century. Yet, he admits, "I know when you factor in inflation, old Barnum kicked my butt."

According to Rose, it was his decision to take the sideshow out of the state fairgrounds and into clubs that created the revolution. "This isn't the sideshow. This is main stage. I played three sold-out nights at Madison Square Garden, and I don't see how I can be called a sideshow. I'm not on the side of anything if I'm playing the Garden. Maybe I took the side out of the show."

Though he had the vision to merge his show with rock 'n' roll, Rose isn't a fan. "I like Neil Diamond. I went to Lollapalooza, and someone pointed over to a crowd and said, 'There's Jane's Addiction.' I said, 'I hope she gets treatment.'" Rose studied MTV's new, fast edits, read through *Rolling Stone* and *Spin*, and figured out his formula. "I grossed my first million dollars basically with a kid that could lift something with his nipples and a guy with a tattoo on his arm," he says. "That's your next-door neighbor today."

The success of the Jim Rose Circus has led to appearances on *The X-Files*, *The Simpsons* (where Homer joins as the Human Cannonball), talk shows, and its own program on The Learning Channel.

Rose still takes the circus on the road occasionally. In addition to show business, he's brought his unorthodox methods to big business. After he was featured in *The Wall Street Journal* and *Fast Company*, major corporations paid him big money to give keynote addresses. "They think I'm smart," Rose concludes. But he isn't eager to bring bally into corporate America. He owns his own public relations company and is now living his dream of playing poker professionally.

DANIEL BROWNING SMITH, THE RUBBER BOY

✶ *Born 1979*

✶

✶ Daniel Browning Smith is a living Gumby. To his knowledge, there is no one alive today who is more flexible.

Smith was born in Mississippi on May 8, 1979. Four years later he discovered his powers of flexibility, after jumping off the top of his bunk bed and landing in a straddle split. He excitedly showed his dad what he could do. Impressed, Smith's father went to the library and collected photos of contortionists to show his son. "I tried to do what was in the pictures until I could," Smith says. "It was a childhood hobby of mine. If you're fast you run track, if you're tall you play basketball. I was bendy, so I bend."

At eighteen, the Rubber Boy left home to begin his career onstage with the Bindlestiff Family Cirkus. After breaking himself in with the troupe, he worked with showman Ward Hall and then with Tim Cridland, aka Zamora the Torture King. The gigs earned Smith enough money to enroll in the San Francisco School of Circus Arts, where he studied body control. He's now performing stunts that would make a pretzel jealous.

Smith developed his extraordinary abilities through intense training, precision, stretching aids (pulleys and ropes), and trial and error. Every trick, he explains, has its own exercise that had to be invented specifically for it. Unlike other contortionists, the Rubber Boy has trained his body to twist in all directions. He can bend forward and backward and dislocate both shoulders and both hips. He twists his torso an incredible 180 degrees—in both directions. By carefully contorting his shoulders and rib cage, he can drop his heart nearly three inches below his sternum. Audiences can see it beat. His body can pass through an unstrung tennis racket sideways—he goes in leg, arm, head, other arm, then slides the rest of himself through. He'll even squeeze his entire five feet, eight inches and 135 pounds into an eighteen-gallon box (13½ by 16 by 19½ inches). He is currently working on rotating his head 180 degrees, as Martin Laurello did in the mid-1900s.

The Rubber Boy also practices the art of "enterology," which is basically the opposite of escapism. This pursuit began as a joke when Smith was disgusted with his job at an amusement park. Intending to get fired, he did his straitjacket escape routine completely backward. His boss loved it. So did *Guinness World Records: Primetime*. The stunt earned him a distinction as World's Only Living Enterologist.

Smith is now based in Los Angeles. His talents have been seen on stages around the world, at NBA halftime shows, in commercials and in films, and most recently as Rollo the Rubber Boy on HBO's *Carnivàle*.

★

★ BRUCE SNOWDON
★ *Born 1946*
★

★ Born on February 19, 1946, in Glen Cove, New York, Bruce Snowdon grew up to become the last of the sideshow Fat Men. A victim of hereditary obesity, and a fan of food, he was destined to be big. His father's struggles with weight were not something Snowdon wanted to experience. "I'd rather have fifty happy years than seventy miserable ones," he claims. "I like being fat."

Before getting paid to be stared at, Snowdon received a college education and earned a living as a maintenance man on an Army Reserve base in New Hampshire. One day he "waddled down" to the library and came across an old circus book. A photograph of a sideshow Fat Man struck him. "He was about 300 pounds, which by my status is chubby," Snowdon says. The image gave him an epiphany—his 400-plus pounds could land him a job in show business.

The ambitious and ample Snowdon found a copy of *Amusement Business* magazine and eventually was put in contact with showman Ward Hall. By the summer of 1977 he had found his dream job. Billed as Harold Huge or Big Jim, Snowdon was often introduced to audiences with an exaggerated description of a typical meal: "This morning for breakfast he had two dozen eggs, two pounds of bacon, six stacks of hotcakes, a gallon of orange juice, a pot of coffee, four strawberry shortcakes—but he wasn't very hungry." Appearing shirtless before the audience, Snowdon wiggled his flab like a giant tub of

Jell-O to show off his advertised 712 pounds. In reality, his greatest mass just broke 600 pounds. Too big for any household scale, his weight is measured at a junkyard.

After twenty-six years of touring with Hall, Snowdon has retired in Gibsonton, Florida, near where he owns property. Despite his enormity, he manages to get around in an old Lincoln and with the aid of a walker. He still enjoys eating, though he claims his diet is nothing unusual: "A couple of hamburgers. Some summer squash. Whatever I can cook in a pan. TV dinners, what have you. A couple of ice cream sandwiches."

With luck, his bulk will still help provide a living. It got Hollywood's attention, landing him a brief spot in the movie *Big Fish*, where he was treated to a bath by Ewan McGregor. Otherwise, Snowdon may seek work at a Wal-Mart. Dieting, however, is not in his plans: "I don't mind being enormously fat."

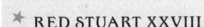

RED STUART XXVIII
Born 1951

John "Red" Stuart XXVIII was born in New Jersey on March 21, 1951. The Roman numerals refer to his status in the Mary Stuart, Queen of Scots, lineage.

When he was four, Stuart's mother put him up for adoption in Philadelphia. He grew up in an orphanage and foster homes until he graduated from high school, in 1967. And then his life took a new course.

After hitchhiking across the country, Stuart found a job at a carnival during Mardi Gras in Louisiana. A gypsy named Toni del Rio had a sideshow and offered to teach him sword swallowing and fire eating.

Red Stuart pushing a needle through his cheeks, 2004. © *Liz Steger*

Stuart accepted. Four tries and fifteen minutes later he swallowed his first sword. His rapid learning applied to fire eating as well. "It was just simple science," Stuart says. "Everyone has a tolerance to pain or heat. I have a high tolerance." Very high. Stuart's repertoire grew to include hot-coal dancing, the human pincushion, the human blockhead, and walking on shards of glass. He also adopted an unusually pointy diet, munching on such snacks as broken glass, razor blades, nails, and tacks.

★ On September 3, 2004, at the Third Annual Sideshow Gathering and Sword Swallowers Convention in Wilkes-Barre, Pennsylvania, Natasha Veruschka earned a place in *Guinness World Records* by swallowing thirteen swords at once.

While Stuart mastered nearly every sideshow art, he took sword swallowing to another level. In 1969 he was pronounced the only sword swallower able to swallow broadswords and car axles. He has put coat hangers, giant screwdrivers, bayonets, neon tubes, and a fifty-four-inch-long, two-and-a-half-inch-wide sword down his throat. The massive blade goes down about twenty-four inches into his body. Some of the swords he has swallowed are on display in the Showmen's Museum in Gibsonton, Florida.

As a jack-of-all-trades, Stuart has skills that extend beyond sideshow stunts. Through four decades and travels around the country, he has helped set up rides, handled electrical and maintenance duties, and run girl shows and reptile shows. In the latter, Stuart found opportunities other than simply exhibiting the scaly creatures. He could swallow them. He learned to swallow an endangered species using an indigo snake, just like a sword. The snake slithered down his throat headfirst, its jaws trapped shut by his esophagus. In an even more intimate stunt, Stuart performed the "Kiss of Death," where he offered his tongue for the snake to strike down on, then brought his tongue and the clamped-down head into his mouth. "I didn't do it too often. It hurt like hell," he recalls. "I'm not sadistic."

After a show, Stuart sells souvenir pitch cards. Anyone who buys a card is treated to one more stunt. He gladly takes dollar bills from the crowd and staples them to his flesh. Now that's value.

Stuart still performs occasionally. He also passes secrets on to younger performers serious about learning. Stuart has taught others to swallow swords as swiftly as he learned to—in the case of Charon Henning, under five minutes.

"Just make up your mind and say you can do it," Stuart explains. "If you say you can do it, you can do it. If you have the slightest amount of doubt, don't ever do it. It's the same thing with the pincushion, the blockhead, fire eating, and hot-coal dancing. The body can reject a lot of things when it's prepared."

Stuart has mastered the mental discipline to endure what most would consider self-torture. That's not to say he's impervious to pain: "You sneak up behind me and poke me in the ass, I'll jump five feet just like anyone else would."

VIVIAN WHEELER

Born 1948

Vivian Wheeler, 2004. *Biff Yeager*

At more than fourteen inches, Vivian Elaine Wheeler's is currently the longest beard of any living woman. The *Guinness Book of World Records* featured her in its 2001, 2002, and 2003 editions, when her beard was eleven inches long, but she was inexplicably denied a fourth entry in 2004, when it was at seventeen inches. Facial hair isn't something unusual within Wheeler's family. Both her mother and her paternal grandmother had beards. Wheeler's growth began when she was born, in Alton, Illinois, on August 9, 1948. Not only was her face covered in an inch and a half of blond hair, but she had both male and female organs. "They were on top of each other inside me, connected by skin, like Siamese twins," she says. Since her father had two sons already and her mother wished for a daughter, doctors were instructed to remove the male organs.

Wheeler's father was humiliated by his redheaded and red-bearded little girl, but it didn't prevent him from capitalizing on her. She spent several years working for Ringling Bros. and Barnum & Bailey. She received all her schooling from teachers who accompanied her on the road. She shaved whenever she returned home.

Around age eighteen, Wheeler stopped shaving and married the first of four husbands. She was bearded each time she married. Although Wheeler's love life sounds impressive, she has no sexual attraction, to men or women. "I married because that's the laws in the Bible. A man is supposed to be married to a woman, and a woman to a man," she maintains. "And you're supposed to be married to have children." Wheeler had a daughter in 1972 and a son in 1976. Her male pelvic bone structure forced her to have both by cesarean section.

Wheeler's religious beliefs have grown stronger since she became a reborn Christian in 2001. She enjoys going to church, but is often asked by the pastor not to. People pay more attention to her than to him. Yet her faith remains unshaken: "God looks on the inside of you, not the outside. And he sees the person that I am. See, we are the church, not the building."

Wheeler's career has been rejuvenated with Ken Harck's Bros. Grim Side Shows. Over the past several decades, she worked for various other outfits, including the Hall & Christ sideshow. She has exhibited herself under her own name and an alias, Malinda Maxey. Onstage, she lectures on herself and answers predictable questions, such as which public bathroom she goes to. (She uses either, although she has been stopped when heading into the ladies' room.)

Fortunately, the many questions aren't a problem for her. She's comfortable with who she is and what she does. "I love doing my job, and I love people," Wheeler says. She also loves her beard. One day, she hopes, it'll flow from her chin down to her waist.

MICHAEL WILSON, THE ILLUSTRATED MAN

1952–1996

✶ In 1986, a fully tattooed Michael Wilson helped launch the rebirth of the Coney Island sideshow. According to Dick Zigun, who hired Wilson on the spot for Sideshows by the Seashore as the Illustrated Man, he was the first person to exhibit a tattooed face publicly since Jack Dracula in the early 1960s. "He was incredibly important to this whole generation as one of the original modern primitives," Zigun observes. "It was very unusual to have your face tattooed. But it was also before every suburban teenage girl in America had a pierced tongue."

Wilson's rise to sideshow stardom began on the West Coast. He was born Michael Whisenhunt in 1952, in a small town north of San Francisco. At the age of eight he was diagnosed with diabetes. During his teen years Wilson spent a lot of time in San Francisco, particularly in Haight-Ashbury. After getting his first marking at thirteen, he became fascinated, even obsessed, with tattoos. Over the years he designed his own, mixing traditional art, tribal patterns, and occult themes.

Michael Wilson posing at the wedding of the Great Fredini and the Combustible Kiva.
Photo by Carl Saytor

By 1980, Wilson had covered nearly his entire body. His face was an empty canvas waiting to be filled, but San Francisco tattoo artists refused to ink it. A determined Wilson headed east to New York City, where underground artists accepted his challenge.

A few years later, Wilson began his tenure as Coney Island's Illustrated Man. A typical show involved his lecture on the history of tattooing, dating back to ancient Egypt. As he spoke, he removed his clothing to reveal his extensive artwork, consisting of some 35,000 tattoos covering ninety percent of his body. "They say that getting tattoos is like eating potato chips, you can't have just one," Wilson often said. In addition to exhibiting his colorful flesh, he lay on a bed of nails and, as a grand finale, hammered a spike through his tongue into a two-by-four. "That was before people knew about tongue piercing," says the Great Fredini, who performed with Wilson. "The first couple of years people were really bugging out." Although he may have been shocking and frightening to some, those who knew Wilson often described him as kindhearted and intelligent.

Outside Coney Island, Wilson was still the Illustrated Man. He was always a celebrity among the tattooing community, and his fame spread through appearances on TV talk shows and in advertisements and fashion magazines. Such extracurriculars supplemented his sideshow income, but he never got the big break to strike it rich.

By 1996, the Illustrated Man was suffering from depression. "He really painted himself into a corner," the Great Fredini says. "After being completely tattooed, what else can you do?" Wilson's wild lifestyle didn't mesh with his diabetic condition, and in the summer of that year it got the best of him. Wilson was found dead in his apartment on July 29, apparently having suffered a diabetic seizure. He was forty-four.

EGRESS

The final exhibit many visitors saw at Barnum's American Museum was the exit. Barnum tricked many eager museumgoers—who wanted to be sure not to miss anything—with a sign reading: "To the Egress." Not realizing the word "egress" meant the exit, patrons found themselves marching right out the door before they were necessarily ready to leave. The only way to gain reentry was to pay again. This helped Barnum make more money by keeping up a steady turnover. Could those who were fooled have been that surprised?

America will never again see human oddities on exhibit as it did in the second half of the 1800s, or even the early part of the 1900s. But what it may see in the future is a new kind of freak. With advances in plastic surgery, and creativity and enthusiasm for radical body modification, we may eventually see performers go beyond the extremes of The Enigma, Katzen, The Lizardman and others. And while medicine has prevented many freakish births, it may lead to greater and greater life expectancies, thus turning the tremendously old into curiosities. Just this year a woman in Brazil made headlines when she was claimed to be 125 years old. She's practically another Joice Heth. Come to think of it, maybe history does repeat itself. And maybe America is headed toward yet another, albeit different, Golden Age of sideshow.

ARMLESS AND LEGLESS MEN
RIDING A TANDEM
Ⓛ EX. SUP. CO., CHGO.

Eli Bowen (steering) and Charles Tripp (pedaling)
on a tandem bicycle. *Author's collection*

From Under the Tent
to Across the Web

The Great Nippulini ★ greatnippulini.com

The Great Throwdini ★ knifethrower.com

Jewels (The Beautiful Jewels) ★ nothingimpossible.net

The Lizardman ★ thelizardman.com

Johnny Meah ★ czarofbizarre.com

Jennifer Miller ★ circusamok.org

James G. Mundie's Prodigies ★ www.missioncreep.com/mundie/images/

Harley Newman ★ bladewalker.com

Pain-Proof Rubber Girls ★ painproofrubbergirls.com

Ratt's Freak Show ★ phreeque.tripod.com

Todd Robbins ★ toddrobbins.com

Jim Rose ★ jimrosecircus.com

The Rubber Boy (Daniel Browning Smith) ★ therubberboy.com

Show History ★ showhistory.com

Sideshow Bennie and His Carnival of Wonders ★ sideshowbennie.com

Sideshow World ★ sideshowworld.com

James Taylor's Shocked and Amazed: On & Off the Midway ★ shockedandamazed.com

Vamphear Circus ★ vamphearcircus.com

Natasha Veruschka ★ home.earthlink.net/~tena11

Zamora the Torture King ★ mindandmatter.net

Selected Bibliography

Listed below are articles, books, and films that have been useful in creating this book. This bibliography is by no means a complete account of all the sources I consulted in my research; other articles, books, and films, as well as websites, old advertisements, and interviews, were also critical.

"Admiral Dot Has a Daughter." *Fresno Weekly Republican*, October 20, 1893.

"African Dwarf Museum's Model for Sculpture." *Coshocton Tribune* (Ohio), August 23, 1925.

"All Midgets in this Circus." *The Daily News* (Frederick, Maryland), October 18, 1915.

Barnum, Phineas T. *Struggles and Triumphs: Or, The Life of P. T. Barnum.* New York: Alfred A. Knopf, 1927.

Being Different. Dir. Harry Rasky. Double S. Productions (Astral), 1981.

The Billboard/Amusement Business, November 21, 1925.

Bogdan, Robert. *Freak Show: Presenting Human Oddities for Amusement and Profit.* Chicago: The University of Chicago Press, 1990.

Bondeson, Jan. *A Cabinet of Medical Curiosities.* New York: W. W. Norton, 1997.

Brahms, William B. *Franklin Township, Somerset County, NJ: A History.* Franklin Township, NJ: Franklin Township Public Library and Port City Press, 1998.

"Circus Folk Mourn 'Best-Liked Freak.'" *The New York Times,* April 19, 1926.

"Circus Folk Mourn the Passing of Zip." *The New York Times,* April 26, 1926.

"Circus Freaks Are Shy and Retiring, but Gay, Happy Amongst Themselves." *Indiana Evening Gazette* (Indiana, Pennsylvania), May 1, 1926.

"Circus Giant Busy on First Day Here." *The New York Times*, April 7, 1937.

"Circus Lore Told by Famous Clown." *The New York Times*, April 6, 1936.

"Circus and Museum Freaks—Curiosities of Pathology." *Scientific American*, March 28, 1908.

Claxton, Michael. "A History of Little People in Magic." *Genii: The Conjuror's Magazine*, vol. 64, no. 9 (September 1, 2001).

"Contesting Col. Goshen's Will." *The New York Times*, March 9, 1889.

Crawford, Kathleen, Dale Swan, and James Taylor. *Anna: A Souvenir Pitchbook*. Baltimore, MD: Dolphin-Moon Press, 1995.

"Curiosities at Leisure." *The Elyria Weekly Republican* (Ohio), June 1, 1882.

"Dead Wives Come In Handy." *The Daily Northwestern*, January 28, 1910.

"Death of Minnie Warren." *The New York Times*, July 24, 1878.

DeGenaro, Stephen A. "The Ohio Big Foot Girl." *Timeline*, vol. 15, no. 5 (September–October 1998).

Delo, Pat. "Gibb Sisters, Famed Siamese Twins, Dead." *Daily Transcript and Telegram* (Holyoke, Massachusetts), January 9, 1967.

Dennett, Andrea Stulman. *Weird and Wonderful: The Dime Museum in America*. New York: New York University Press, 1997.

"Doubt Boy Was Son of Siamese Twin." *The New York Times*, April 3, 1922.

Drimmer, Frederick. *Very Special People*. Repr. New York: Citadel Press, 1991.

"Dwarf Stories." *Newark Daily Advocate*, December 18, 1889.

"The Dwarfs and Giants—Who Some of Them Are and How They Live." *The New York Times*, October 23, 1881.

"Famous Dwarf Dies in Massachusetts." *The Deming Headlight* (New Mexico), November 5, 1920.

"Famous Dwarfs." *Coshocton Morning Tribune* (Ohio; from *Kansas City Star*), January 7, 1916.

"The Fat Bride's Death." *Evening Observer*, October 31, 1883.

"Fattest Man at 800 Marks 25th Birthday." Associated Press, June 25, 1951.

Fellows, Dexter, and Andrew A. Freeman. *This Way to the Big Show: The Life of Dexter Fellows*. New York: Viking, 1936.

Fiedler, Leslie. *Freaks: Myths and Images of the Secret Self*. New York: Simon & Schuster, 1978.

Flemming, Frank M. " 'Sympathy' Scheme of a Little Armless Girl to Get Million Dollars from Americans." *The Constitution* (Atlanta), March 25, 1906.

"Fortunes in Deformity." *Freeborn County Standard* (Minnesota), January 20, 1886.

Freaks. Dir. Tod Browning. Metro-Goldwyn-Mayer, 1932.

"Freaks Bequests." *Newark Daily Advocate* (from *Philadelphia Times*), April 2, 1885.

"The 'Freaks' of the Circus." *The Washington Post*, May 12, 1907.

"Freaks at Hotel Fire." *The New York Times*, April 5, 1904.

Freaks Uncensored! Dir. Ari Roussimoff. Bohemia Productions, 1998.

"Funeral of Giant Goshen." *Trenton Times*, February 15, 1889.

Geyer, Celesta, and Samuel Roen. *Diet or Die: The Dolly Dimples Weight Reducing Plan*. New York: Frederick Fell, 1968.

"Giants and Dwarfs." *The Strand Magazine*, October 1894.

Gilliams, E. Leslie. "Side-Show Freaks as Seen by Science." *Illustrated World*, October 1922.

Gould, George M., and Walter L. Pyle. *Anomalies and Curiosities of Medicine*. 1896. Repr. New York: Bell, 1956.

Gregor, Jan T., with Tim Cridland. *Circus of the Scars*. Seattle: Brennan Dalsgard, 1998.

"Grief over Loss of Brother Leads to Death of Midget." *Sheboygan Press* (United Press), April 26, 1937.

"Had Two Hearts, Lost One, Lived Two Weeks." *Colorado Springs Gazette*, July 29, 1906.

Hall, Ward. *My Very Unusual Friends*. Published by the author, 1991.

"Hannah Battersby Dead." *The New York Times*, April 16, 1889.

"Harris' Nickel Plate Circus." *Freeborn County Standard* (Minnesota), April 14, 1886.

Hartzman, Marc. "42nd St. Is Alive on the Inside Again with the Bindlestiff Family Cirkus." *Backwash*, no. 18 (2003).

———. "'The Ill-Advised and Downright Dangerous' Life of the Lizardman." *Backwash*, no. 17 (2002).

———. "94 and Still Banging Away: The Original Human Blockhead." *Backwash*, no. 17 (2002).

———. "Sword Swallowing, Spike Hammering and Freaks at Johnny Fox's Freakatorium." *Backwash*, no. 15 (2000).

History of the Life of Unzie: The Australian Aboriginal Beauty. New York: Dick's Publishing House, 1893. Becker Collection, Special Collections Research Center, Syracuse University Library.

Hoffman, Renoda. *Yesterday in White Plains: A Picture History of a Vanished Era*. 2nd ed. White Plains, NY: 1984.

"Homeliest Woman." *The Bismarck Tribune*, April 6, 1929.

Howard, Martin. *Victorian Grotesque*. London: Jupiter Books, 1977.

"In the Interest of Science: The Hairy Family Under the Eyes of the Doctors." *The New York Times*, March 28, 1887.

Jay, Ricky. *Learned Pigs & Fireproof Women*. New York: Warner Books, 1986.

"The Jewish Giant: A Sound Portrait." Prod. Stacy Abramson. Sound Portraits Productions, 1999.

"Jonathan R. Bass, The Ossified Man." *The Buffalo News*, August 30, 1998.

"King Theebaw's Mascots." *The New York Times*, December 4, 1886.

Kirby, Irwin. "What, Sideshows Ought to Be Banned?" *Amusement Business*, August 10, 1968.

Klever, John E., ed. *The Kentucky Encyclopedia*. Lexington: University Press of Kentucky, 1992.

Kunhardt, Philip B., Jr., Philip B. Kunhardt III, and Peter W. Kunhardt. *P. T. Barnum: America's Greatest Showman*. New York: Alfred A. Knopf, 1995.

Kunzog, John C. *One-Horse Show: The Life and Times of Dan Rice, Circus Jester and Philanthropist*. Published by the author, 1962.

Lewis, Arthur H. *Carnival*. New York: Trident Press, 1970.

The Life & Adventures of Capt. Constentenus, The Tattooed Greek Prince, Written by Himself. New York: New York

Popular Publishing, 1881. Becker Collection, Special Collections Research Center, Syracuse University Library.

"Life History of Francesco A. Lentini, Three-Legged Wonder." Becker Collection, Special Collections Research Center, Syracuse University Library.

"Life of Isaac W. Sprague, the Living Skeleton." 1892. Becker Collection, Special Collections Research Center, Syracuse University Library.

"Lilliputian Star Is Buried." *Nevada State Journal*, April 28, 1937.

Lindfors, Bernth, ed. *Africans on Stage: Studies in Ethnological Show Business*. Bloomington: Indiana University Press, 1999.

Little, Carl Victor (United Press). "Famous Twins United in Death As in Lifetime." *Sheboygan Press-Telegram*, March 30, 1922.

Lord, Priscilla S., and David J. Foley. *The Folk Arts and Crafts of New England*. Philadelphia and New York: Chilton Books, 1965.

Mac, Beth, and Jen McCaffery. "Eko and Iko: The Remarkable Life of Willie Muse." *The Roanoke Times*, 2001.

Mannix, Daniel P. *Freaks: We Who Are Not As Others*. New York: Pocket Books, 1976.

———. *Memoirs of a Sword Swallower*. 1950. Repr. San Francisco: V/Search Publications, 1996.

———. *Step Right Up!* New York: Harper & Brothers, 1950.

———. "Strange People." *True*, September 1948.

Martel, Joanne. *Millie-Christine: Fearfully and Wonderfully Made*. North Carolina: John F. Blair, 2000.

Martin, Douglas. "Frieda Pushnik Is Dead at 77; Turned Her Deformities into a Career." *The New York Times*, January 7, 2001.

Martin, Jack. "Sideshow Performers Bring Happy Memories to a Fellow Member." *The White Tops*, January/February 1985.

McCullough, Edo. *Good Old Coney Island*. New York: Charles Scribner's Sons, 1957.

McKennon, Joe. *Circus Lingo*. Sarasota, FL: Carnival Publishers of Sarasota, 1980.

McWhirter, Norris, ed. *Guinness Book of World Records*, 17th Edition. New York: Bantam Books, 1979.

Mitchell, Joseph. *McSorley's Wonderful Saloon*. New York: Duell, Sloan and Pearce, 1943.

"Morris, the 'India Rubber Man.'" *Scientific American*, July 9, 1898.

"Mr. Nellis, Born Without Arms." Freaks Clipping File, Billy Rose Theatre Collection, New York Public Library for the Performing Arts.

Niedershuh, Karl J. "Remarkable Baby Ruth." www.dimensionsmagazine.com/images/circus/ruth, 1997.

"Odd Human Freaks." *New Oxford Item* (Gettysburg, Pennsylvania), September 30, 1892.

"Once Famous Freaks." Freak Clipping File, Billy Rose Theatre Collection, New York Public Library for the Performing Arts.

"An Ossified Man Dead." *The New York Times*, March 20, 1892.

Our Heritage 1883–1890. Published under the auspices of the Sheyenne, North Dakota, Historical Society

"The Passing of the Once Popular Sideshow Freak." *The New York Times*, February 26, 1911.

"People of Tiny Height." *New Oxford Item* (Gettysburg, Pennsylvania), February 10, 1893.

"Problem for Jailer." *The Helena Daily Independent,* November 1, 1936.

Rasky, Frank. "Skin Game: Tattooed Lady's Marital Rapp as Thousands Flea (Circus)." Freak Clipping File, Billy Rose Theatre Collection, New York Public Library for the Performing Arts.

Rich, Louis. "Tattooing Enters on Machine Age." *The New York Times,* September 4, 1930.

Rose, Jim, with Melissa Rossi. *Freak Like Me: Inside the Jim Rose Circus Sideshow.* New York: Dell, 1995.

Rosen, Fred. *Lobster Boy.* New York: Pinnacle Books, 1995.

"'Rotating Head' Leads to Arrest of Man for Abandoning Wife." Associated Press, May 1, 1931.

"Roy Bard." *Variety,* August 18, 1937. Freak Clipping File, Billy Rose Theatre Collection, New York Public Library for the Performing Arts.

Rusid, Max. *Sideshow.* New York: Amjon, 1975.

"Secrets of the Showmen." *The New York Times,* October 8, 1882.

Sideshow: Alive on the Inside. Exec. prod. Tim Miller; dir. Lynn Dougherty. Big Chief Entertainment, 1996; Shanachie Entertainment, 1999.

Sideshow Newsletter. Ed. Bob Blackmar. 1999–2003.

"Slump in the Freak Market." *The Washington Post,* April 2, 1910.

Stencil, A. W. *Seeing Is Believing: America's Sideshows.* Canada: ECW Press, 2002.

"Strange Freaks of Nature." *Freeborn County Standard* (Minnesota), March 25, 1880.

Stumbo, Bella. "Two Lives Remembered; Eulogy: Family and Friends Recall the Conjoined Twins' Grace, Cheerfulness and Perseverance." *Los Angeles Times,* January 17, 1993.

Sturtevant, C. G. "Who's Who Among the Governors." *The White Tops,* Christmas 1944.

Taylor, James. *James Taylor's Shocked and Amazed: On & Off the Midway,* vols. 1, 6, 7. Baltimore: Dolphin-Moon Press and Atomic Books, 1995, 2001, 2003.

"Theebaw's Hairy Family." *The New York Times,* December 26, 1886.

Thompson, C. J. S. and M. B. E. *Giants, Dwarfs and Other Oddities.* New York: Citadel Press, 1968.

Thorp, L. Ashton. *Manchester of Yesterday.* Manchester, NH: Granite State Press, 1939.

"Unzie's Marvelous Hair." *The Fort Wayne Gazette* (Indiana), March 6, 1895.

"Wages of Curiosities." *Marion Daily Star* (Ohio; from *St. Louis Post*), June 6, 1883.

Wallace, Ed. "Circus Freaks Measure Up to Normal Life," April 11, 1959. Freak Clipping File, Billy Rose Theatre Collection, New York Public Library for the Performing Arts.

"What We Know About Waino and Plutano, Wild Men of Borneo," 1893. Becker Collection, Special Collections Research Center, Syracuse University Library.

Willis, Steve, with Charles Fattig. "Major Mite." *The White Tops,* September/October 1992.

Wilson, Earl. "Behind the Scenes at Coney." Freak Clipping File, Billy Rose Theatre Collection, New York Public Library for the Performing Arts.

Wood, Gaby. *Edison's Eve.* New York: Anchor Books, 2003.

About the Author

Marc Hartzman is of average height and average weight, and is in possession of ten fingers and ten toes. As the freaks might say, he's a norm.

His fascination with human oddities began at an early age. He saw the movies *The Elephant Man* and *Time Bandits* numerous times and avidly read the first twenty-five pages of each year's *Guinness Book of World Records* (especially the Robert Wadlow pages).

Hartzman has written about sideshow performers for *Backwash*, a zine he founded in 1996, and *Bizarre* magazine. His passion for all things unusual and quirky also led to his first book, *Found on eBay: 101 Genuinely Bizarre Items from the World's Online Yard Sale*.

Other than freaks and strange objects, Hartzman writes about various goods and services as an advertising copywriter in New York City. He lives in New Rochelle, New York, with his wife, Liz; their baby, Lela; two cats; and a bearded dragon named Steve.